BREAK 'EM
UP

ALSO BY ZEPHYR TEACHOUT

Corruption in America

BREAK 'EM UP

RECOVERING OUR FREEDOM from BIG AG, BIG TECH, and BIG MONEY

Zephyr Teachout

Foreword by Bernie Sanders

ALL
POINTS
BOOKS

NEW YORK

First published in the United States by All Points Books, an imprint of St. Martin's Publishing Group

www.allpointsbooks.com

Designed by Meryl Sussman Levavi

Library of Congress Cataloging-in-Publication Data

Names: Teachout, Zephyr, author.
Title: Break 'em up : recovering our freedom from big ag, big
    tech, and big money / Zephyr Teachout ; foreword by
    Senator Bernie Sanders.
Description: First edition. | New York : All Points Books, [2020] |
    Includes bibliographical references and index.
Identifiers: LCCN 2019058373 | ISBN 9781250200891 (hardcover) |
    ISBN 9781250200907 (ebook)
Subjects: LCSH: Monopolies. | Big business. | Corporate power. |
    Corporations—Moral and ethical aspects.
Classification: LCC HD2757.2 .T43 2020 | DDC 338.8/2—dc23
LC record available at https://lccn.loc.gov/2019058373

First Edition: 2020

10 9 8 7 6 5 4 3 2 1

To Lissarette, Merita, Cristina, Ariella, and Mama Rosa,
the owner and providers at our son's daycare.
Thank you for the joy, care, and warmth you have
given our baby, and the peace of mind you have given me.
Without you this book could not have been written.

Contents

Foreword

by BERNIE SANDERS

When we turn on television or listen to the debate in Washington, we are so often told that the economy is "booming." And yet, most of us are well aware that the economy today is not working for working people. Yes, a handful of billionaires and large corporations are doing better than they ever have—but at the same time, millions are struggling to secure the most basic necessities needed to survive.

Today, the richest 10 percent of Americans own an estimated 97 percent of all capital income—including capital gains, corporate dividends, and interest payments. Since the 2008 Wall Street crash, 49 percent of all new income generated in America has gone to the top 1 percent. The three wealthiest people in our country now own more wealth than the bottom 160 million Americans. And the richest family in America— the Walton family, which inherited about half of Walmart's stock—is worth $200 billion and owns more wealth than the bottom 42 percent of the American people.

While the corporate profits that presently go to a small number of ultra-wealthy families are at or near an all-time high, wages as a percentage of our economy are near an all-time low.

This did not happen by accident. We must understand that the move toward oligarchy has occurred in conjunction with a level of corporate consolidation and concentration not seen since the Gilded Age.

In the last four decades, nearly every single industry in America has become more concentrated. Monopolies and oligopolies rule over every aspect of American life, from the food we eat,[1] to the airlines we fly,[2] and even to the eyeglasses we wear.[3] And with less competition, these corporate behemoths are able to rip off consumers, extort suppliers, stifle innovation, drive down wages, and buy elections.

The monopolization of America is not some esoteric issue—it is one of the trends that has created an economic crisis for working people all over our country.

If that seems familiar, that is because this dangerous trend similarly threatened our nation in a past era—and our government took action to stop it. Indeed, at the turn of the twentieth century, Congress empowered regulators to break up monopolies and halt consolidation—and those antitrust laws helped workers gain a larger share of the economic pie.

However, in recent years, the courts and regulatory agencies have been taken over by corporate ideologues determined to weaken antitrust laws and accelerate the consolidation of industries across the country. And so here we are again—in a new Gilded Age and a new era of monopolies dominating our economy and writing our laws.

We have seen giants like Amazon grow to control more than half of all e-commerce.[4] The company employs various anticompetitive tactics to harm small businesses, all while it pays virtually no taxes in the communities where it operates and also pays zero federal income taxes after making billions in profits.

We have seen the consolidation of large hospital systems, which command higher prices and deliver worse service. Indeed, one analysis found that after major hospital mergers, local communities saw hospital prices rise by between 11 and 54 percent.[5]

We have seen media mergers and Silicon Valley mergers that create a handful of news and technology conglomerates that control more and more of what we read, watch, and listen to in our democracy.

We have seen mega-mergers like the one between T-Mobile and Sprint, which represents a gross concentration of power that runs counter to the public good. Americans deserve affordable wireless access. This kind of merger will not only lead to fewer options and higher prices for consumers, but it could lead to 30,000 jobs lost and reduced wages for thousands more.

And in rural America, we have seen giant agribusiness conglomerates extract as much wealth from small communities as they can, while family farmers go bankrupt and, in many cases, are treated like modern-day indentured servants.

In too many rural communities there is only one buyer of crops, which means farmers and ranchers are at their mercy. They are forced to use one corporation's feed and livestock. They are forced to accept one corporation's costs, and they are forced to accept one corporation's lower and lower payment rates.

The numbers are stark: today, just four large companies control 82 percent of the beef packing industry, 85 percent of soybean processing, 63 percent of pork packing, and 53 percent of chicken processing.[6] At the same time, Monsanto controls 80 percent of U.S. corn and more than 90 percent of U.S. soybean seed patents—a situation that has only gotten worse after the Trump administration approved Monsanto's disastrous merger with Bayer.

The result: today, for every dollar Americans spend on food, farmers earn less than 15 cents—which is the smallest share in the modern-day history of our nation.[7]

None of this is random or inevitable—it is happening because our government is allowing it to happen. But it doesn't have to be this way.

We can rediscover our American tradition of controlling corporate power and promoting fair competition through antitrust.

We can halt the consolidation and concentration of our

economy, and reverse the trend in the same way that we did a century ago.

We can halt anticompetitive mergers, break up existing monopolies and oligopolies, and appoint federal regulators ready to take action on behalf of workers and consumers—not massive corporations. We can also use regulatory agencies to crack down on anticompetitive business practices, and we can institute new guidelines for proposed consolidation that makes sure mergers are approved only if they will not harm workers and consumers, or our economy as a whole.

We can do all of this—but it will not happen by itself. It can happen only through a grassroots, bottom-up movement that understands the challenge in front of us, and then organizes against monopoly power in communities across this country.

This book is a blueprint for that organizing. In these pages, you will learn how monopolies and oligopolies have taken over almost every aspect of American life, and you will also learn about what can be done to stop that trend before it is too late.

Let me be clear: this book is not designed to make readers experts in the legal minutiae of antitrust. It is designed to empower people from all walks of life to join the movement to break up the power of these mega-corporations that are threatening our communities.

This will be no easy task. The effort to break up monopolies will be opposed by those very same corporations that are benefiting from the status quo. They will spend unlimited sums of money to try to preserve the current system that provides them so much wealth and power.

But I am more confident than ever that if we stand together and do the kind of organizing described in this book, we can pass the laws we need to defeat them—and finally create an economy that works for all of us, not just the top one percent.

Introduction

For all power tends to develop into a government in itself.

—Former Supreme Court Justice
William O. Douglas

For most of world history, we have understood that humans are political animals. The urge to socialize, to love, and to fight runs deep in us. What's more, we are not laissez-faire in our socializing. We are creatures who concentrate and wield power to get what we want. It is a basic, universal human trait, like sexuality, or hunger, or compassion. It is the stuff of heroism, and, if it goes unchecked, of tyranny. We know this from Aristotle, Shakespeare, James Madison, Frederick Douglass, Hannah Arendt, and every James Bond and Marvel movie ever made. Tyrants have arisen in every age because the taste for power informs every human institution and resides in every human being; how we harness it is the question over which nations live or die.

For the last few decades, political scientists and economists have been living in a collective delusion, a fantasy that the owners of private corporations belong to a different species from most people, that they are driven by the profit motive alone, that (with a few negligible exceptions) they have no designs on the rest of us. All the average tycoon wants, we are told, is to make as much money as possible and to be left alone by those who are in the messy business of governance.

This fantasy may lead to some satisfying, even justified, accusations *(The CEO is greedy! The profit motive has destroyed our forests!),* but by painting the richest investors of our day as if they lived and moved somehow strictly within the world of money, separate from the world of politics, we blind ourselves to the extraordinary political power that they have amassed, and enjoy.

These people wield vast control over both our civic and our individual lives. When Facebook CEO Mark Zuckerberg announced his views about privacy in the spring of 2019, you'd think some kind of national privacy czar had spoken: his words were more potent than any law. The policies adopted by the corporation he controls impact hundreds of millions of people. Mark Zuckerberg is a human being like the rest of us: he eats, sleeps, sometimes he quarrels with his wife, sometimes he's sententious, sometimes he's annoying, sometimes he's scared, sometimes he may even be funny. But unlike the rest of us, Facebook has the power to determine which newspapers thrive and which go bankrupt; when Zuckerberg changes his mind he changes what we read, and even how we think. When Werner Baumann, CEO of Bayer—formerly Monsanto—decides to try out a new form of crop rotation, tens of thousands of farmers must go along with his experiment or face bankruptcy. Pfizer exercises a capricious power that we would never permit in a government agency; when it decides to hike up insulin prices before an earnings report, or just to test a theory, people die. Google has gained power so vast as to be nearly invisible; we accept the power of Google almost the way we accept the weather. Google can make or break any company or idea according to where it appears on a search result. When Google decides, for whatever reasons—selfish, or altruistic, or both—that children should learn one form of addition rather than another, millions of children, using apps favored by the Google for Education tools, will learn that new method.

Two corporations control office supplies. Four corporations control wireless. Five corporations control food. Two corporations dominate retail. Five corporations control defense contracting. Four corporations control home internet, and in many parts of the country, people have no say at all about which provider they use. One corporation dominates books. Five oil corporations control contracts at 50,000 gas stations. The entire pharmaceutical business model is a monopoly. Three corporations dominate the market for voting machines. A decade after they helped trigger the Great Recession, too-big-to-fail banks are bigger and more concentrated than ever.[1]

In the last eleven years we have allowed over 500,000 mergers worldwide; mergers in the last five years were valued at an annual average of $4 trillion.[2] As mergers have grown, so have mega-mergers. Microsoft recently bought LinkedIn, and AT&T bought Time Warner. While James Comey and Donald Trump dominated the headlines, DuPont and Dow continued plans to become DowDupont, Amazon merged with Whole Foods, and Walmart announced that it would buy the popular men's apparel brand Bonobos. While Robert Mueller publicly empaneled a grand jury to investigate Trump, Monsanto consummated its marriage to Bayer.

These monopolies extract wealth from people directly, through price-gouging and wage theft, and indirectly, by causing regional inequality and closing off opportunities to start businesses. They then extract political power too, so they can keep it that way.

At the same time, data harvesting and analytic tools have become ubiquitous. As a result, the very nature of work is changing: surveillance, isolation, and fear are becoming a daily fact of the workplace. The 2010 Supreme Court case *Citizens*

United struck down long-standing limits on corporate political speech. Corporations are using the leeway given them by *Citizens United* not only to spend money on super PACs, but to let their workers know how they should vote.

The highest and best goals of America—equality and freedom—require government to protect citizens from any group or any person wielding too much power. We used to do this pretty well, using antitrust, campaign finance laws, public utility regulation, labor laws, and other anti-monopoly tools. But in recent years, our government has failed on all these fronts. Meanwhile, corporations have disabled key institutions designed to protect against arbitrary power.

The rule of law depends on transparency, reason giving, and each person being treated equally by the law, regardless of how much money or power they have. After the crash of 2008, the impunity of elite networks was on full display when no banker was jailed for lawless activity. Pharmaceutical and big tech corporations regularly get away with laughably trivial fines for their major violations of the law. And corporate monopolies are not just avoiding individual prosecutions—itself a major affront to the rule of law—but building the architecture of a new system without protections for the powerless. Open, public courts are a vital tool of political equality and liberty, the essential institution that recognizes each person as rights-bearing. Public courts have been replaced by arbitration in which judges are paid by corporations, reasons aren't given, and no one knows what happens. As a result, justice is disappearing.

A vibrant news system can provide a check on private power and corruption in public institutions. For news to play this democratic function, it needs to be decentralized; ownership needs to be widely dispersed, and newspapers need to be able to survive on either ads or subscriptions. But failure to regulate and break up the advertising duopoly of Facebook and

Google has allowed them to grab control over media and centrally edit the flow of information.

Economic democracy requires workers to be able to bargain for decent benefits, and business owners to freely compete. But as we have given the green light to monopolies, big corporations have been setting the terms—not negotiating for them. Corporate goliaths are increasingly managing the entire economy for consumer goods from their perch on top of the market, deciding which companies succeed and fail.

Until recently, even many people who grasp the problem passively accepted corporate consolidation as a fact of life and did not respond with the indignation they bring to, say, redistricting or labor rollbacks. The danger of monopoly had not been an issue in presidential debates until 2019, nor had it been a question for most congressmembers. Although there are tens of thousands of community activist organizations dedicated to campaign finance, climate change, and gender equality, I know of no local antitrust leagues—unlike 120 years ago, when there were thousands. No board meetings have been disrupted by demands for divestiture. There've been no sit-ins at the Federal Trade Commission (FTC) or the Department of Justice demanding that a big corporation be broken up. This is rapidly changing, but no politician has lost their job for their silence on the merger wave—yet.

For decades, instead, the left has failed to understand the magnitude of the concentration problem, how it limits freedom in so many areas of life, how it drives inequality and empowers racism. We have focused on petitioning public government to redistribute wealth or provide social services, ignoring the creation of new, private systems of government that run our day-to-day lives. When progressives do fight private power, therefore, we often do so on the terms set by the right, in which one's role as a consumer is more centrally important than one's role as a citizen. Our main tool has been naming and shaming with the goal of persuading corporate boardrooms to change behavior, not persuading *Congress* to act. You've heard the phrases: *Vote with your feet. Vote with your wallet.* You may even have internalized them so completely that you feel guilty when you use Amazon or Uber after protesting their treatment of workers, as if it were hypocritical to demand the destruction of a service you use every day. A well-organized strategic boycott is a powerful tool, but the degree to which the left has internalized ethical consumerism is frankly dangerous. It means that when a progressive hears about Facebook accepting lies in paid political ads, they think their job is to stop using Facebook, when they should really call their congressmember and demand that she sponsor legislation that would make social media companies liable for paid lies. Because this anti-political ideology has infiltrated leftist politics, even progressive politicians are rarely asked to address monopoly problems; meanwhile, monopolies are lining the pockets of most Democratic and Republican candidates to make sure they look the other way.

It is a profound project, to reshape our politics and win back our freedom. But we can break these concentrations of power as soon as we set our minds to the task. We already have the tools at our disposal. Using no more than existing statutes, a new president can demand that the FTC and Department of Justice stop mergers, and implement industry-specific anti-monopoly rules across the executive branch. State attorneys general can—and are starting to—investigate big trusts, block mergers, and force divestiture. A new Congress could certainly help to speed the process, by passing laws that overturn decades of bad Supreme Court precedent and return us to the jurisprudence developed prior to 1981, when it was much easier to stop corporate concentration. That same Congress—and statehouses—can pass anti-monopoly laws directly targeting this modern threat.

With a major, grassroots anti-monopoly movement, we can radically reshape our economy and democracy in the service of human needs. We can have affordable drugs. We can have a wide-open seed market that isn't connected to a fertilizer market. Farmers can reclaim the right to fix their own tractors, and taxi drivers can get a decent wage. We can have an economy where business owners make a profit but aren't governed by profit maximization. We can have a basic communications infrastructure that doesn't rely on targeted ads and surveillance. We can even have an economy made up of worker-owned co-ops and unionized corporations, small- and medium-sized businesses, and substantial local ownership, if we so choose. We can have a moral economy. But none of this will happen until we end government by private monopolies.

*

I want to get a few misconceptions out of the way: first, you may think that a single corporation is not a "monopoly" unless it controls an entire market. That's just not true. When Standard Oil was broken up, it controlled 65% of the market, not 100%. Until 1980, we used anti-monopoly law to block mergers of corporations that had even 5% or 6% market share. Monopoly, as used throughout this book (and frequently used in American history), means any company that has so much power that it sets the terms of an interaction—like drug companies that don't compete with one another, but just make up whatever prices they want to charge. In other words, a monopoly is a kind of little government, in which the monopolist makes the rules.[3]

Second, sometimes people present anti-monopoly and strong regulation as two opposing strategies, as in: *Do you want to break up big banks, or regulate them?* This is a silly, if widely used, query, designed to divide progressives. We need to tax wealth, for instance. But while we are taxing wealth, an after-the-fact redistribution, we should change the rules so that grossly unfair wealth accumulation can't happen in the first place, or we'll be permanently fighting ultra-powerful billionaires determined to gut any effective wealth tax. We need to change the rules for how data is collected. But while we are regulating data, shouldn't we also make sure that the market for data isn't owned by three or four companies? If not, we can't even have a reasonable conversation about big data, because Google has too much influence on government. We need to break up big banks precisely *because* the law passed in the wake of the financial crisis, Dodd-Frank, regulated banks but didn't limit their size or interconnectedness. It is being gutted by a juggernaut of lobbying by the too-big-to-fail banks that we allowed to persist. Monopoly is a rival form of government burrowing its way into democratic government, so we must always strike at the root of its power, and not leave anti-monopolism for later.

Third, you may think that stopping mergers and breaking up companies are the only anti-monopoly tools. That's too narrow. Anti-monopolism is a broad philosophy standing in opposition to unaccountable private power. Campaign finance law, predatory pricing law, public utility regulation, laws that make co-ops easier to organize, and the right to sue big companies all count as ways to break up power.

Finally, you may have been told that all market systems inevitably lead to big, quasi-governmental corporations. Not so. We can build any kind of corporate law and market structure we want. We can limit corporations by size, break up corporations by function, clarify rules for unfair business practices, demand neutrality for intermediaries, change the maximizing-profit model of businesses, outlaw certain forms of surveillance capitalism, and structure finance so that it can't overtake commerce, for starters. We can force Google Search to divest from Google

Shopping and Google Maps. Spectrum can be broken up into several component parts so that labor unions can meaningfully negotiate with the corporation again. Uber can be broken into five different corporations, regulated, and stopped from having more than 20% market share in any given city. Amazon Marketplace can be separated from Amazon Web Services, AmazonBasics, and Alexa. We used to do this kind of thing pretty regularly, and by the 1970s, income and wealth inequality was at an all-time low. These policies will be forcefully opposed by big corporations, but they aren't actually that hard to enact.

How did we get here? The bottom line is that for decades, economists and courts and policy makers have treated monopoly in one way: if consumers get low prices, there is no monopoly problem. This is known as the consumer welfare standard. If Amazon provides a multibillion-dollar consumer surplus by lowering prices, this is a world-changing boon, and we shouldn't ask about any possible political and economic side effects. This argument is short-sighted. When Amazon exercises power over its suppliers, forcing them to pay their workers less, those "suppliers" are actually your fellow citizens.[4] So while you may save $3 on an Amazon-sold product, those savings come from Amazon having forced its seller to pay your neighbor $1 less an hour.

Taken together, these and other false narratives have quietly—but quickly—eroded our understanding of freedom, to a point that would shock the progressives of the last century. Freedom isn't just having enough food, shelter, education, and healthcare; it is also having the ability to look someone else in the eye and say "no thanks" to a job, because they aren't the only employer out there; it is having the space to be creative and start a new company without fear of being crushed by incumbents; it is the comfort of knowing that even if you have unpopular political views, your boss can't control every part of your life. Without these freedoms, it is no surprise that Americans regard the political process with skepticism. To have choice within the privacy of the ballot box means little if that's the only choice, the only privacy you have. If that choice does not impact the entities that have real power over your life, there is something deeply wrong with our democracy.

✳

This book has two arguments to make.

First, I will argue that monopoly is tyranny: that no democracy can survive for long once a few corporations have amassed governmental power in such a massive form and scale. Those corporations use isolation, surveillance, experimentation, and fear to extract value from workers, silence political dissent, exploit users, and regulate all of us. They don't hide their ambition, but because they are corporate, instead of military, we can be blinded to their lust for power, understanding it only as a rational desire to maximize profit—or, in the case of big tech, as a kind of boyish utopianism that shouldn't be dampened.

Amazon, Google, Facebook, Monsanto, AT&T, Verizon, Walmart, Pfizer, Comcast, and CVS represent a new *political* phenomenon, a twenty-first-century form of centralized, authoritarian government. They regulate, tax, extract, and terrify. They thrive on radical discrimination, treating each of us differently and isolating each of us according to our differences. After *Citizens United*, monopoly powers can use their money to influence policy in unlimited ways (so long as they don't directly coordinate with candidates). They spy on workers and tell them what to think. They fund foundations that shape editorial boards. They are the biggest lobbyists. They don't pay taxes. They embed themselves in federal, state, and local law enforcement. They build moats around their power and use predatory pricing or mergers to keep out competitors—or at least all competitors that aren't within their special class of quasi-governmental corporations.

When a handful of CEOs and Wall Street financiers have subverted our democracy, destroyed our individual liberties, and stolen the value of our labor—all in the name of freedom and progress—then we should think of them not as economic actors but as tyrants: little would-be Alexander the Greats. So the first part of my book examines today's monopolies as part of a new form of political structure and shows how they exert control over our everyday lives. As the citizen has turned into a consumer, the manufacturer and farmer into a feudal tenant, and the worker into a serf, corporate monopolists have begun to charge whatever prices they want, pay whatever wages they want, *and* dictate politics however they see fit. The attendant unchecked concentrated power leads to a cancerous egotism that takes over people and institutions. As the great Supreme Court Justice Louis Brandeis said early in his legal career, while giving an address advocating for antitrust, "[a]bsolute power leads to excesses and to weakness: neither our character nor our intelligence can long bear the strain of unrestricted power."[5]

The first eight chapters make this argument by looking at how monopolists have captured and corrupted different sectors of the American political economy, and how they are using their powers in ways that reduce your freedoms and well-being, and subvert our democracy. I start off by describing the new economy of farming, and how it works. Then I show how the same basic approaches developed in farming are now being applied to many other sectors. Chicken farmers, taxi drivers, restaurant owners, dry cleaners, TaskRabbiters—all are working inside a quasi-economic, quasi-political system that depends upon isolation, arbitrariness, fear, and a deep loss of agency and vitality. I then look deeper into the features of this new regime. Who are the rulers? What is their relationship to media? How do their courts work? How do they organize in campaigns? What are their racial politics? And what does all this mean for inequality?

My second argument concerns strategy; we need to organize an antitrust movement for our time.

We can't rely on consumer boycotts. Big corporations know the ethical consumer sensibility, are comfortable within it, and play to it. In fact, boycotts—because they include carrots and sticks—can help reinforce the authority of corporations. When we threaten to boycott Facebook for not taking down white nationalists, we reinforce the idea that Facebook has the authority to decide what constitutes acceptable speech in social media, and signal our acceptance of Facebook as the editor of everything.

Instead, we should be stopping mergers, breaking up big corporations, regulating aspects of big tech as a public utility, enabling cooperatives, changing the way we fund elections, banning forced arbitration, strengthening unions, and demanding that states and the federal government use their existing power to regulate and investigate the corporate usurpers.

The second part of this book lays out the concrete steps we need to take and shows why our current approaches will keep failing until we change. It will require a change in leftist protest. Instead of protesting Pfizer on Tuesday for hiking drug prices, Comcast on Wednesday for suppressing union voices, and Amazon on Thursday for getting billions in subsidies, we should unite behind a coherent agenda, demanding that antitrust authorities break up Pfizer and Comcast, Amazon and Facebook, Monsanto and Tyson.

We need to build an anti-monopoly movement, the likes

of which has never been seen before. In so doing, we can confidently call on the tools of the past, augment them, and use them to regain our power. We can replace the modern monopolists with a more decentralized set of worker- and producer-owned co-ops, and medium-sized companies with unionized workforces, supplemented by local banking. We must all embrace an anti-monopoly vision in order to achieve the moral economy that we deserve.

✳

There is some good news. Over the past few years (and even months), the nearly extinct movement against monopolies has grown into a major political force once again.

In 2014, Tim Wu and I ran on a joint ticket for governor and lieutenant governor of New York on an anticorruption and antitrust platform. We called ourselves "old-fashioned trust-busters." While the race got some national attention because of our anticorruption themes and our unlikely high vote count against an incumbent governor and his running mate, we found that people were thrilled when we mentioned that we wanted to break up big corporations. At our campaign events people ripped up their cable bills to protest the cable monopolies, and we heard countless stories of small-business owners who felt they had been crowded out. That same year, with the looming merger of Comcast and Time Warner Cable, protesters rallied at the yearly Comcast board meeting in Philadelphia, shouting to shareholders, "We vote no!"[6] The Comcast–Time Warner merger failed when the Department of Justice announced it would sue to stop it—after a massive coalition of 56 groups across the country organized against it.

Towns around the country have banned big-box stores. Jersey City has a law on the books banning chain stores altogether, which it recently used to keep out CVS.[7] Tulsa, Oklahoma, is putting a limit on Dollar Stores; and there are efforts in almost every state to take back control of electricity from corporations that have swallowed local utilities.[8] Seven hundred and fifty different communities have built their own broadband service providers, built local internet cooperatives, or made some of the local fiber network public for all—breaking the stranglehold of big telecom.

In 2017, SumOfUs, Friends of the Earth, and the Open Markets Institute delivered over 1 million signatures in opposition to the Monsanto-Bayer merger.[9] Farm organizers testified against it. A poll showed that 93% of farmers shared the organizers' views.[10] Months later, a ground-up, grassroots movement in Queens, New York, defeated Amazon's effort to build a new headquarters there—a movement fired by antipathy toward Amazon's monopolistic business model.

Chris Hughes, the billionaire co-founder of Facebook, called for breaking up Facebook in the pages of the *New York Times*.[11]

The House Judiciary has started a major investigation into antitrust violations.

The attorneys general in 47 of our 50 states have launched investigations into Google and Facebook.

In one of the largest worker protests in recent history, "The Walkout for Real Change at Google" led to the corporation changing its arbitration clauses—a monopoly governance tool, as I explain in chapter 4.

These were extraordinary moments.

Globally, the anti-monopoly movement is even stronger. Europe has cracked down on Google and Amazon with heavy fines (albeit not heavy enough). In 2017, anti-merger activists stood in the rain in France, shouting "Non à la fusion!" (no to the merger)[12] in an attempt to persuade the European Union to stop Bayer from joining with Monsanto. The previous year in Bonn, protesters and politicians descended upon the Bayer general board meeting, calling the fusion with Monsanto a "marriage of death" and a "crime against nature."[13]

A million Indian bank workers walked off the job in opposition to bank mergers in 2018. The general secretary of the largest union involved in organizing the strike fumed: "All the alibis raised by the government in justification of the mergers, like 'economies of scale,' 'better efficiency,' etc., are all superfluous, baseless arguments and can only be termed as mere jugglery of words."[14] Small traders and manufacturers held mass rallies against the proposed merger of Walmart and Flipkart in India that same year, claiming that the merger threatened their survival and self-governance. A representative of the traders explained, "Walmart will go the Uber way. They will sell goods at cheaper rates initially, and then start hiking their prices once small traders are wiped out." He said, "We are protesting for our future generations."[15]

What if a million workers protested here? Direct action on a massive scale has effected major change before. A company considered in its day the largest company in the world has been broken up at least three times—Standard Oil, then AT&T, then IG Farben—all despite plutocratic resistance, because of persistent, strategic activism. Unfortunately, breaking up the biggest company in the world, or even the biggest five, will not be sufficient today. For the sake of our future, we need to build the most powerful and effective antitrust movement the world has ever seen. This goal is urgent and ambitious, but it is also surprisingly practical; let's begin with a sample list of companies that should no longer exist in their current form two years from now. If you read nothing else, tear out this page and tack it to your refrigerator:

Amazon
Alphabet
Google
Monsanto/Bayer
Spectrum
Pfizer
Uber
Visa
Unilever
Verizon
Exxon
Bank of America
Citibank
Common Spirit Health
Disney
CVS
Nestlé
UnitedHealthcare
Blue Cross/Blue Shield
Comcast
Boeing
Walmart

Join me, and let's break 'em up!

1

The Chickenization of the American Middle Class

For 40 years, Dean Pierson cared for and milked his dairy cows on High Low Farm, in a pretty valley at the foot of the Taconic Mountains in New York's Hudson Valley. One morning in 2010, he woke up, went into his barn, carefully shot each of his 51 cows in the head, and then shot himself. His friends bore his coffin to the graveyard on top a John Deere tractor.

A thousand miles west, on the plains of Iowa, Matt, a corn and soybean farmer, confessed to his wife that he was worried about the planting season. He never came home, and the next day she found a suicide note that she describes as a "love letter," urging her to ask a family friend for help with the farm.[1] On a cold, gray April Fool's Day a few years later, Keith Gillies, a Minnesota soybean farmer, killed himself, leaving his wife— the president of the state's soybean growers' association— bewildered and lost.[2]

Farmers and farmworkers are killing themselves and drug-ging themselves to death at terrifying rates.[3] Three-quarters of farmers or farmworkers say they are close to someone with an opioid addiction and have been "directly impacted" by the epidemic.[4] The mental health crisis in farming is so serious that one big corporate distributor sends a letter listing mental health

resources twice a month to its farmers, along with their checks
and price listings.[5] As a new farmer tweeted recently, in response to a new mental health outreach program, "All my life,
literally all I wanted to be was a farmer. Now I'm an adult a
year from diving into an industry so bad that you get suicide
prevention help with your paycheck. How are you even supposed to deal with that?"[6] Farmer organizers I talk to describe
the weeping and terror of men and women who run farms or
work on farms, who feel totally lost while they know they are
supposed to feel free because they run their own businesses.

To understand the gig economy and the future of work,
it helps to understand what is happening in farming, and to
understand farming, it helps to start with chicken farming. We
tend to treat rural and urban problems as if they existed in two
separate worlds. In fact, a new immigrant in a big city faces
the same challenges as a family who has lived in the same rural
community for generations. One struggles with Uber, and the
other with Tyson, but these monopolies operate in strikingly
similar ways, and they provide a dystopian roadmap for the
future of business in America.

CHICKENIZATION

The chicken industry is booming. If you squint at it from a distance, it also looks cheerful: 25,000 independent family farmers dotting America's landscape. Each farmer owns at least one
chicken house. Each sells chickens to a distributor. Many have
employees. Given the number of chickens raised in the United
States, and the number of people engaged in raising them, one
might assume the owners make a decent living. They don't.
Chickens are a $90-billion-a-year industry, but many farmers
make poverty wages, and live with debilitating debt.[7]

"I get phone calls continually about suicide," Jonathan Buttram, a third-generation farmer and president of the Alabama Contract Poultry Growers Association, tells me. Two farmers he knew had killed themselves in the past. Buttram wanted to make sure I knew he was not suicidal, but his health was in terrible shape. At sixty-three, he was taking three heart medicines, and he was overwhelmed with stress and anger and fear. "The only problem with me is I have a heart, that causes a problem," he said. "If you have no heart maybe you can survive in this world."

The world Buttram means is the world of big processors.

Three processors—Tyson, Pilgrim's Pride, and Perdue—are responsible for buying and selling almost every chicken in America. They are the ones who slaughter the chickens, pluck and gut them, chill them, and ship them to groceries and restaurants. There is growing evidence that the processors secretly coordinate with each other and do not compete with each other.[8] They stay off each other's turf. So in most parts of the country, farmers have no choice but to sell their chickens to one buyer. And in order to sell to that buyer, the farmer has no choice but to sign an arbitration contract, so that any dispute with his processor stays secret (I talk more about arbitration clauses in chapter 4). The same contract forbids him from talking to his neighbors about how much he makes per chicken, or any other aspect of farming. He must build his chicken houses to the processor's exact specifications. And inside any given farm, you'll likely find a million-dollar bank mortgage for that chicken house, meaning that, if the processor refuses to sell his chickens, the farmer will go bankrupt.

The processor's control extends to every part of a farmer's business. If he is in a Tyson region, he must use the medicines from Tyson and the lighting and watering schedule recommended by Tyson. He must use the advisors that Tyson recommends.

He must agree with Tyson that there will be no fixed payment for his chicken. Tyson instead holds what they call a "tournament," promising to pay farmers more when their chickens produce more meat than their neighbors' chickens. The farmers, who are already forbidden to talk to each other, know that there is not a single price for a pound of chicken, but a changing one, and while they can see their own paycheck, they can't compare it to others'.[9]

Farmers are liable if something goes wrong, and they must shoulder the full cost of failure, but they lack the freedom to make decisions. They lack insight into how the processor makes decisions, and they have to accept a high degree of uncertainty about how much they will get paid and why their payments change. It is a structure reminiscent of Jeremy Bentham's panopticon, a vision of a jail designed to maximize control and quell dissent, where a jailer can see all the inmates, but the inmates cannot see each other. All contracts also give the processor the right to gather data from farmers and use it. Almost all contracts can be terminated with 90 days' notice, though some farmers I talked to said that the companies ignore the 90-day rule when they want to get rid of someone.

Tyson—or Perdue or Pilgrim's—is then in a position where it can experiment on farmers without their knowledge. If Tyson wants to try out a new kind of feed, it could force 5 out of 50 farmers in a region to use that feed. None of them will know the nature of the experiment because the terms of the contract keep them in the dark. If those five farmers produce skinnier chickens, the farmers will bear the cost of the experiment, and Tyson will simply pay them less. If Tyson wants to experiment with new dimming techniques (chickens are frequently kept in dark pens so they don't destroy each other through stressed pecking), it can demand that half the farmers use the new techniques. It can use the results of the experiment for any purpose, but it does not have to share them with the subjects in its experiment. It can study the breaking points of farmers—when do they earn so little that they quit—and structure contracts to keep farmers just barely in business. While the chicken farmers are radically transparent to Tyson, Tyson's choices are totally opaque. Buttram's theory is that they purposefully keep 15% of the chicken farmers doing well and starve the other 85% so that they have enough examples they can trot to Washington, DC, the "15 percenters," who can speak glowingly about their experience.

The political result is a transformation of citizens into subjects of experimentation and arbitrary power. The farmers are isolated from their neighbors by contract, are experimented and spied on by their processors, and live in fear of speaking out. Their situation involves a permanent precariousness; they know they can be devastated by one wrong move. They have no assurances that their chickens will be sold, no ability to bargain, and no solidarity or friendly—or unfriendly—rivalry with their neighbors. Forbidden from talking to the other businessmen and -women in their own industry, they are stuck in a state of deliberate paranoia and suspicion that can never be confirmed or put to rest. If they have a bad six months, was it punishment, luck, or a downgrade across the board? How would they know? A chicken farmer who speaks frankly and openly about the system, or his processor, risks all he has. While farmers may be free to argue about national scandals or international trade wars, they are silenced when their voices might matter the most to their own livelihood.

The social, political, and informational isolation makes people suspicious, fearful, subservient, and very angry. One farmer I talked to told me that more than one friend of his had dreamed about going on killing sprees against processors. In 2010, the Department of Justice held hearings around the country to investigate problems in the chicken industry. At first, some farmers lined up to testify. At one meeting in Normal, Alabama, with Department of Justice Chief Christine Varney, a long line of farmers formed, men and women, ready to tell their stories. But after the hearing, farmers who spoke out started getting bad chickens and bad paychecks, and many were forced out of business. After that, farmers kept silent because they were scared that if they spoke out, they'd be punished. Contract farming might as well have cut out the farmers' tongues.

Buttram started a gas cooperative to bring down costs for farmers in his area, but he says this angered the local processor, who tried to get rid of both the co-op and Buttram. They terminated his contracts. When he moved into a related business, cleaning out chicken houses for other growers, they banned him from going on anybody's chicken farm and threatened termination for anyone who used him.

This processor-control model—called chickenization, because the innovators came from chicken processing—has spread to almost all poultry and pork production. It is not driven by technological change. It is, rather, a direct result of changes in our antitrust laws. For most of the twentieth century, chickens were raised by farmers who bought feed from independent feed mills, bought chicks from hatcheries, and sold chickens to one of many different local processors. Each type of company sold their product on an open market. Farmers made choices about how to build their chicken houses, how to treat their workers, how to treat the animals, how big or small to grow, how much risk to take, what breeds to look into, and how to spend their Sundays.

Ronald Reagan changed all that. In the early 1980s, Reagan transformed antitrust policy and appointed hundreds of judges who gutted antitrust law. Under the direction of Bill

Baxter, Reagan's head of the antitrust division of the Justice Department, prosecutors stopped blocking horizontal mergers. A horizontal merger is the joining of two companies in the same market; today that might mean Nike merging with Adidas. Prosecutors also announced a radical change in the policy regarding vertical mergers—mergers between a company and a related company in a different field. A vertical merger today would be Adidas, the shoe company, buying a rubber manufacturer that they use to make shoes. Prosecutors adopted the stance that vertical integration, once looked on with trepidation, would lead to great efficiencies and lower consumer prices. In the rare case where the Justice Department sued to block a merger, Reagan-appointed judges interpreted the major antitrust statutes so narrowly that the statutes became little more than dead letters.

Chicken processors seized the chance to consolidate power. Tyson, Perdue, and Pilgrim's went on a buying spree, horizontal, then vertical: first they bought up all the processing plants in a region, then they collected every company that had anything to do with chicken distribution. They bought feed mills, hatcheries, transportation systems, packagers, and marketers. Live chickens die if they travel too far, and dead chickens rot. Therefore, chicken farmers can only sell within a certain radius; if all the processing plants in that radius are owned by one company, a farmer has no choice but to follow the dictates of the processor to get the food to market.

We call them small-business owners, but a recent 2018 review of lending to chicken farmers concluded that the farmers should not be categorized as small-business owners (and therefore eligible for billions of dollars, collectively, in loans), because the processor, now vertical integrator, controls almost all aspects of the production. "We found integrator control exercised through a series of contractual restrictions, management agreements, oversight inspections, and market controls. This control overcame practically all of a grower's ability to operate their business independent of integrator mandates," the inspector found.[10]

Lately chickenization has spread to beef, bringing with it fear and dismay. Joe Maxwell, a former Missouri lieutenant governor who now works with contract farmers, describes it as an erosion of civic freedoms. "When there is just one buyer," he says, "you don't have any rights." Farmers cannot make choices about the treatment of their animals, the treatment of their land, or the treatment of their workers. They are stripped of moral agency. In Maxwell's words, they are forced to choose between "giving up the values they have for the land, or los[ing] the land." Some leave. Many go bankrupt. Others stay on as serfs.

There's a particular moment that Maxwell has come to recognize, the moment when a chickenized farmer realizes the full extent of his impotence. It comes a few years after the excitement and joy of building a chicken farm or taking over a family operation. Maxwell describes it as a terrifying awakening. "The scaffolds have been built and you can see them from your cell . . . the other folks are in prison hearing the nails being driven."[11] Even if the farmer is still making a living, he can see the ways in which the corporate structure takes over all the decisions and stands ready to cut him out of his livelihood if he makes a wrong step.

The rest of agriculture is starting to hear those same nails. Unlike the chicken farmer, stuck with a carcass that needs to be handled within a narrow geographical radius, the commodities farmer—think corn, rice, wheat—can easily ship outside their region. One might imagine, therefore, that the corn, soy, wheat, and rice farmers might have substantially more freedom: their crops are nonperishable, storable, transportable.

But while the commodities farmer in America faces different choke points, monopolies are still in charge. The lords of grain are Monsanto (which provides the seeds and fertilizer); Archer Daniels Midland (ADM) and Cargill (the big buyers); and John Deere and Caterpillar (which provide the equipment).

In theory, prices are set by the market. In practice, these merged companies have the power to set prices. After Reagan's judges upended the old market rules, Monsanto followed the same process as Tyson: first it bought up all the seed companies, then it started buying vertically, in fertilizer and pesticides. In a new twist, Monsanto offered farmers huge incentives to buy Monsanto seed, but the contracts came with lock-in mechanisms, making it financially ruinous to use seeds from any other supplier.

Like Tyson, Monsanto now makes decisions that used to be the farmer's. If a family wishes to switch to a non-Monsanto seed company, first they have to leave the field fallow for at least a year—not an option for farmers who live from paycheck to paycheck. Furthermore, a family isn't allowed to use Monsanto seeds if they harvest those seeds themselves. Instead, they have to keep buying new seeds every year. Once a farmer stops buying a seed, they are not allowed to use it even accidentally, and Monsanto has been aggressive about policing accidental use, making it safer for farmers to stick with Monsanto, instead of switching to a different seed and risk getting sued.[12]

These contracts have depressed farmer income and increased Monsanto profits: to plant an acre of corn in 1990, it used to cost $100 for everything, including the fertilizer and the seed. Now it costs over $400 per acre.[13] That figure does not cover the human cost of servitude, when a family is no longer allowed to make the most basic decisions for itself, or the material cost when a farmer is forbidden to innovate—to try for a higher yield or a better crop—or the environmental

cost when farmers are reduced from true investors in the land
to little more than inmates.

Even on his tractor, a farmer has no freedom: John Deere
contracts require that the tractors be serviced by affiliates of
the companies. In other words, you're not allowed to fix your
own tractor. And John Deere's power is built on over 20 mergers, and the fact that it has made itself the fifth-largest agricultural lender in the country. It can issue credit to farmers on the
condition that they buy tractors from Deere and not the competition. A third of Deere's profits are now in lending, and it
leverages its dominance in each arena to increase its dominance
in the other. John Deere's profits are up, farmers' are down;
during a recent downturn, when farmers struggled, Deere was
doing just fine.[14]

To be clear, farming is not a business rocked by technological change, as whaling was rocked by natural gas, or typewriters
by the personal computer. Farming, as an industry, is bigger
than ever. People are eating lots of food—more than we ever
have, per capita—and you would expect, just from going to a
grocery store, or perusing the number of full restaurants on a
Tuesday night, that farmers would be flush. They aren't. Some
of the biggest Fortune 500 companies may be in agriculture
and are making huge profits, but farmers are poor and insecure.

I grew up in a rural community where people have been
farming, typically on a small scale, for hundreds of years. My
family raised sheep and chickens—and the rare pig and calf—
for our own consumption, while neighbors on all sides made
their living as dairy farmers, waking up to milk cows first thing
in the morning and selling that milk to cooperatives. It was
never an easy living. When I worked as a farmhand over college summers, the farmer I worked for was up before dawn and
still running his tractor when the sun went down. To make
ends meet, he drove a UPS truck in winter. But in certain basic

ways he was free. He could choose what seeds to buy and how to plant them. He could fix his own tractor. He could sell to buyers he trusted. He had a passionate love of his land, of science, and of good crops. In the winters, along with driving a UPS truck, he would read up on all the newest developments in farming and science magazines, trying to grow a better product.

That was in 1985, when farmers were paid nearly 40 cents for every dollar we spent on food. Farmers in the same position today make less than 15 cents.[15] Where has the rest of it gone? To those same few corporations, depriving farmers of security, dignity, and the freedom to be full citizens.

GIGOPOLIES

One hundred miles south of High Low Farm, in July 2018, four coffins sat out on the steps of New York's city hall. They represented four taxi drivers, family men who had killed themselves after their taxi medallions—the expensive permits that allow a New York cab to operate—lost their value, thanks to the new tide of unregulated Uber cars on New York streets.

If you don't live and work in a rural community, you may not have heard of chickenization, but like those taxi drivers, you may have been chickenized yourself. In cities and towns, we call it the "gig economy"—but it's based on the same principles of monopoly. Seamless and Amazon are, to restaurants and to publishers and writers, what Monsanto is to growers of corn or soybeans. The real difference is cosmetic. In farming, monopolies usually justify their existence on the grounds of "efficiency"; in the service sector and the media, the false god is technology.

For that reason, before we turn to Uber, it's worth examining the two ways people usually talk about the gig economy.

Both describe giggism in essentially technological terms. Both are wrong.

One view is that the gig economy has freed the American worker as never before. The office worker is released, at last, from the nine-to-five grind of a Dilbert. The home cleaner is emancipated from a singular, tyrannical, and cruel boss. These workers are now free to sell their skills and experience to the highest bidder, creating an online reputation based only on their work. The freelancer chooses her own vacations and sets her own timeline. Where the old economy was closed, the gig economy is open. Where the old economy left few choices to the worker, the gig economy gives them options. Under this view, the gig economy unlocks unused potential and (in the extreme form of gig-boosterism) increases equality, because the middleman between seller and buyer is removed.

A second view holds that the gig economy is a tragedy, but a technologically foreordained one. Gig workers are necessarily atomized and powerless. They are lonely, isolated, and stuck, because the internet has inevitably led to a world where you can isolate particular needs and match them to a particular skill, where people's skills are priced individually and sold separately. This disambiguation—the shift from jobs to tasks—has inevitably led to the isolated, powerless worker. A sympathetic *Atlantic* article on the rash of driver suicides led with the statement, "Technology has pushed a vulnerable, largely immigrant, population into an economically precarious position." In this telling, technology is the agent of change and has removed the middleman at great cost.[16]

The first perspective is not only mistaken, it is upside down. Freedom is not given to workers, but to the monopolies that control their work. The second view, while more sympathetic and realistic about the nature of modern work, is also mistaken, and is arguably more insidious, because it invests technology with a superhuman, inexorable power of its own. Both views wrongly imagine that the function of technology is to *remove* the middleman, when in fact gig platforms *replace* a large set of regulated middlemen with a single intermediary. The purpose of these new intermediaries is to establish positions of power, choke points of control, after which they can identify ways to maximally extract wealth from any transaction, while taking minimal responsibility.

The modern gig economy is neither glamorous *nor* inevitable, and it hides monopolies behind the rhetoric of technology, just as contract farming hides a feudal technique behind the language of efficiency. The words you hear most frequently when reading about the gig economy are *tech* (which suggests newness), *platform* (which implies neutrality), and *disruption* (which implies taking down centralized power). As we shall see, all three terms are misleading. To quote Bhairavi Desai, the co-founder and executive director of the New York Taxi Workers Alliance and one of Uber's most tireless opponents: "Our fight was never about the technology, it was about the business model."[17]

Taxis were introduced to New York City in the late nineteenth century; they became affordable for working men and women—thus, part of the city's infrastructure—in the late 1920s, when cars with unskilled drivers flooded the streets and desperate drivers actually fought each other for fares. The city was a snarled mess. Transportation became unsafe: an overworked driver in a poorly maintained car could kill you.

Enter Morris Markin, president of Checker Motors. In a bold effort to corner the New York taxi market, Markin bought up dozens of cab companies and created the biggest fleet the city had ever seen. Markin was also deeply embedded in local politics. He persuaded his friend Mayor Jimmy Walker that, in the name of safety and efficiency, the city should "sell a single franchise to one company to operate all the cabs."[18] This sort of private-public partnership was very fashionable during the administration of Herbert Hoover, a former engineer who believed passionately in centralization. The single-franchise model—with one big business controlling traffic and wages— gained traction, and Checker Motors flourished until a state-led anti-corruption investigation revealed that Markin's associates had bribed Walker's administration to get the monopoly.[19]

Mayor Fiorello La Guardia took over in 1934 with a promise of cleaning up corruption. He created a new legal regime for taxis, a version of which New York City lived with for 80 years. It was grounded in six principles: providing reliable service, keeping out monopolies, stopping corruption, preventing congestion, promoting safety, and ensuring that drivers could make a decent living. It introduced licenses, which protected passengers by ensuring that all cabs were certified and regulated. It protected the city by restricting the total number of cars on the street. And it protected drivers from monopoly bosses like Markin, dividing medallions (taxi permits) between those who owned the car they drove (42%) and those who owned fleets of cars (58%).[20]

As the new law declared, "The taxicab industry must be safeguarded against the ultimate possibility of monopolistic control."[21] The medallion system spread power among a wide range of taxi owners. This gave the drivers bargaining power. A driver unhappy working for one fleet owner still had hundreds of other fleet owners to whom he could sell his services. Although the system was far from perfect and could be open to abuse by medallion moguls like "taxi king" Gene Friedman, it led to the cheapest taxis in the country, a relatively uncongested city, and decent pay for drivers. Then Uber came to town.

Uber arrived in New York City in 2013, and in the early

years—echoing a Monsanto tactic—paid big bonuses to attract drivers. At the same time, Uber undercut New York City taxi rates, which at the time were the lowest in the country. Drivers flocked to Uber. So did riders. In less than three years, Uber displaced cabs and became the dominant mode of for-hail transportation in New York City.

How did they get around city regulations, so ingeniously designed to balance the interests of drivers, customers, and everybody else?

First, Uber simply broke the laws. CEO Travis Kalanick encouraged drivers to engage in what he called the "criminal misdemeanor" of hacking without a permit. And not just in New York. "Uber Policy Whitepaper 1.0" of 2013 made it company policy to test local enforcement by breaking local laws wherever Uber opened up shop.[22] At the same time, Uber openly developed software whose only purpose was to evade law enforcement, to make it harder to bust unlicensed drivers.

Second, Uber leveraged their new market share to push through new laws. It spent millions on lobbying mayors and city councils. It also gave heavily to nonprofits, including the New York Urban League and the National Action Network. Uber even hired a consulting firm that bullied drivers into arguing against their own interest. As the drivers described it, you'd get a call that you were about to be "patched through" to a city council member, then you'd be told what to say. "It felt like a company town," Biju Mathew, a co-founder of the Taxi Workers Alliance, told me. "Everywhere you could sense their power."[23]

Finally, Uber engaged in predatory behavior. Predation, in the legal sense, is when a company tries to drive out competition in order to monopolize, either by undercutting prices or by overpaying for assets, including workers. Uber has been losing money hand over fist for years—nearly $3 billion in 2016, and $4.5 billion in 2017. It does so to dominate the market—that's

why Wall Street gives it a long leash. Predatory behavior used
to be illegal, it is the classic stage one of any monopoly bid, but
Uber isn't that worried about lawsuits. Post-Reagan prosecutors rarely bring predation cases, and the post-Reagan judiciary
makes them hard to win.

Uber set out to own the territory of New York City the
way Tyson owns swaths of Arkansas. Once you control a market, you can set prices, extract wage value, and vertically inte-
grate with other companies to create more control and more
extraction. In the case of Uber, that means paying workers
less and charging passengers more. Desai explains it this way:
"Once you monopolize, you don't ever need to show up at the
table."[24] Because you own the table. That is why investors are
willing to risk so much, for so long, if a CEO can persuade
them that a monopoly is on the horizon.

Uber hasn't succeeded in making money yet. After its IPO
in May 2019, its value plummeted. Unfortunately, it is bringing drivers down with it. Within five years, Uber had managed
to reduce drivers' pay from an average of $14 per hour to less
than $12 per hour, all while driving up the price of a taxi
ride.[25]

The drivers who switched to Uber found themselves in a
situation very different from a taxi driver's. Technically, the
driver was a free and independent contractor. At the same
time, he was wholly subject to company decisions and whims.
The driver was responsible for the car, for insurance, and for
any criminal or civil infraction, but the company called all
the shots. Drivers could be "deactivated" for a single, unin-
vestigated complaint or for no reason at all. One driver was
deactivated because he was attacked by a passenger and called
the police. The company described this as a "safety issue" and
kicked him out of the network.[26]

When the company first came to New York, it offered

drivers an 80% cut on every fare. Driver value was tied to the value they created. No longer. Now, a passenger agrees to a base fare (set by Uber), and drivers are paid a fee according to their distance and time (also set by Uber), but—just as in contract farming—the ratio between these two is hidden and constantly changing. Growing evidence suggests that Uber is sometimes keeping not 20% or 25%, but up to 60% of the fare. Just as in contract farming, Uber hides all the data it collects from its drivers and experiments on them without their knowledge or consent.[27]

And it all happened so fast because the technology was dazzling. *Is* dazzling. You push a button and a car appears? Those of us who remember trying to hail a cab in the cold and rain will never get over the marvel of it. The technology is genuinely innovative and great. But despite public relations that might make you think otherwise, the idea for this application wasn't invented by Uber. Most car services—including New York taxis—were moving in the direction of e-hailing before Uber entered the scene. At the most, Uber hastened the adoption of e-hailing by a year or so. You don't need monopolistic control for an application to work. It can easily work inside a regulated, licensed medallion industry: either all drivers use one app that a city buys into, or regulated, licensed drivers choose among different apps. Uber successfully sold the idea that, if we wanted to use our phones to get a taxi, we needed to destroy 80 years of anti-monopoly laws. This was a giant lie.

For those thousands of taxi drivers who put their life savings in city-issued medallions, the result has been ruinous. For the rest of us, it's meant lower wages, higher fares, and longer driving times, with whole arteries of the city reduced to twice-daily traffic jams.[28]

For-hail drivers in New York City are a hardheaded, politically active group. When Donald Trump passed his travel ban

targeting Muslim countries, for example, the New York Taxi
Alliance immediately began picketing at JFK Airport (94% of
the workforce is made up of immigrants). In my experience,
taxi drivers have no sentimental affection for traditional fleet
owners, or for Lyft or Uber. Each one is just another boss.

Yet the drivers I talked to—Uber drivers, taxi drivers—all
describe Uber's recruitment as a bait and switch that left them
feeling fleeced, angry, and more than a little depressed by the
focus of the left. The left has been concentrating very hard on
raising the minimum wage while ignoring the rise of a company like Uber, which is explicitly designed to extract all value
and power from drivers. Drivers worry that winning policy
fights but losing power fights will lead to the long-term decimation of both power and policy.

One day in particular stands out to Biju Mathew, the taxi
driver quoted earlier. It was a perfect midsummer day in New
York City. Highs in the low 80s, lows in the 70s, sunny, with
thousands of workers jubilant at a mass rally, many of them
weeping in triumph. After years of walkouts, six a.m. rallies,
and heart-wrenching testimonies before lawmakers, the state
legislature announced that it was abolishing the $8.75 per hour
poverty wage for fast-food workers and would raise the minimum to $15. The Fight for $15 victory was a turning point,
one of the greatest labor victories in decades. It showed how
non-unionized workers could win hard fights.

On the same day—July 22, 2015—at almost the exact
same hour, in the streets of every borough of New York City,
in yellow and green taxis, in Ubers and Lyfts, there was a collective cry of anguish—texts and calls buzzed from driver to
driver. The same morning of the epic Fight for $15 victory,
Mayor Bill de Blasio announced that, after a yearlong fight,
there would be no cap on the number of Uber drivers. The
principles La Guardia championed had lost. Uber had won.

The supposedly progressive mayor had sold the drivers out. And he had done so under cover of the Fight for $15 victory. As when the Supreme Court recognized marriage equality in the same week that it struck down the key provisions of the Voting Rights Act, the timing did not seem accidental.

Mathew sees the fight with Uber as part of a larger fight in our economy: in the new model, when it comes to wages, we may be able to win minimum-wage fights, but those numbers could also come to represent the maximum wage, because the new platforms squeeze everything out of every worker once they have monopoly control. "The floor is becoming the ceiling," he says.[29]

THE CHICKENIZATION OF EVERYTHING

This is the future of work, not just for food and taxis, but for huge swaths of our economy.

Consider the growing chickenization of restaurants. The future of eating is home delivery. Digital ordering has grown 300% faster than sit-down eating since 2014, according to one report. Today, delivery accounts for 10% of restaurant sales. As of 2016, 64% of restaurant food was eaten somewhere other than the restaurant. Increasingly, those off-premise meals are ordered through an app.[30] Delivery apps have become a crucial part of the restaurant business—in 2013, Grubhub merged with Seamless, and they too have been in a race for market domination. Their two main competitors are DoorDash and, yes, Uber.

The platforms charge between 15% and 30% commissions, taking away money that used to go to the restaurants, and justifying it on the grounds that they are expanding the customer base. The platforms keep the data on customers' names and phone numbers, leaving restaurants with no way to build direct relationships with customers. Restaurant owners have no real choice but to comply. "Grubhub has such huge market share that to say no, a lot of them feel like they'd be missing out on a lot of business," Melissa Autilio Fleischut, president of the New York State Restaurant Association, told a *New York Times* reporter. "I don't know of any restaurant who says, 'I'm not going to do it through these apps.'"[31] As the market calcifies, and the ratio of delivery to sit-down rises, the rates may rise.

To stay in business, restaurants may pay their own workers less. They may cut corners on food. If Seamless vertically integrates with a ketchup company, restaurants may find that access to Seamless depends upon using Seamless Ketchup, or sharing sensitive data. If they protest, they may find themselves delisted from these central platforms. Customers don't benefit either; Grubhub already charges restaurants higher commissions in exchange for better visibility on the platform, meaning that restaurants are spending their narrow profit margins competing with each other for space on Grubhub, instead of competing on quality.

Tens of thousands of tiny nodes of small-business owners in America are facing similar threats. For decades, Korean American families have run dry-cleaning small businesses in American cities. Now, they face competition from well-funded startups, like FlyCleaners and Cleanly, who are racing to become the middlemen—the platforms putting themselves between the dry cleaners and customers, and taking a cut from the dry cleaners, while forcing them to obey the new platforms' standards.[32]

At the same time, franchising is increasingly looking like a version of chickenization. The franchise model in America— used by McDonald's, IHOP, Quiznos, and others—was once a way for business owners to use the value of a national chain to create their own business, with autonomy. Here too the model gives increasing control and profit to the franchisor, leaving the franchisee with more risk and responsibility. The franchisee takes on the debt, but McDonald's tells the franchisee precisely how to run their restaurant, with temperatures, layout, and prices all dictated from above. The one area of freedom given franchisees is how much—or rather how little—to pay their workers. McDonald's micromanages the work, and has the information capacity to be able to experiment on franchisees, but blames the franchise owners for poverty wages. When Fight for $15 organizers protested McDonald's, the company argued that it was not responsible for the choices of its tens of thousands of franchisees.[33]

Silicon Valley likes to call this decentralization. It is, in fact, the opposite. Power is centralized. Money is centralized. Decision making is centralized. The only things decentralized are labor and risk, and these take place under constant one-way surveillance. As a farmer innovates, that innovation is no longer something he can take advantage of, but something that Monsanto can. One former Monsanto engineer put it this way: "If you inadvertently teach Monsanto what it is that makes you a better farmer than your neighbor, it can sell that information to your neighbor."[34]

All models of chickenization rely on intensive collection of data. Seamless collects data on deliverers. Bayer/Monsanto has made purchasing data companies a priority and has spent billions to acquire data analytics firms. John Deere uses its tractors to spy on farmers, collecting information on crop rotations, weather patterns, soil nutrients, and yields. With growing concern about data, some people are suggesting that we need to establish a clear premise of data ownership. There are good reasons to do so, but it will not and cannot change the contract model. Even if a contract stipulates that the farmer, driver, or merchant "owns" the data, the company (Deere, Monsanto,

Uber) will always make sure it can use that data however it likes. And because the company's surveillance is all one way, it is the only one in a position to connect the dots between one farm or car and a million others.

Surveillance and power go hand in hand, each reinforcing the other. The surveillance is already extreme—following every turn of a taxi driver, or every heat change of a chicken house—and is on track to cover all aspects of independent work, as censors listen to conversations, gather keystrokes, judge emotion, and identify ways to extract more value from the business that depends on them.[35] In 2018, the largest education company in the world, Pearson, a monopolist in testing and education software, proudly released a study that showed that they had been using students as guinea pigs to test products. The company randomly embedded different psychological messaging in some versions of its software programs, but not in others. At 165 colleges and universities, 9,300 students were unknowing subjects of the Pearson experiment during the spring of 2017.[36] All the students used MyLab Programming, a product that is supposed to help students learn material tied to a computer-programming textbook. Some students received "growth-mindset" messaging; others did not. The students were totally unaware of their involvement in the test, which gave an advantage to some and a disadvantage to others.

The National Chicken Council, the official lobbying arm for Tyson, Perdue, and Pilgrim's, is proud of the contract farming structure. They hold up the broiler industry as a model that will "characterize U.S. agriculture in the future." Its chickens are, as the council likes to put it, "cage-free," meaning that they are "raised in large, climate-controlled and ventilated barns, where they're free to move about, interact with other chickens and have 24-hour access to fresh food and water."[37] It is a low standard for freedom, and not only if you're a chicken.

2

Big Tech's Governmental Ambitions

> From our earliest days, Mark used the word 'domination' to describe our ambitions, with no hint of irony or humility.
> —Chris Hughes, co-founder of Facebook[1]

In March 2018, the *New York Times*, the *Guardian*, and the *Observer of London* published an astonishing story. A private company, Cambridge Analytica, had used weaknesses in Facebook to access the private information and psychological profiles of 87 million people. It was one of the largest data leaks in American history, and, because Cambridge Analytica sold its data to be used in election campaigns, it called into question the integrity of the election processes. It meant that Facebook had been systematically violating user agreements and sharing people's private information, and that these violations might have changed the outcome of several very important elections.

Congress demanded an investigation. Facebook CEO Mark Zuckerberg reluctantly showed up, agreeing to answer questions for exactly one day, no more. He sat on a booster seat, pale, rigid, vaguely impatient. Over one hundred cameras surrounded him, surveilling and documenting the surveiller and documenter. Two centers of power confronted each other: the slight, 33-year-old billionaire and the 40 senators. Of the two adversaries, the billionaire was the more formidable, the more famous, and the more influential in the lives of the citizens of the country. The recent policy choices he had made about privacy, journalism, and anonymity were treated by most journalists as more weighty than many, if not most, of the recent policy choices made by the men and women questioning him.

According to one study, half of 18- to 24-year-olds go on Facebook when they wake up, before they do anything else. At least 350 million photos are uploaded to Facebook every day. Every day, over 1.1 billion people use Facebook on their phones, spending on average 20 minutes per visit.[2] Like the post office or the telephone in the nineteenth and twentieth centuries, Facebook and its subsidiaries Instagram and WhatsApp are not only ubiquitous, but necessary for participation in modern life. You cannot operate a business, you cannot run a charity or a political campaign, you cannot publish a magazine or make a public argument without them. Zuckerberg's editorial choices currently shape the lives of most Americans.

Just because it is ubiquitous does not mean Facebook is good for you. Frequent users are three times more likely than nonusers to feel isolated and to struggle with their mental health. And for good reason. In the words of programmer Tristan Harris, social media is "a race to the bottom of the brainstem," because the ad-based business model trains the company to find every reason—shame, anxiety, fear of missing out—to keep people on the website as long as humanly possible. Facebook designers program the website to make it more likely that you'll scroll on Facebook than sleep.[3]

Facebook has built its power by spying on and killing its rivals. For instance, Facebook was caught paying teenagers $20 per month, plus referral fees, to install spyware that let Facebook observe their online activity—including chats, videos, even encrypted material. Participants were also asked to share their purchase histories, via screengrabs. As TechCrunch reported when it broke the story, Facebook engages in this sort of spying in order to spot potential competitors and swallow them up.[4] In 2012, Facebook paid $1 billion for Instagram. In 2014, it paid $22 billion for WhatsApp, a five-year-old company with roughly 50 staffers. This was the largest amount paid out by any venture capital–backed firm in the nation's history;[5] it was not spent on talent, or on data, but purely on power. Facebook needed to stop WhatsApp from posing a threat to its dominance.

This strategy—possible only because we have not been enforcing our antitrust laws—has made Facebook untouchable. When the news of the Cambridge Analytica data leak came out, people threatened to boycott Facebook. But where to go? Leaving Facebook to use Instagram or WhatsApp would be like walking from one room of Zuckerberg's house to another.

For all these reasons, one might have assumed that Zuckerberg would be greeted in the Senate as a usurper. After he finished the opening statement, a thousand reporters around the world sat, fingertips on keyboards, waiting to see what would happen when the senators bore down on the young man who owned most of our personal information and profited off deciding what we should think about, read, and buy.

Democratic Florida senator Bill Nelson asked the first question. Leaning over his desk in an avuncular power pose, he warned Zuckerberg that if Facebook did nothing to self-regulate, Congress would have to act.

This opening sally set the tone. One after another, senators made speeches of concern, asking Zuckerberg for his help in restraining Facebook's bad practices. Many used the word "support," as if addressing a fellow lawmaker. Senator Amy Klobuchar thanked him for "the support that you have given to the Honest Ads Act bill that you mentioned." Senator Ed Markey asked him to support a child online privacy bill of rights. Senator Todd Young asked him to support a universal privacy platform. Later in the hearing, Nelson said, "I think you are genuine. I got that sense in conversing with you. You want to do the right thing. You want to enact reforms." Needless to say, "enact reforms" is the language of government, not corporations.

The senators were treating Zuckerberg as the governor of a separate country: Facebook. They came in peace.

As I watched this hearing, I kept thinking of the 1950 Kefauver hearings on the Mafia. When the Senate hauled the mob boss Frank Costello before Congress, they most pointedly did *not* ask him whether he would support enhancing RICO (Racketeer Influenced and Corrupt Organizations Act) penalties or the use of wiretaps to expose criminal conspiracy. They asked about money. They demanded particulars. When they insisted that he reveal his net worth, and he refused, he was found guilty of contempt of Congress and he went to prison.

In contrast, Zuckerberg was treated like the Senate's own boy king, a slightly unseasoned monarch whom they wished would curb his rasher tendencies. It felt less like an investigation and more like a scene from *Game of Thrones*.

Even before the hearing began, the terms of power had been set. Zuckerberg was not there on the people's terms, but his own: one day only, 40 five-minute questions, and an assurance that no single line of questioning could take hold—as if there were not any other way to conduct an investigation. Fractured and confused by design, the hearing was a beautifully calibrated performance, put together by Joel Kaplan of Facebook, to show that Zuckerberg, not Dick Durbin or Lindsey Graham, held power in America.

At one point, Senator Graham—who understands the TV spectacle of a hearing as well as anyone alive—asked Zuckerberg whether Facebook was a monopoly.

Zuckerberg said that he didn't "feel like it" was.

When Shakespeare's Richard III was asked by his old friend Buckingham for a promised favor, the king answered that he was "not in the giving vein today." When one is a monarch—or tyrant—hard questions can be answered by sharing feelings, not facts. As data journalist Julia Angwin put it, "Mark Zuckerberg isn't going to run for President, he is *already* President."[6]

And this is not by accident. Indeed, Zuckerberg is so open about his governmental ambitions that it's confusing, like a dinner guest who enthusiastically mentions that he's planning to rob you after eating your meal. "In a lot of ways Facebook is more like a government than a traditional company," Zuckerberg said, explaining in a March 2018 interview with *Vox*'s Ezra Klein that he thought the task of Facebook was to "set up a more democratic or community-oriented process that reflects the values of people around the world."[7]

These ambitions go back years. In 2009, Zuckerberg claimed that new terms were more than just rewriting the terms of use, but were "designed to open up Facebook so that users [could] participate meaningfully in our policies and our future."[8] He then launched a series of failed "referendums," importing the language of government to describe how he asked customers questions.

In early 2019, he announced plans for a global digital currency, Libra, an effort to transform financial services and payment systems around the world. Libra would be backed not by a formal government, but by over two dozen major companies, including many of the biggest monopolists—Visa, Mastercard, Lyft, and Uber. Facebook and other members of the Libra Association would earn interest off the money that users kept in reserve.[9]

In the fall of 2020, Zuckerberg plans to install a judicial department of Facebook, an oversight board that will make binding decisions about what content should and shouldn't be allowed.

In initial form, there will be between 11 and 40 board members who will serve a fixed term. The board's announced contours keep shifting: as initially proposed, it will be able to request information from an advertiser or customer, interpret Facebook standards, ask Facebook to take content down, and issue written explanations for its decisions.[10] While these forays into formal, quasi-legal procedures might seem salutary—at least Facebook may start to explain why it takes things down—they show the degree to which Facebook sees itself as a parallel, independent power, equal or superior to that of the governments of the countries in which it operates.

To explain these decisions in terms of money is to miss something important. The will to power is connected to the desire for material accumulation, but it is made of something different, and Zuckerberg clearly has it. The ability to affect the lives of everyone on earth, to know everything about them, to shift elections, to change the practice of democracy—these are not unforeseen by-products of a business plan. They are not accidents. They are the point.

It is crucial that we understand Zuckerberg, and monopolists like him, as seekers of political power, for it is only through political action that they can be tamed. It also helps us understand their behavior, which can impress us with its lordliness and make us feel that they are, indeed, in on a secret, imbued with a genius, afflicted with a condition that makes them somehow *different* from the rest of us. They are different. And it isn't a matter of genius. The psychological literature is clear on this point: People in power are more likely to interrupt, to look away when others speak, to touch others inappropriately, to say what they want, to take risks, "to eat cookies like the Cookie Monster, with crumbs all over their chins and chests."[11] They are more likely to be rude, hostile, and humiliating. They are more impulsive, more self-centered in their choices, which they make obliviously, because they are less able to read other people's reactions. People in power rely more on stereotypes when making judgments about others, with less awareness of unique or individual traits. They aren't good at describing the interior life of others, and are bad at guessing what others want and feel.

It isn't simply that aggressiveness helps a person become powerful, or that rudeness helps you rise to the top. Power changes us; even those of us who are, by nature, loving, sympathetic, and nurturing. As one researcher put it, "The experience of power might be thought of as having someone open up your skull and take out that part of your brain so critical to empathy and socially-appropriate behavior."[12] When a leader is elected for his social intelligence, the very fact of being elected can leave that intelligence damaged and bruised. But when leaders receive their power through a democratic election, they at least have to try to understand the wants and needs and pain of their electors. Power acquired by chance—by business smarts, by inheritance, by merger—has no need of these niceties; it answers to no one.

AMAZON

Perhaps the psychopathies of power help explain how Amazon can treat its workers so badly. Bathroom breaks are so short that workers tell stories of having to pee in bottles, making the trash cans reek of piss. Warehouse workers have reported both extreme heat—over 100 degrees—and extreme cold—below zero.[13] The National Council for Occupational Safety and Health lists Amazon as one of its "Dirty Dozen" most dangerous places to work in America, detailing how workers "suffer injuries—and sometimes lose their lives—in a work environment with a relentless demand to fill orders and close monitoring of employee actions."[14] One worker described how the monitoring "created a constant buzz of low-grade panic, and the isolation and monotony of the work left me feeling as if I were losing my mind."[15] Part-time workers get no health benefits and are subject to strict quotas for time off: one woman was allegedly fired for taking just an hour more than her allotted three-day bereavement quota after her mother-in-law became severely ill and died.[16]

Jeff Bezos is less publicly poetic than Zuckerberg about his ambitions to govern. What he *has* said is that he likes to be depended upon. "I have realized about myself that I'm very motivated by people counting on me," he told an interviewer. "I like to be counted on."[17] To achieve that end, he is repurposing American infrastructure.

Until 1972, Wilmington, Ohio, was a military town, home to Clinton County Air Force Base. Wilmington was and is small, but the base had eight industrial buildings, some bigger than one million square feet, and room for a fleet of 747s. In 2019, Amazon turned that old base into an "air gateway," with thousands of semitrailer trucks and at least 50 commercial airplanes. Amazon is making itself at home where government used to be. As everyone knows, Amazon is developing drones that will fly at 400 feet, detect obstacles in the air and on the ground, and deliver packages. Less well known is that these same drones will gather data, and that this data will be sold to local and state police departments. Ever since the U.S. government started hosting data and computing resources on a cloud, Amazon has dominated the provision of cloud services to the government; 62% of the highest-level authorizations go to Amazon.[18] And throughout the last five years, the scope of its cloud computing services has exploded. It runs between 1.5 and 1.6 million servers, used by companies like Reddit, Pinterest, and Expedia. Netflix competes with Amazon for video streaming audiences, but depends on Amazon for the cloud.

Amazon is not just a store. It is not just an internet company. It is not just a platform. It is not just a transportation system. It is a vast infrastructure machine with an ambition to take over the body and soul of the country: the postal service, the trains, the trucking operations, the places we store our data, and our politics. "Bezos has designed his company for a far more radical goal than merely dominating markets," Stacy Mitchell, the executive director of the Institute for Local Self-Reliance, wrote in 2018. "He's built Amazon to replace them. His vision is for Amazon to become the underlying infrastructure that commerce runs on."[19] Writer Josh Dzieza went deep into the world of Amazon sellers in a story for *The Verge*, and found that Amazon is a "quasi-state" for its six million sellers: "They rely on its infrastructure—its warehouses, shipping network, financial systems, and portal to millions of customers—and pay taxes in the form of fees. They also live in terror of its rules, which often change and are harshly enforced."[20] Using data taken from its sellers, Amazon even competes against them with its own set of brands, called AmazonBasics.

One way to understand the Amazon marketplace is as a big chicken processor, where all the sellers are chicken farmers. But the scope of Amazon's chickenization regime is at another level of magnitude. While only one group, chicken farmers, relies on Tyson to get to market, almost every producer of consumer goods needs to be on Amazon. Sellers on Amazon have no choice but to sign the contract Amazon puts in front of them, use the techniques Amazon demands, and share all the information Amazon wants. Over 60% of searches for products begin on Amazon.

Of every dollar spent on Amazon, 30 to 35 cents goes back to the company in the form of commissions and advertising.[21] How can it get away with taking a third of the profits on any sale? Simple: Amazon controls the search results. When a customer types in a search term, Amazon decides where a seller's product shows up. The most important search result for any seller is the buy box: If a product is listed in the buy box, it will sell. If a product is buried in search results, it will not sell.

Amazon has total control of that box, and has refused to share its methods for determining what goes there (beyond the usual handwaving about it being "what people want"). One thing sellers have learned, however, is that buying Amazon-provided "advertisements" makes search results go better, and makes access to the buy box more likely. That sounds, at first blush, like the normal market: if you advertise, things go better. A closer examination reveals that "advertising" on Amazon is essentially just paying for placement. One seller of a well-reviewed air hockey table told the *Washington Post* that he was consistently in the top three search results for years, until Amazon introduced sponsored ads. Then he saw his product plummet in placement, even in the free, unsponsored placement. He ended up spending $5,000 to $10,000 a month in advertising to get back where he had been before.[22]

The resulting system is the opposite of a competitive market—it's a kickback regime. Amazon sets up an allegedly neutral system, and then charges fees to game that system, calling those fees "advertisements." Sellers compete over how much they can pay Amazon to get access to consumers. Recently, Amazon has launched a new means of extracting value from its vendors. For several thousand dollars per month, Amazon offers them a 1-800 number to help deal with everyday problems like fraudulent orders. If you sell through Amazon, this is the only way to get a live person on the phone. Many sellers, and independent experts, suspect that those who pay this fee get a leg up in search results, too.

The same model may be at play when it comes to Amazon shipping: a business that sells on Amazon recently sent a 62-

page letter to lawmakers laying out the case that Amazon forces sellers to either use its shipping service—at significantly higher cost and worse performance—or be punished in search results. The same week, the Institute for Local Self-Reliance released a report showing how Amazon rigs its own algorithms to force sellers to use fulfillment-by-Amazon.[23]

There is too much we don't know. The uncertainty creates fear and anxiety among sellers, and a cottage industry of experts whose job it is to navigate this simulacrum of a market. Since nobody knows how Amazon does its rankings, many vendors have decided that the safe bet is to pay up, even it if means participating in a grand-scale protection racket.

What we do know is what Bezos has said about competition— that "[y]our margin is my opportunity."[24] He has consistently applied that principle to the companies that depend on him, using his position to suck up the margin of any company whose goods are sold on Amazon. Amazon has also sucked up the margins of power, and can now tell America what kind of businesses it can run. In an open retail market, merchants or manufacturers can choose to pay workers decently. They can weigh profits against other interests, like giving workers additional benefits or supporting local community projects. But if Amazon knows how much a company *can* make if it pays minimum wage and exploits workers, it can set fees for prime access at the breaking point for that company. Not only does Amazon follow the bare minimum of all labor laws, and pay the bare minimum of taxes; because it is the primary regulator of most consumer products in America, it can require the same of the merchants who use its service.

A few years ago, Amazon got in a fight with the publisher Hachette. To punish Hachette for objecting to terms in a contract, Amazon shifted the web displays for Hachette-published books and made sure they arrived two weeks later than other publishers' books. As Lina Khan and I wrote, a single seller of books is "capable of exercising arbitrary power over the content of our books—akin to censorship power of government."[25]

During another contract negotiation, Amazon punished the publisher Macmillan by turning off its "sell" buttons altogether. One might have thought that other publishers would have loudly objected, but they had already been chickenized by Amazon and kept their mouths shut out of fear.

If Bezos treats his vendors as competitors, he refuses to tolerate any actual competition. When Zappos threatened Amazon in the shoe market, Amazon sold shoes at such low cost that Zappos was forced to sell out—and merge with Amazon. When Quidsi, the parent company of Diapers.com, started developing a strong market for diapers, Amazon bought Quidsi and shut it down.

If we see things through a strictly economic lens, we see Amazon as a company, separate from Jeff Bezos, the man. But that lens fails to understand human nature. Although there is every reason to believe that *Washington Post* editor-in-chief Marty Barron is honest when he says that Bezos has never pushed a story, there is something very troubling about the most powerful monopolist in America also owning the newspaper of record in the capital city of the United States. Sooner or later, when the stakes are high enough and when the issue is sufficiently divisive, the owner is the one who calls the shots.

There is perhaps no better symbol of Bezos' governmental ambition than his space project, Blue Origin. It even has its own coat of arms. When Alan Shepard and John Glenn went to space in in the early 1960s, they did so working for NASA and piloting rockets built by the public. By the end of 2020, Amazon will send paying customers into space on the rocket ship New Shepard. The air force has already paid Amazon

$500 million toward the development of its next passenger rocket, New Glenn.[26] The last time "new" was being thrown around this way, it gave us New England, New York, and New Hampshire—and a new government for a new world. Bezos wants to go to the moon in the next five years, but that's just the beginning: he wants to build colonies for future generations to live, orbiting in space.

Once we look at things through the lens of power, we see that the Wilmington project that I mentioned at the start of this section is not a separate commercial gambit from Amazon Web Services, AWS, or from Amazon's chickenization project or Blue Origin; it is part of the massive game of Risk—of power—that Bezos is playing out across the country. In 2017, Amazon ran a tournament, asking cities to make the argument for why they should be the next Amazon headquarters. It promised 50,000 jobs and $5 billion or more in investment to the winning city. In response, over two hundred cities put on dog-and-pony shows for Amazon. In the process, the cities opened up their vaults of data, sharing with Amazon executives precious information that few companies have access to—all the key information about their infrastructure and transportation, employment and patterns of commerce. The 20 finalists shared even more information, using countless public hours to break down every detail for Amazon's perusal.

After Amazon reneged on its promise of a single headquarters, instead picking both New York and Virginia and demanding massive subsidies from both, New York balked and Amazon suffered a very public fit of pique. But if we see Amazon as seeking information with which to govern us, the point may not have been the headquarters; it may have been the top-level access to the keys of all the cities of the country that it seeks to govern. Access and obeisance. Amazon watcher Stacy Mitchell astutely noted that one goal of the exercise was, clearly, to force a massive public display of subservience: the cities were all putting on shows for royalty.[27]

GOOGLE

Of the big three tech giants, Google is already the most embedded in the power structures of our country. Google's power lies in its ability to manipulate the flow of information, to shape what we know and learn about the world. It shapes and surveils our thoughts through the questions we ask, whether those are questions about ideas or about routes to a destination. Most of the time, Google has every incentive to make sure that the search results are as neutral as possible, and that they meet the needs of the searcher. But not all the time. Whether it is 1%, 5%, or 10% of the time, Google is not operating as a neutral search engine, but as a conglomerate, interested in preferring its own content.

Google search uses its power to prefer Google products. The European Union has fined Google three times since 2017, most recently $1.7 billion for imposing unfair terms on companies that used its search bar on their websites in Europe. Google apparently chooses to pay the fines instead of following the law.

Google, more than even Facebook and Amazon, is an agglomeration of companies. In 2001, Google snapped up one company per week. Most companies it buys, often for billions—like YouTube, Android, DoubleClick, and Waze. Others, it simply copies. A few years ago, Google approached a company that had been meticulously scraping data to determine celebrity net worth. The company had 12 employees and decent traffic; Google asked the owner for permission to use their findings. The owner was puzzled. As he told reporter Adrienne Jeffries, "It's a big ask. Like, 'hey, let us tap into the most valuable thing that you have, that has taken years to create and we've spent literally millions of dollars, and just give it to us for free so we can display it.'"[28] He said no. Google went ahead and did it anyway. The data company collapsed.

In 2017, Google spent more on federal lobbying than any company in the United States, and in 2018, it spent even more—*$21.2 million*.[29] That's more than enough to saturate the society of DC. Lobbyists are everywhere: at the office buildings, at parties, talking to journalists, forming a massive social and information network seeping into the structure of the city.

Indeed, more than either of the other two giants, Google has burrowed deeply inside the intellectual leadership of the country. As a result, its power can seem natural instead of artificial. It funded Harvard's Berkman Klein Center for Internet and Society in the mid-2000s, gave $2 million to fund the Stanford Center for Internet and Society in 2006, and has funded countless conferences and events. It has recruited and cultivated hundreds of law professors who support its views.[30] And it does not react kindly when those views are questioned. In 2017, a group of eight researchers working with the New America Foundation—a think tank heavily funded by Google founder Eric Schmidt—issued a brief statement praising the European Union for having fined Google on antitrust grounds. Google lost no time in making its displeasure known: within 72 hours, Anne-Marie Slaughter, the director of New America, had written a letter demanding that all eight team members resign. (I know: I was one of the eight.) This was a gross enough violation of intellectual freedom that it made the *New York Times*, and New America got a black eye for kowtowing to donors. But Google may not have minded the publicity. After all, it put a body on the street. Google may want to be loved by academics, but like Machiavelli's prince, it will settle for being feared.

And like all would-be tyrants, Google takes an existential

interest in the education of its future subjects. At least 30 million children use Google products in schools. Google Classroom is so pervasive that Google can elevate or demote pedagogical practices around the country by making decisions about what apps to feature. Chromebooks are dumped into classes en masse. These donations are not profitable, but they do serve a purpose: they exist to collect information, just like that other "free service," Google Maps. In 2019, Google for Education partnered with Pearson, a monopolist in testing, giving Pearson preferred status and Google a way into hundreds of millions of children's homes.

Google has already created a new kind of public infrastructure based on surveillance: Google Search. Now it is trying to embed surveillance into the old forms of public infrastructure—including our public spaces. In New York City in the last four years, a private consortium, discreetly backed by Google, installed 1,600 kiosks. Each kiosk has android tablets, phones for calls, and charging systems that any member of the public can use. Each one also has three cameras and 30 sensors, plus a huge, 55-inch display that shows ads—based on the information that the kiosk extracts from its users. The service is ostensibly "free," but the cost is people's information.

These kiosks are permitted to collect personal information to the extent "reasonably necessary to provide the Services," and to provide this information—even the identities of passersby—to government authorities. New York City streets, once the heart of free speech, are being taken over by a privately owned Big Brother that makes money based on the scope of its surveillance and that also has a political interest in surveillance. The devices ping the cell phones of people who pass by and the phones tell them who has been there. The scope of non–personally identifying information collected is enormous. The LinkNYC kiosks can collect political information: who was at the Women's March, what kinds of things they were talking about. What if LinkNYC learns that people are plotting against Google? Even if the information is not personally identifying, surely it will be of interest and could be used to blunt or foil any movement that Google didn't like. If you're a New York pedestrian, there is no such thing as an opt-out.

There are good reasons we don't want the government spying on us. Those same reasons apply to public-private partnerships—and then some. One of the few ways we have to protect our autonomy as citizens is to leverage the tension between government and private companies. In theory, government should have an oversight interest in curbing data collection by private companies. In theory, Google should have a competitive interest in keeping its data to itself. When the interests of government and business are fused in the interest of surveillance, what becomes of the individual who wants to speak her mind freely, think out loud, wander without being tracked, investigate the world without fearing private or public retaliation? The freedom of that person is a threat to the power of both Google and the formal government, and both benefit from taking that freedom away.

If the United States government spied on us as a condition of our freedom to use the mail or phone, we'd be worried. We would worry about a government that allowed us to use public squares or public transit only if we gave up access to the thoughts and conversations we had there. We would worry that this information could be used against us personally—or in aggregate, to sow confusion and undermine dissent. We would worry, because we know that the mere possibility of surveillance stunts free thought and chills free expression. And yet, for the first time in our history, we have allowed our essential infrastructure to be based on surveillance, not by the government but by Google.

MAFIA, OR JUST GOVERNMENT?

These big tech companies dominate all aspects of choice, controlling markets, picking winners and losers, listening in on conversations, directing purchases. They have gone beyond responding to consumer needs to dictating them. All are building systems that suggest what we might want before we've thought of it, prompting desires, not just gratifying them. They are finishing our emails for us. In his dystopian nonfiction book, *World Without Mind*, Franklin Foer showed the ways in which Google, Facebook, Amazon, and Apple are hollowing out the human mind, replacing individually- and community-created will and desire with algorithmic anticipations of will and desire.[31] Their quasi-governmental, quasi-business model is designed to strip freedom from both purchasers and producers—from all citizens.

How should we think about these three companies?

Private Regulators

Amazon, Google, and Facebook are so powerful and have such a long leash from Wall Street that they are no longer market participants. They *are* the market, which is the point: why be inside a market when one can control it? They all use their dominant position to promote their own products. Google Search results show Google products. Amazon search results show Amazon products. They have replaced the newspaper, the atlas, the phone book, the post office, the bookstore, the travel agent. They all use two techniques that are particularly dangerous for democracy: monopoly power and targeted ads. Monopoly power removes them from the market. The targeted ad business model encourages intensive surveillance, promotes addiction, and isolates us from each other, making collective action harder.[32]

In 2018, Denmark appointed a career diplomat, who has worked in Afghanistan and Kosovo, to a new position. Casper Klynge became the world's first foreign ambassador to the technology industry. The Danes had concluded that Google, Facebook, and Amazon had amassed the power of governments, and needed to be dealt with directly. "What has the biggest impact on daily society? A country in southern Europe, or in Southeast Asia, or Latin America, or would it be the big technology platforms?" Mr. Klynge asked in an interview with the *New York Times*. "Our values, our institutions, democracy, human rights, in my view, are being challenged right now because of the emergence of new technologies."[33]

The big tech companies certainly act like governments in other ways, regulating and taxing all the businesses that depend on them. Regulation occurs when a company has sufficient dominance that it can force changes across an industry or even, in the case of something like these tech giants, across society. For instance, Tyson has so much power that when it decides that a certain feed hormone is acceptable, its decision becomes the industry standard. The reverse is also true. In 2013, it took exactly one week for Merck to suspend sales of the drug hormone that Tyson stopped allowing, as suddenly as if the FDA had taken it off the market. Similarly, Walmart has so much power that when it decided that paper boxes around deodorant were unnecessary, and ordered suppliers to eliminate them, it was as if a new federal law against paper boxes had been passed.[34]

Amazon, Google, and Facebook regulate entire swaths of the American market, not just deodorant or beef hormones. As regulators, these companies also do the research that regulators used to do. To understand the shape of work in America, we used to rely on the public reports of the FTC. Today, the most important new information on labor is hidden away in private hands. John Deere embeds surveillance tools in its combines, then uses its data not only to sell more combines but to regulate farmers. Its regulatory decisions are not made with the public in mind. Private regulation operates independently of Washington and the statehouses, yet it has the same impact, even though it has not been debated and reviewed in the public sphere. Unlike government regulation, it has no need to be reliable or transparent or fair. It is accountable to no one except the corporation that put it in place.

This new form of government shares some features of constitutional monarchism—centralized control bound by norms set by a leader. But unlike monarchism, it gives controlling power to multiple monopolists, not one individual, and the companies' constitutions are constantly subject to change. Larry Page and Sergey Brin, the co-founders of Google, once argued that no search engine could have integrity while it was driven by ads—but that constitutional commitment has gone the way of Do No Evil, without any process except the whims of leadership. Instead, as Columbia University Law School professor Tim Wu argued in *The Curse of Bigness*, this new form of control echoes the fascism of the last century.[35] Mark Zuckerberg offers a vision of a strong leader, a centralized economy, and tools that allow for quick centralized decision making under a unified ideology. Unlike the fascism of the 1930s, however, Facebook's fascism is not state based, and it is not unitary. The modern monopolists may not be allied with Hitler or Mussolini, but, as Wu has pointed out, there are close parallels between how the fascists defended their economic model and how the modern monopolists do.

Mafia

The Mafia may be the closest analogue to these tech monopolies, because, like the Mafia, corporate monopolists coexist with democratic forms of government, so citizens are dual subjects: of the country, and of one or many monopoly bosses. The Camorra, a large organized-crime group, has controlled the garbage industry in Naples for over 30 years. Garbage was an attractive industry because it affects everyone; as the crime family showed, once you controlled all the garbage collectors, you could hike up the prices with abandon. No one was going to choose to go without garbage collection, even when the price was high. For the scheme to work, the Camorra needed to buy up all the garbage collectors and build strong relationships with the police departments to limit criminal exposure. They allowed some non-Camorra garbage collectors, as long as they paid a tribute to the mob. They spent lots of money on politics, making sure that politicians got some of the value of their monopoly, and worked on personal relationships. They pushed for leniency in law.

Like the Mafia, big tech companies make sure they have friends in high places. They spent a combined $64 million in federal lobbying efforts last year. Amazon spent the most, at $14.2 million, with Facebook close behind at $12.6 million.[36] Amazon has hired Jay Carney, the former press secretary under President Obama; Anne Rung, the former procurement chief under President Obama; Michelle Lee, former U.S. Patent & Trademark Office director; Jeff Miller, the Trump-allied lobbyist and campaign bundler; Bryson Bachman, former senior counsel to the Department of Justice's Antitrust Chief; LaDavia Drane, former chief of staff to Representative Yvette Clarke; Victor Gavin, former deputy assistant secretary of the Navy; and Scott Renda, chief of strategy, policy, and communications under President Obama. Facebook's leadership includes Joel Kaplan, former deputy chief of staff, policy, under President George W. Bush; Jennifer Newstead, former Trump and Bush administration official; Sheryl Sandberg, former chief of staff for U.S. Treasury Secretary Larry Summers; Ted Ullyot, former chief of staff for U.S. Attorney General Alberto Gonzales; Kevin Martin, former Federal Communications Commission chairman; Sarah Feinberg, former special assistant to President Obama; David Plouffe, former campaign manager for President Obama; Ken Mehlman, former campaign manager for President George W. Bush; Joe Lockhart, former White House press secretary under President Clinton; Joel Benenson, the former chief strategist, Hillary for America 2016; and Meredith Carden, of the Office of First Lady Michelle Obama. I could go on. These high-powered former federal officials lend shine and legitimacy to the tech industry and provide access to formal government at the highest levels.

The modern corporate power centers are like the Mafia in another way as well: power is divided among different families. They may fight over turf, but they share a desire to protect each other from regulation. Within each sphere, one company, or a tiny club of companies, controls access to the market. Like the Mafia, they keep close ties to the enforcers.

Unlike democracy, or monarchism, this form of mafia-corporate governance has no serious intellectual pedigree. Unlike democratic or monarchic models of government, there is no implied moral obligation of these companies to look out for the welfare of their subjects. Facebook owning WhatsApp and Instagram and dictating the terms of modern journalism serves no one but Zuckerberg and his shareholders. No political theory can justify such companies' existence, so it is defended—or at least explained—on the grounds that it is not in fact political, but economic. The cognitive confusion exists on such a massive scale that almost everyone, even the new rulers themselves, largely believes that their role is economic and philanthropic, not political. Clearly, you don't have to know you are a tyrant to be one.

THE GREAT TECH BREAKUP

In March 2019, Elizabeth Warren called for breaking up the big tech companies, unwinding the hundreds of mergers that have fed Google and Facebook. She proposed legislation that would prohibit any tech platform from both offering a marketplace for commerce and participating in that marketplace. She argued that platforms had become essential infrastructure, like roads, buses, mail, telephones, and water. An individual might opt out of one particular service or another, but it is nearly impossible to live outside the grid that these new utilities order and control.[37] At the time, Warren was taken as an earnest, but not serious, candidate; this proposal caught fire, however, and was part of what propelled her to the front of the presidential primary pack. It was an electrifying moment.

In the summer of 2019, anti-tech monopoly energy was growing, and the House Antitrust Subcommittee started holding hearings on big tech companies. Congressman David Cicilline of Rhode Island chairs the committee, and has been dogged in his investigations. The committee sent a list of 150 questions to Amazon, including this one: "Does Amazon's algorithm take into account any of the following factors: a. Whether a merchant is enrolled in Fulfillment-by-Amazon; b. Whether a merchant has purchased ads on Amazon; or c. Whether a product is private label sold by Amazon?"[38]

Among academics and writers, calls to break up big tech have come from left, right, and purportedly nonpartisan capitalists. In 2017, a 27-year-old then law student, Lina Khan, wrote a law school note on how Amazon's dominance was breaking American competitive markets. Her note, "Amazon's Antitrust Paradox," caught fire, and was featured in the *Washington Post*, the *New York Times*, and *Wired*. In the last four years there have been several major books on the subject. New York University professor of marketing Scott Galloway began writing his book *The Four* (about Apple, Google, Facebook, and Amazon) as a book of admiration, and ended concluding that they needed to be broken up, because they inhibit competition. Since then, Galloway has kept beating the drum about how tech giants are bad for innovation and a thriving economy. An early investor in Facebook, Roger McNamee, has written witheringly in *Zucked* about Facebook's irresponsibility.

University of Virginia Law and Media Studies Professor Siva Vaidhyanathan has been sounding the alarm about Google in particular for over a decade.[39] Tim Wu has argued that former Supreme Court Justice Louis Brandeis' ideas about monopoly and power would require breaking up big tech. Maryland Law professor Frank Pasquale argues that the FTC has been astonishingly negligent in refusing to oversee big tech.[40] Franklin Foer's book *World Without Mind*, which I mentioned earlier, called for breaking up big tech to stop them from taking over our inner lives. Other notable arguments come from Jonathan Tepperman and Denise Hearn in *The Myth of Capitalism*, making the conservative case for antitrust.

Kara Swisher, an influential tech writer and podcaster, has openly lamented the failure to prevent big tech mergers and the baffling refusal of regulators to see how these mergers prevent competition.

Federal and state regulators are finally starting to do their job. Fifty of the countries' state attorneys general are currently investigating Google for anticompetitive behavior, and forty-seven are looking into Facebook. The Justice Department, the

FTC, and the House Judiciary Committee are all actively investigating big tech.[41]

In the fall of 2019, a year and a half after the hearing I described at the beginning of this chapter, Zuckerberg appeared again in front of Congress, this time to answer questions about his proposed currency, Libra. This time, the mood was different. California congresswoman Maxine Waters, the chair of the Financial Services Committee, ran the hearing, and began with a line of brutally direct questions. She asked Zuckerberg to explain precisely how lies in political ads benefited him, and systematically dismantled his pretensions to leading on civil rights. Following Waters, Congresswomen Alexandria Ocasio-Cortez, Katie Porter, and Joyce Beatty subjected him to withering questions, many of which he could not, or would not, answer. At one point he even stopped speaking for a few seconds, struck dumb by their assertion of authority. "I think lying is bad," he blurted, at a loss for defending his company's paid promotion of lies.[42]

Zuckerberg still holds more power over the 2020 elections than any person in the country, and makes changes in the architecture of our public space on a near daily basis, toying with our democracy. Bezos is still consolidating power over all consumer goods sales in the country while dreaming of life in space. Google is aggressively expanding into the traditional public sector.

Dismantling their power will be no small task. They are ramping up lobbying at the state and federal levels, hiring antitrust lawyers from attorneys general offices, spending more in political campaigns, and pushing laws that appear to regulate their sector, but do little, while strong-arming state and local officials to comply with their wishes.

But the hearing showed that the tables are turning: people understand that the government of Zuckerberg, Bezos, and

Google is not inevitable. We can break them up, and work toward banning their poisonous business model.

The risk, at this point, is not that government won't act, but that it will act just enough to make it look like it is doing something, but not enough to break up big tech's power: that's part of the point of being so embedded in government. For instance, although the FTC has started investigating big tech, it tends to treat them as wayward teens rather than as Mafia-like rivals to public government. In 2019, the FTC fined Google for baiting children with nursery rhyme videos, and then using the data it collected to send targeted advertising to those children, in direct violation of the 1998 Children's Online Privacy Protection Act (COPPA). Google's defense was risible: it said it didn't know it was reaching children. This, after telling Mattel that YouTube, Google's video property, "is today's leader in reaching children age 6–11 against top TV channels," and telling Hasbro, the maker of My Little Pony and Play-Doh, that YouTube is the "#1 website regularly visited by kids." It told advertisers that "93% of tweens visit YouTube" and that YouTube is the "new Saturday morning cartoons." Google then collected information about these children and used it for marketing. It was a flagrant violation of the law.[43]

In its settlement with the FTC, Google did not even admit wrongdoing. It was required to pay $170 million, an amount so trivial to Google that it did not even warrant a letter to investors. FTC commissioner Rohit Chopra wrote a blistering dissent, explaining that the practice didn't just hurt children, but also built up Google's dominance, quashing competition. As Chopra argued, the FTC too often "brings down the hammer on small firms, while allowing large firms to get off easier." This is the company that, more than any other, we have entrusted with the education of our children.

Whether left or right, we tend to ascribe too much intelligence to those who wield great power. It's a simple cognitive error; Zuckerberg is in power so he must have some special qualities. But power does not mean intelligence. Think of Ford's Edsel or Coke's New Coke, or the hundreds of armies that have marched for weeks in the wrong direction, or NASA's Mars orbiter that disintegrated because its software used the imperial system instead of the metric system.

Monopolists are especially prone to disastrously bad judgment because they are accountable to no one: not to the market, and certainly not to the people they govern. When Zuckerberg regulates in his own self-interest, he may well get it wrong. But it does not matter whether Facebook's all-out decimation of local journalism was the product of a self-aware capitalist like Google's Sundar Pichai, simply looking for the big buck; a self-important philosopher-king like Zuckerberg, looking to control conversation; or simply two wildly lucky and irresponsible young men playing with too much power. What matters, as I describe in the next chapter, is that all of local journalism now lies in the hands of Zuckerberg and Pichai, who have shown no interest in supporting *independent* journalism—that is, independent from themselves.

3

Oh, Journalism Was Murdered?
Too Bad!

> The hand that rules the press, the radio, the screen
> and the far-spread magazine, rules the country.
> —Learned Hand, "Proceedings in Memory
> of Justice Brandeis," 1942

Most of us have a profound attachment to the idea of a free press. "Democracy Dies in Darkness," as the *Washington Post* likes to remind us. To many of its readers, this motto conjures up the *Post*'s biggest story ever, the Watergate scandal, which turned Bob Woodward and Carl Bernstein into national heroes. We like the idea of newspapers holding a president to account. But the strongest sinews that connect the public to policy and power are the quotidian stories of car accidents and Boy Scout trips. Local daily journalism, like doctor's visits, provides preventive care: reporting on small scandals prevents big scandals; it tells officials that they're being watched. It builds solidarity by connecting people to each other in their shared daily struggles, and maintains accountability by holding a mirror up to the community. It is the glue that makes self-government possible. In this chapter I explain how those sinews are being torn apart by big tech.

✳

OH, YOU WERE RAPED? TOO BAD!, blared the front page of the New York *Daily News*. Below the headline, a picture of a young boy gazed out from newsstands across the city with gentle, open brown eyes. Now an adult in his thirties, the victim had come forward to tell a harrowing story of being anally raped by one Catholic cleric and forced to perform oral sex on another.[1] The paper excoriated the Catholic Church for blocking a law that would make it possible for adults to bring civil cases against their rapists, and they pressed their attack through the spring and summer of 2016, with in-depth investigations that showed how much money the church was donating to local politicians. DEVIL'S AD-VOCATES, read one headline. Another: BISHOP TRIED TO BRIBE ME TO KILL SEX ED BILL. One morning, the *Daily News* printed the phone numbers of the three most powerful politicians in New York on the front page, with the headline, CALLING THEM UP. This was newspaper journalism at its most vital: dogged, brave, labor intensive, influential. And popular—the *Daily News* stories reached tens of millions, in print and online. And now its best days are a thing of the past. Two years after it exposed the corruption of the New York diocese, the *Daily News* investigative team has ceased to exist. Its entire newsroom staff was slashed in half. What happened? The answer is simple: Facebook and Google.[2]

As a matter of professional pride, reporters are loath to write about themselves. This may explain why the destruction of daily papers, along with the essential value they provide to society, has been greeted with relative quiet until recently. You don't see a bunch of laid-off reporters staging sit-ins or storming the gates of the Facebook campus. The protective ambition—and fear—of senior publishers and editors no doubt makes protest more complicated: speaking out against the entities that most control their future may seem unnecessarily self-sabotaging at a delicate time. Add in a heavy dose of shame: the business rooms of the papers were fooled by the tech giants in the early 2010s, as were publishers, editors, and reporters. But these explanations are not wholly satisfying: it isn't as if journalists and publishers haven't advocated on behalf of their own industry in the past. If papers are slighted by politicians who refuse Freedom of Information Act (FOIA) requests or don't take questions, you'll hear a howl. Journalists advocate for sunshine laws and lobby against even hints of censorship. So why has big tech's appropriation and destruction of journalism's power been met with general acceptance?

Facebook and Google have succeeded in convincing most of America that journalism has died a natural death. That the end of daily journalism is a tragedy of technology, something we must all accept as sad, but unavoidable. In fact, it is nothing short of murder. This chapter tells the story of that murder, and what we must do—quickly—to bring journalism back to life.

When the church abuse stories hit, the *Daily News*, the paper of the workingman and -woman, was in the middle of a major revival. After a low decade in which it had acquired the nickname "The Daily Snooze" given by its right-wing rival, the *New York Post*, the paper had woken up. In 2016, the *Daily News* social media audience grew 75%, set record traffic numbers, and was at the center of local and national debates on police violence, gun violence, and Catholic Church abuse. *Daily News* reporters won the Pulitzer Prize for Public Service for their 2016 in-depth reporting on evictions. The paper was one of the ten most widely circulated daily papers in America.

Jim Rich was the editor in chief of the *Daily News* during this successful run. An energetic, hungry-looking man in his midforties, with a blend of exhaustion and permanent excitability reminiscent of Harrison Ford in *Indiana Jones and the Last Crusade*, Rich has a low threshold for dullness. As he told me when we met for coffee, "You can't bore your way to profitability." Rich and his team of 230 journalists, editors, photographers, and designers set out every morning to "call bullshit" on power and to light the city on fire, telling the stories of the little guy, for the little guy, and with the righteous anger of the little guy.

When it came to reporting on the Catholic Church, the "little guy" was children, mostly working-class children, who had been abused by priests. The *Daily News* put its reporting muscle into uncovering these stories. The paper sold cheap—$1—but production was expensive. It took skilled reporters following leads and building relationships and checking facts. The paper committed as many as 20 staff members at a given time to reporting on the abuse and responses to it. This was gumshoe work, and it required compassion and an incredible drive to be accurate. Not just for the kids or for the law: if the reporters carelessly got something wrong, the *Daily News* could be bankrupted by libel suits.

Power doesn't like to be called out, and some people high up in the Catholic Church were livid. The Catholic League, which styles itself as a Catholic anti-defamation league, organized a boycott of the paper. Hate mail poured into the newsroom. The journalists, and the management at the paper, kept the stories coming and the headlines sharp. One day, the *Daily News* went too far for the church. The paper's cover was an image of a priest from the neck down, wearing a gold cross necklace. The headline was, THEY PROTECT PREDATORS. The "T" in "protect" was the cross of the church.[3]

The Archdiocese of New York acted quickly and unambiguously, canceling a million-dollar contract with the *Daily News* for its printing services. That's a lot of money in publishing. As Rich recalled, CEO Bill Holiber came into his office. They both knew why the contract was canceled, but they didn't consider backing off. "What are we going to do? We're talking about kids being molested," Rich recalled them saying. They knew that while it would really hurt the bottom line, they could survive. "You are always pissing people off in journalism," Rich said. "If you're not pissing someone off, you're not doing your job."

The Church and its allies failed to stop Rich: instead, those stories led to significant changes in state law, and awards for the great work.

But Rich was fired in July 2018, along with 93 employees, including 45 journalists. The massive layoffs shocked New York City. Rich wants people to understand who is responsible: not any enemies they picked up in reporting, but Facebook, Google, and the politicians who refuse to use antitrust to stop them. As a lifelong tabloid journalist, he chooses his words carefully, and is only unhappy if they aren't controversial enough. Journalism isn't dying a natural death, he said, nor is the internet killing journalism. This is neither suicide nor old age. Journalism is getting killed. "Murdered," he said. "Poisoned," he said. "Choked." Facebook and Google are "thieves," he said. "Thugs. Mafia." He wants to be clear that the murderers are Mark Zuckerberg and Sergey Brin and Larry Page. And the people responsible for letting this happen are the politicians who refuse to enforce ancient antitrust principles.

✳

There are basically four ways to pay for journalism: advertisements, subscriptions, the government, and private funders willing to lose money. Some of those private funders make small contributions (think the NPR membership drive); some are what you would call philanthropic; and some are publishers proud to have their name on a cultural institution. Today, many big national news organizations are financed by some combination of all these. NPR is a blend of some government funding, low-dollar and high-dollar philanthropy, and corporate ad-like sponsor-statements. ProPublica, the investigative journalism organization, is wholly funded by high-dollar philanthropy. The *Guardian* is increasingly funded by low-dollar philanthropy, people chipping in a few dollars when they read an article. The *Wall Street Journal* is funded by subscriptions and high-end advertisements. Like many other traditional vehicles of print journalism—the *Atlantic*, the *Washington Post*, the *Financial Times*, *Harper's*—the *New York Times* traditionally depended on a blend of advertisements and subscriptions but increasingly relies on subscriptions. The paywalls work for these publications, and they will likely survive.

Not all of these options are available to all kinds of journalism. The *Daily News* sells for $1 on the newsstand—that's normal for a daily paper that serves working-class readers. These papers stay alive by selling ads. There are a few exceptions: the *Boston Globe* is owned by a billionaire, John Henry, who allegedly loses $25 million a year. The *New York Post* is funded primarily by Rupert Murdoch, who operates it at a major loss (some speculate he loses as much as $100 million a year).[4] But for the most part, even billionaires willing to operate at a loss like to keep that loss within a certain range: a million dollars a year, not $25 million. In other words, if newspapers can't make money off digital ads, there are no—or few—working-class daily papers. And without working-class daily papers, there is no democracy.

Ad-funded newspapers go back 200 years. In 1833, the *New York Sun* made its debut, charging only a penny per paper, unlike the six cents the elite papers charged. It covered issues that mattered to working men and women and provided a sharp contrast to the elite financial news in what were called the "Wall Street papers." The *Sun* sold advertising to merchants, who wanted their wares to reach people. At the top of every issue of the *Sun* was this somewhat wordy but straightforward motto:

The object of this paper is to lay before the public, at a
price within the means of every one, all the news of the
day, and at the same time offer an advantageous medium
for advertisements.

The very first hire was a court reporter. The *Sun* became
popular, as did the business model. For 180 years, versions of
this penny press enabled democracy, giving rise to a democratic
consciousness where the perspective of the little guy mattered
and the powerful were not given special admiration. The *Sun*
and its ilk reported on murders, affairs, sports, and scandals, and
held powerful people to account. They printed trial transcripts
and presidential speeches verbatim. The valiant, corruption-
busting prosecutor, a staple in modern American life, was arguably a product of the penny press, which valorized the crime
fighter. Mayors, congressmen, and senators rose and fell on its
reporting.

The *Daily News* is a direct descendant of the *Sun*, a classic
tabloid, thriving on human interest, sports, and politics, hitting
the powerful over the head—and in the gut—as often as possible. The *Daily News* was at every deli, its headlines splayed all
over the subway. It was the most likely daily paper to be read
by poor and immigrant communities in New York. It relied
on get-out-of-the-office reporting; journalists for the *Daily
News* left what staff reporter Chelsia Rose Marcius called the
"Manhattan bubble" every day. If you're in Manhattan, Chelsia
said, "a lot of people can't name the streets in Queens or South
Brooklyn," but at the *Daily News*, the reporters were always
going to people's homes, going to every neighborhood, and
seeing the problems that people face on a daily basis. It held the
city council to the fire, grilled the police commissioner and
the mayor, and just kept showing up. It offended everyone (including me) on a pretty regular basis. It didn't have the glamour

of the big investigative-only outlets like ProPublica but was more "like a grunt in the war," Rich told me. "We never let go." You could rely on the paper always being there the next day, still bothering the same politicians. They didn't just ask the question once, or investigate the story once, they investigated it every day. As Marcius said, the *Daily News* was a complicated, imperfect place, but there was no doubt whom it served: "the marginalized class, the working class," the people who were "so easily overlooked" by national papers.

Take construction accidents: that's classic *Daily News* coverage. Construction workers are often undocumented and non-union; accidents are not covered by national outlets. But if a worker fell from a scaffolding, the *Daily News* would send a reporter to cover the incident. The reporters chased leads every day, partly because "you get to the big stories by reporting on so-called small stories," as Marcius said, but also because just telling people what is happening in their own world, whether or not it connects to a big scandal or big policy, is what people want. It is also essential to creating a citizenry.

And all of this—the whole architecture of the paper—depended on selling ads: ads for shoes, for sofas, for divorce attorneys, for cars—and now, for iPhones. When Craigslist appeared in the late 1990s, it began to cut into a big section of these ad dollars. The classifieds, where jobs, apartments, and used consumer goods were shared, were replaced in a decade with Craigslist, and apartment hunts now happened in a different place than police reporting. The loss of classifieds was a blow to local journalism, a big blow, but it was not fatal; it meant the loss of one particular kind of advertising that did not need the news to connect people who were selling to people who were buying. It did not, however, mean the end of ad-based journalism, because people still wanted to read the news, and advertisers still wanted to be where the people were. Jim

Rich has no anger toward Craigslist because, as he said, Craig Newmark "figured out a better way to do what we were doing." Craigslist made it harder to sell ads, not impossible.

THEN CAME FACEBOOK AND GOOGLE

Facebook and Google now make money on *exactly* those ads that local papers used to make money on—not similar ads, the same ones, ads placed next to the stories. In 2017, Google made $95 billion from selling advertising, enough to pay 300,000 reporters $100,000 each.[5] Facebook made almost $40 billion that same year just from selling digital ads.[6] Google consistently has profit margins above 20%.[7] To compare: Walmart's profit margin is 2.1% and big oil's profit margins hover around 6%. Facebook and Google account for approximately 70% of all digital ads sold in the country, and almost all new ad revenue goes directly into their pockets: Google and Facebook accounted for 99% of *new* digital ad sales in recent years.[8]

As the *Columbia Journalism Review* described it dryly, "This is exceedingly bad news for the balance of the digital publisher ecosystem."[9] Not only do Google and Facebook suck dry the resources of newspapers, but innovative ideas or new ways of reporting can become wildly popular, and the value goes to Facebook or Google, not to the journalists or publishers.

To understand how they did it, we must realize that Google and Facebook are, first and foremost, advertisers. We call them "platforms," a word that suggests neutrality, but they are not neutral. We call Facebook "social media" and Google a "search engine," but "social" and "search" are means to one end—making money in digital advertising. As digital advertisers, they sell targeted access to the people they purportedly serve. Content has one use in this business model: it keeps people clicking on ads. If Nike wants to reach 10,000 people who are in the target demographic for shoes, it will go to Facebook and buy ads on Facebook to connect Nike ads and Facebook users—perhaps users who are reading, sharing, and commenting on links to the *Daily News*, and to the iconic covers. Or Bayer will go to Google and buy ads so that Google can connect Bayer advertisements to *Daily News* readers.

The new digital advertising companies are not like traditional advertising companies, who were brokers, connecting platforms (like television, newspapers, and radio) with sellers (like Nike and Bayer). Instead, the new companies—Facebook and Google—are both ad brokers and platforms at the same time: it's as if CBS owned the advertiser Ogilvy.

Unlike a broker, Facebook and Google do not buy information and then resell it; they collect the information and use it themselves. Because the quality of their granular information about people is so much better than that of their digital ad competitors, Facebook and Google ads are far more expensive than most digital ads. They can charge more to Nike, or to Bayer, because they know more about the people being reached. While most data brokers know things like what you bought, Google knows what you searched for. While most data brokers know your credit score, Facebook knows more about you than you know about yourself. Not only does it know who your friends are and how you interact with them, but it also knows the number of interactions you have with products and ideas every day. Nothing is more valuable for businesses who want to sell their goods.

To be sure, Facebook and Google are not the only companies that spy on their customers. At this point, every company of a certain size makes data collection and data sale part of its business. Domino's Pizza, airlines, shoe companies—they all collect data on their customers. They sell the data to aggregators, who in turn sell it back to those same companies and others who are trying to reach customers. The ads based on this data are the cheapest in the business. They make up at most 40% of the digital ad business.[10]

Much more expensive ads—and data—are available from Google and Amazon. These two companies do not sell data. Instead, they buy data from the exchanges, and then use it to augment their own high-quality data. What they sell to other companies is access. When you search for "green shoes" and Google serves up Target in the right-hand column, that means Google has sold access to you, using your data. Amazon works essentially the same way, only instead of selling traditional advertisements, it sells product placement in the world's biggest store.

The most expensive ads and data of all come from one company alone: Facebook. Facebook's data is of a different category for two essential reasons. First, Facebook knows who you are. It has your name. Second, Facebook knows who your friends are, and there is no more valuable piece of data than knowing your cohort. I may know what teams you support, who you vote for, where you were yesterday, and what toppings you take on your pizza, but if I want to sell you shoes, that information pales in comparison with knowing who you hang out with.

What your friends do, and what they buy, are the best predictors of what you will do and buy. Not surprisingly, Facebook ads are astronomically expensive. And the price keeps going up—proof, if proof were needed, that Facebook has no competition in this field.

Three activities—surveillance, discrimination, and addiction—define the Facebook and Google operations. Surveillance is the art of extracting as much information as possible from every person and every interaction. Discrimination is providing different information and different advertisements to each person, based on indicators. The goal is to maximize the amount of money Facebook and Google can make off of knowing who you are. Addiction is the best mechanism for ensuring that you spend as much time as possible hooked up to a machine that will send money to Facebook and Google.

A cynic might say that Facebook is just a sophisticated version of the *New York Sun*—an ad-generating machine that uses journalism to reach people—but there are key differences. Unlike the *New York Sun*, Facebook and Google did not write, edit, or fact-check the stories that they make money from. They did not create the videos that they make money from. And unlike newspapers, Facebook and Google have become essential communications infrastructure: not only do all newspapers go through them, most people need to use them to get jobs, communicate with friends, and talk about politics.

Facebook and Google didn't figure out a better way to report stories, or take pictures, or make headlines: they just figured out a way to make money off of other people's labor. Here is where Rich gets apoplectic: "Where else would this make any sense?" Imagine a world, he says, where GM doesn't try to make a better or cheaper car than Ford, but where it gets all the money every time a Ford drove off the lot. He points at the cash register of the diner where we're eating. Imagine a world where Grubhub came along "and promised access to millions more eaters, but the only cost was that the restaurant couldn't make any money off the food anymore!" It isn't capitalism, he says, but theft.

Because Facebook has so much control over the places most people go for information, it has a vise-like grip over public access to newspapers. It can feature any individual newspaper story it wants. It can bury a publication by pushing down its relevance in feeds and searches. It controls the levers over much of the communications infrastructure of the country, and it has leveraged that control to make profits off those industries that rely on reaching people when they seek information.

CHANGING THE SETTINGS
OF DEMOCRACY

In the early days of Facebook's News Feed, the content that people saw was purely chronological. If a friend posted dog pictures at 10:15, 11:15, and 12:30, and a cousin posted a story about Mitt Romney from the *Boston Herald* at 11:30, the user would see dog, dog, Mitt Romney, and then dog again. As it grew, however, Facebook started ordering the posts that people saw in a nonchronological fashion. Facebook started making quasi-editorial choices, similar to those that a news publication makes, picking which content a user would see and in what order. They used algorithms to do so.

The early editorial algorithms prioritized the content coming from news organizations, preferring stories about Mitt Romney to pictures of a friend's dog. So the user would see, Mitt, dog, dog, dog, dog.

Newspapers rushed to use this new tool. Having taken a major beating by Craigslist, they believed that if they made social media the center of their growth strategy, they could radically increase their numbers of readers and recover revenue. This is because for more than a century, newspapers had equated eyeballs with revenue, not to mention influence. Newspaper managers encouraged journalists and readers to share articles, and built their web presence around the platform. For its part, Facebook offered incentives to news organizations to bet big on their site, offering tools that would allow revenue sharing. Nearly everyone took the bait. They did not realize that Facebook didn't have any long-term need for the newspaper publishers (or magazines, or other content providers) to make money.

Change 1: Bury the News

After scandals implicated Facebook in spreading Russian propaganda, the company changed its algorithm, and in so doing, changed the entire ecosystem of news in America. In 2018, the new algorithm created a personalized score for each piece of content posted. We don't know all the details, but the new system devalued any content from any organization's page, and gave higher scores to posts that came from individuals. That meant that any institution—be it a political campaign or a news organization or rock band or a shoe store—could still post, but unless they spent money to boost their visibility, that content was unlikely to be seen. Facebook's publicly stated motive in making this change was to reduce the power of propaganda, because the Russians used Facebook pages as the primary way to push their stories in the 2016 election. But the side effects of the change were not bad for Facebook's bottom line; the organizations that had previously been able to easily engage in public conversation now had to pay for interactions. If the *Daily News* wanted a huge readership in 2018, it suddenly had to pay for it. Newspapers were suddenly in an impossible position: in order to make their money off digital ads, they had to spend money on digital ads. Since most news organizations are not wealthy or funded by big donors, they could not afford this, and news suddenly disappeared from view for millions of Americans. People didn't necessarily notice the change, because they had become accustomed to thinking of Facebook as neutral. But newspapers were furious: they had helped build an audience for Facebook, and then were shut out of revenue after it became dominant.

How did news organizations make the mistake of over-committing to a Facebook strategy? The CEO of BuzzFeed, Jonah Peretti, explained in an interview that although they at BuzzFeed knew they were dependent on Facebook, they believed the dependency went both ways, and that Facebook would actively work to make sure that journalists and publishers got a sustainable piece of the revenue. BuzzFeed bet big on making money using the platform, and that bet started to look less stable after they realized how little Facebook cared. Peretti told ReCode's Peter Kafka in an interview that

> I was completely wrong about the degree to which Facebook would help publishers. . . . It seemed to me that it was in Facebook's interest to create sustainable models for quality content that lived directly on its platform. Sure, the company would be giving up a slice of its revenue, but the impact on the overall user experience generally and establishing Facebook as the center of not just the consumption of content but the monetization of content specifically would be powerful moats. The truth, though, is that the short-term incentives to maximize revenue, primarily through News Feed ads that Facebook kept for itself, were irresistible.[11]

The new structure meant that when journalists' hard work—like that by those twenty *Daily News* journalists investigating child sex abuse—generated revenue, that revenue did not go to the newspapers. That revenue went to Facebook (and Google).

Peretti at BuzzFeed at least understood the bargain they were making to share revenue. But others did not; many publishers thought they weren't competing against Facebook.

They considered Facebook a social media company, whereas newspapers were in the journalism business, which led them to believe that the two were synergistic: the *New York Times* reports news, and Facebook creates a place for the news to be shared and discussed. They eventually realized that Facebook is a digital advertising company and the *New York Times* is a news company that depends on advertising to survive: they are not synergistic but antagonistic. Facebook is directly competing with the news media that it is allegedly serving. For example, they are deliberately angling to maximize the profits they earn from *New York Times* reporter Jodi Kantor's work. If a blockbuster story about Harvey Weinstein generates $10,000 of digital advertising revenue, Facebook's goal is to pocket as much of that money as possible. If one of the effects of this is that the *New York Times* goes out of business, then Facebook has one less competitor. Because of this dynamic, the *New York Times* has shifted its business model toward subscriptions, not wanting to rely on a parasitic partner. But most local and working-class newspapers don't realistically have that option, and they can't build a subscriber base that supports their work. They have to choose between not going on Facebook, and being starved to death; or using it, and being robbed to the point of starvation.

Change 2: Feudalism

Just before this book was published, Facebook changed its algorithm again. In late fall 2019, Mark Zuckerberg announced that he understood that he was taking revenue from journalists, and wanted to "fix" the problem with a new architecture for news.[12] The solution sounds good: Facebook is now paying certain major publications for their content. However, a

Facebook-controlled team makes editorial decisions about which part of their partner content to feature. It leaves publications dependent, and creates a feudal system. It does nothing for the working-class papers like the *Daily News*. Zuckerberg hoped to appease some critics, but while he has created a new funding scheme, the structure of power has actually gotten worse, not better. Now a Facebook-selected team works in tandem with news publications, creating a nightmare scenario in which most news is centralized and sharing of information is centrally coordinated.

At first blush, this new arrangement may not seem unfair or worrisome: What's wrong with another layer of accountability? The problem is that unlike Facebook, traditional newspapers are held responsible for what they publish. The *Washington Post* has an editorial team that decides when stories are of high enough quality to publish, which stories to feature on the website, and what order you will see them in. The editorial team must keep the company afloat, but also has journalistic responsibilities, both legal and cultural: if they get something wrong, or print something that causes an outrage, the editorial team has to answer for it. When the *Daily News* ran those stories about the Catholic Church, they had to run every word by a tough team of lawyers. One wrong word, and they could be sued for hundreds of millions of dollars. When Gawker Media had to pay $140 million after a jury verdict on its decision to post a sex tape involving Hulk Hogan, it went bankrupt. But Facebook does not share this risk. No matter what stories are posted, and even if it knows a story is false—no matter what laws are broken by landlords, employers, and others who use it—Facebook lacks liability. This is because of a law passed in 1996, Section 230, that gives Facebook and Google and other platforms immunity from the content that is shared on their sites.

LOSING THE BALANCE

Our free press now depends on the goodwill, even the whims, of a few men and women. The News Feed algorithm has now changed multiple times after a conversation between Mark Zuckerberg and Sheryl Sandberg, and it can change again. A paper can build up an entire business model based on one of Zuckerberg's algorithms, only to have it shift a few months later. Blogger Josh Marshall writes that the journalist's relationship to social media is like a serf's relationship to a landowner.[13]

A few months from now, they could decide to bury the *Boston Globe* and to build up the *Boston Herald*. Overnight, Bostonians would find themselves in a new media landscape. Or Zuckerberg could decide that Boston doesn't need a local paper at all. For the ultimate act of gross power would be to shut off news altogether. As the *Columbia Journalism Review* recently opined, "As imbalanced and abusive as the relationship between publishers and Facebook is, the nightmare scenario is if Facebook decides to shutter access to its members, leaving a news outlet to starve. This level of power in the industry is dangerous and unacceptable."[14] There is nothing in our current system that would stop this from happening. In the Facebook model, there is no protection for publishers. There is also no protection for readers—or for those who are in the news itself.

In American life, public judgment has never been swifter or more absolute. Today, if someone is accused of a crime, it can destroy their dignity and livelihood overnight. If a politician is falsely accused of taking a bribe, the accusation can instantly end her career. It has been said that there are no second acts in American life; in Facebook's America, there are no second thoughts. False stories about public figures and public policy matter because, in addition to damaging individual reputations, they lead to terrible decision making in a democracy. As we saw in the 2016 election, false stories move quickly through Facebook, and truth lacks any real protection.

Over hundreds of years, American common law developed a balance between protecting the free expression of ad-funded newspapers and protecting individual people, and the public at large, from lies and scurrility. Newspapers can be sued for libel—a false statement, printed negligently (or knowingly), that harms someone's reputation. They can be sued for invading privacy, or for intentional infliction of emotional distress. A story can't just be fascinating gossip; according to our laws, with some exceptions, it has to be true and newsworthy. In other words, although we've allowed ad-based industries in the past, they operate within the context of other regulations that protect against the likely degradation of information that can come along with the hunt for eyeballs. And we've never allowed essential communications infrastructure to be ad-based. The crisis of false news (spread by Facebook) and the crisis of no news (journalism killed by Facebook) are two branches of the same rotten tree.

Instead of tossing the ad model, or admitting its central role, Facebook used the propaganda scandals to consolidate power in four steps. First, it demoted the role of all news, giving itself a greater role and starving newspapers. Second, it selected a few news organizations to partner with, giving them a funding stream but also creating a feudal codependency. Third, it announced the creation of a Facebook supreme court to analyze the veracity of stories and take down requests, separating itself from the traditional responsibility of a newsroom. Fourth, it is flooding journalism nonprofits with cash, buying up goodwill. I called several old friends in journalism to talk about the restructuring of power. Two of them had projects funded by Facebook or Google.

Facebook is telling us it wants to be government, to become

the uber editor of all publications, *and* to become embedded in the watchdog group culture by supporting the watchdogs. This is like the Mafia promising Congress that it has created an alternate legal system to punish the most violent offenders, so we should just send criminals their way—and that it's been giving money to charities.

Two-thirds of counties in America now have no daily newspaper. While the number of daily newspapers dropped 10% from 2013 to 2016, Facebook's profit margins went from 9% to above 30%.[15] From 2001 to 2016, newspaper publishers in the United States lost more than half their employees. We now have 174,000 journalists in America, down from nearly half a million. Some papers have contracted, becoming thin and reprinting wire services. Others have folded altogether. There are 1,300 communities that have no newspaper at all. Queens, a county of 2.3 million people, has plenty of crime but no court reporter.[16]

In July 2018, the *Daily News* announced huge cuts. Marcius was laid off, Rich was laid off, the team that did in-depth reporting on opioids was laid off. Instead of 230 staff, the newspaper had 80, total. There was no way they could put 20 reporters on a beat, let alone spend the hours to cultivate sensitive witnesses. The paper could no longer aim for big investigative pieces like the investigations of child sex abuse, let alone show up at construction accidents. "Do the math," Rich said. "There is no way to cover what is happening in the city with 80 [people]."

In less than a decade, we have shifted from being a democracy with reporters in most courtrooms to one with a national elite press and a big void filled with unchecked gossip and propaganda. Facebook and Google have deliberately, radically poisoned the way we read and the way we relate to one another. They have devalued the very idea of news. Those changes won't reverse themselves easily.

We do have the power to reverse them. We can break up
Facebook into its component parts, leading to competition between social media providers, creating choices for publications.
We can break up Google into component parts too. We can ban
the targeted ad–based business model for essential communications infrastructure. All that would mean is that social media
and search companies would have to fund themselves with fees
for service, instead of "for free" services paid for by our liberty.
Phone companies and postal services have charged customers:
social media can too. When platforms get out of the ad business, local papers stand to gain, because they will no longer
compete against their distributors.

Facebook and Google will always try to use crises to amass
their own power, but it is up to us to demand the structural
transformation that will make a free press possible.

4

Replacing Justice with Power

> It is procedure that spells much of the difference
> between rule of law and rule by whim.
> —Supreme Court Justice William O. Douglas, 1951

The right to open courts, public trials, and independent judges is the basis of the American justice system. It is central to our very idea of fairness before the law. It goes back to thirteenth-century England. For the last 800 years, the existence of public courts has meant that any peasant has been able to wander in off the street to watch proceedings, and everyone has to make their case in public, meaning that sometimes unsavory practices are exposed. Because of the truly beautiful and bizarre jury system, any person can have a complaint heard by 12 randomly chosen people, an assembly with no stakes in the fight and no ties to powerful interests. The very first bribery statute, from 1384, prohibited judges from being paid by anyone but the king, and certainly not the parties to a dispute. The long-established right of appeal means that power is distributed among decision makers, and that a judge's reasons should be sound. The judicial requirement that judges must follow precedent and explain themselves publicly means that judges have to articulate reasons for their exercise of power, which often forces them to explore their own prejudices. The right to bring class actions means that less-wealthy people can band together against powerful interests. In other words, the Anglo-American legal system is a remarkable anti-corruption edifice, built up over half a millennium, that makes it possible for people to have rights.

White-shoe lawyers at fancy firms, realizing the difficulties for their corporate clients embedded in this system, started pitching an alternate court system nearly 40 years ago. Because of their work, we are now deep into a sophisticated and terrifying project: replacing American law with a parallel court regime, using the language of peace to explain it and the tools of Anglo-American law to defend it. The system is known as arbitration. Or, as one experienced litigator described it, "It's trial for the one percenters is the way that I think about it."[1] Arbitration resembles law the way that margarine resembles butter. It has a similar shape and color, but it is made of something entirely different. It has echoes of the Star Chamber, a sixteenth- and seventeenth-century English court that temporarily replaced public courts and became known for its arbitrary rulings and abuse of power. The Star Chamber was designed to give judges enormous flexibility, ostensibly to ensure that powerful people were held accountable, and it justified the break with the tradition of public courts on grounds of its speed and efficiency. The Star Chamber became a tool of oppression, and was eventually shut down in the seventeenth century. Today as well, arbitration is built on secrecy and the myth of efficiency, and allows big banks, big tech, and big agribusiness to control court proceedings.

In arbitration, arbitrators rather than judges make the decisions in a case. As in a court, the parties pay for their own lawyers, and are responsible for getting their own witnesses to appear. However, unlike in court, where the judge's salary is paid by the state, in arbitration, the parties pay the arbitrators directly. Companies that frequently appear, therefore, repeatedly pick and pay arbitrators, whose judgment may be influenced by these repeat employers. There is no right to a jury, and there is no right to appeal. One website advertises the advantages of arbitration this way: "A jury can create stomach-turning stress for a business defending a lawsuit." The whole thing happens in secret. Instead of following publicly developed rules of evidence, or rules governing what information must be disclosed through discovery in a given case, arbitrators make case-by-case decisions about what is admissible. Instead of relying on precedent and prior cases, the arbitrators make individual determinations, and since it is all secret, fewer precedents are created. These variations mean that big corporations have far more control over decisions and outcomes than in a public court proceeding: there's none of the uncertainty of jury trials and far less fear of an unsympathetic judge.

The terms of arbitration—also known as *alternative dispute resolution*—have a calculatedly anodyne, almost therapeutic sound, as if they've been borrowed from a textbook on couples counseling. *Can't we all just get along?* the language calls out. One of arbitration's biggest promoters, the mission of which is "to bring together corporate counsel and their law firms," calls itself the International Institute for Conflict Prevention and Resolution. The title makes you want to donate, as it sounds as if the group is resolving conflicts like the Syrian civil war. In reality, the role of arbitration is to beat down workers and consumers, especially the least powerful and wealthy.

ARBITRATION BASICS

The typical arbitration agreement will be full of legal terminology that will mean little to a lay reader. For instance, when the hundreds of millions of people who use Amazon Prime sign up for it, they agree that:

By using any Amazon Service, you agree that the Federal
Arbitration Act, applicable federal law, and the laws of the
state of Washington, without regard to principles of conflict
of laws, will govern these Conditions of Use and any dispute
of any sort that might arise between you and Amazon.[3]

Further into the contract, you might find something like
this, excerpted from the current Wells Fargo bank arbitration
clause:

You understand and agree that you and the bank are waiv-
ing the right to a jury trial or trial before a judge in a public
court.[4]

Some arbitration clauses go further and limit the degree of
discovery and whether discovery is allowed, minimize the role
of depositions, and ask the signer to waive oral hearings, opening statements, and closing arguments. Arbitration agreements
can limit how many pages can be submitted and the number of
exhibits allowed. While the worker signing a contract or the
purchaser buying a hair dryer might not be thinking about a
future dispute, the big companies are building a wall against future lawsuits. For big companies, the threat of collective action
has been the biggest headache, so from their perspective, the
most important provision in almost all arbitration agreements
is a waiver, like this one from Amazon:

We each agree that any dispute resolution proceedings will
be conducted only on an individual basis and not in a class,
consolidated or representative action.[5]

Arbitration agreements effectively throw out the old system: they dispense with the jury, take away the right to appeal,

and require no rules of evidence, all while installing a judge paid by the people he or she has power over. Even if the company has treated hundreds or thousands of others the same terrible way, you are on your own.

When talking about arbitration, much is made of the fine-print problem—the indisputable fact that nobody reads these contracts. Businesses do not compete over the fine print, because neither workers nor consumers pay attention, understand, or have the time to engage.[6] However, the focus on the small size of the fonts used, and the cultural habits around signing documents, has obscured an important point: in concentrated markets, where all the companies use the same arbitration model, few people would reject goods or services on the grounds of these terms even if they *did* read them. Reading the contract is not, as the fine-print debate imagines, the first bid in a negotiation. Can you honestly imagine emailing someone at Verizon with amendments to the contract, threatening to go to T-Mobile? Can you imagine a low-paid worker threatening to reject a job because they want the future right to a jury trial for a hypothetical lawsuit against the employer? Of course not. The waivers are not choices, but tools of coercion and power leveraged by monopoly government.

Defenders of these terms implicitly imagine consumer choices and a sufficiently dynamic market in which companies are competing to provide the best court system. That is risible in consumer contracts with banks and phone companies, and cruel in low-wage employment contracts. UCLA law professor and arbitration expert Katherine Stone points out the impossible position someone would have to be in to consider rejecting these terms in an employment context. The only person who would walk away would be someone with a big rainy-day cushion in their bank account (so they wouldn't need a salary), a lot of job options (so the employment offer wouldn't be their only choice), *and* a fear that their future employer was going to abuse them (which would make them see arbitration as particularly unhelpful). That's a rare hat trick. In other words, forced arbitration clauses, jury waivers, and collective action waivers are made possible *because* of monopolies.[7] When only a few companies control most sectors, and all of the companies use the same terms, there is no choice, regardless of whether the disclaimers are printed in a 20-point font, with exclamation points, or hidden.

A TALE OF TWO CASES

How did we get here, and so quickly? For most of American history, arbitration agreements simply didn't exist between individuals and big companies. Case law from the Supreme Court made it seem impossible that arbitration would ever be used broadly. In 1966, just two years after the Civil Rights Act of 1964 was passed, Harrell Alexander, a 28-year-old black man in Denver, Colorado, got a maintenance job for the Gardner-Denver Company. The company was—and remains today—one of the giants of industrial production in America. It has invented speed controls for steam engines and is the lead seller of several industrial products. Alexander worked maintenance for two years, was promoted to be a drill operator, and then was suddenly fired. The company said they fired him because too many of the parts he produced were defective and had to be tossed. Alexander said he was discriminated against because of his race. He produced evidence that other drill-bit operators made just as many unusable parts and that the typical response to similar bad parts was demotion, not firing.

Alexander first brought a claim under his union's collective bargaining agreement, which prohibited racial discrimination. When that failed, he followed the general procedure available to anyone: he first brought a complaint with the Equal Employment Opportunity Commission and then brought a federal lawsuit. He claimed job discrimination on the basis of race, which is illegal under Title VII of the Civil Rights Act. Gardner-Denver, seeking to avoid a trial, successfully argued in lower courts that Alexander's use of binding arbitration, under the collective bargaining agreement, foreclosed bringing a suit. Essentially, via his union contract, he had picked one route to seek redress (arbitration), so he couldn't pick another (federal court). The company relied on the 1925 Federal Arbitration Act (FAA), a law pushed by then secretary of commerce Herbert Hoover, which allowed some businesses to waive their rights to a jury, to review, and to the rules of evidence in business-to-business disputes. In the 1960s, the Court had blessed using arbitration for labor disputes, and Gardner-Denver argued that under the FAA, Alexander had waived his rights.

Today it seems unimaginable, but the Supreme Court decision in Alexander's favor was unanimous—and written by the corporate-friendly Justice Lewis Powell. The arbitrator, the Court concluded, has the authority and capacity to resolve questions of contractual rights between the parties. But arbitration could not be the sole forum for the full scope of federal rights that an employee might have: Alexander had the right to bring his civil rights argument to open court. There are two key passages in Powell's decision worth pausing on: these are the passages that have worried corporate lawyers. First, Powell was very skeptical of the idea of a waiver of legal rights, because of its potential to undermine the very purpose of civil rights law:

> Title VII's strictures are absolute and represent a congressional command that each employee be free from discriminatory practices. *Of necessity, the rights conferred can form no*

part of the collective-bargaining process since waiver of these rights
would defeat the paramount congressional purpose behind Title VII.
In these circumstances, an employee's rights under Title
VII are not susceptible of prospective waiver.[8]

In other words, forcing arbitration would undermine the
basic purpose of civil rights laws. While Powell acknowledged
that Alexander could agree to a post-conflict private settlement whereby Alexander waived his rights—after the fact—it
would be against the purpose of Title VII to allow Alexander
to *prospectively* waive his right to bring the case to trial.

Second, Powell made sweeping statements explaining why
arbitration is a poor replacement for federal courts when it
comes to vindicating civil rights. Arbiters are not competent,
he argued, to deal with the interpretation of broad public statutes like Title VII. "*The fact-finding process in arbitration usually is
not equivalent to judicial fact-finding.* The record of the arbitration
proceedings is not as complete; the usual rules of evidence do
not apply; and rights and procedures common to civil trials,
such as discovery, compulsory process, cross-examination, and
testimony under oath, are often severely limited or unavailable."[9] Arbitration may be cheap and effective, he said, but that
is all the more reason that it should be used *only* to resolve the
unique disagreements between parties that concern their particular contractual obligations, not essential federal laws.

That case was decided in 1974. In its wake, a small group
of lawyers realized that the big corporations they wanted to
work for had a growing problem, and they could make their
reputations by solving it.

In 1977, the anodyne-sounding Center for Public Resources
(CPR) came into being.[10] The first act of the CPR was a dec-
laration of its agenda: reduce the costs of business litigation.
They planned, they announced, to identify and develop new

forums for conflict, communicate the value of these new tools, and implement these new methods. They called them "experiments and new resources to decrease the costs of litigation and regulatory disputes."[11]

CPR built an active legal team over the next decades, funded by a national coalition of 200 major companies and the top 100 law firms. It set up headquarters in a posh building on Park Avenue in New York City. The board of CPR has always been big business; today it is a who's who of monopolists: Bayer, Visa, Amgen, and Shell are all represented, making CPR a genteel version of the American Legislative Exchange Council (ALEC). Like ALEC, which provides model legislation for lawmakers, CPR provides model arbitration agreements—semi-bespoke forms for companies creating their own private legal regimes. The goal is to erase access to open federal and state courts, to replace public courts, juries, and judges with secret corporate court look-alikes. These arbitrations were initially called "minitrials" by advocates, as if to say, it is the same thing, just *smaller*. But these minitrials were not smaller versions of the old tradition; they were different, and had a transformational goal. According to arbitration expert Stone, CPR's "real mission was to facilitate overturning *Alexander v. Gardner-Denver* or make a carve-out for employment arbitration that arose outside the collective bargaining agreement."[12]

Looking back, one is struck by the audacity of the early CPR. It did not hide its mission: clearing out the courts. It argued in briefs and in public that in the wake of federal civil rights law and fair labor laws, there were too many cases being brought to court. The increase in employment discrimination claims brought in federal court might make one worried about employment discrimination and what to do about it, but CPR argued the opposite: we don't need to get rid of discrimination, we need to get rid of these cases. While many people—even on the left—were uninterested in the threat posed by alternative dispute resolution, there were early, loud critics sounding the alarm bell, including Yale Law professor Owen Fiss, who argued that the structures being created were incapable of protecting public rights and would lead to replacing public values and justice with "private interests" and private regimes.[13]

Within 12 years after CPR was founded, it had succeeded in overturning *Alexander* in spirit, if not in fact. A big moment came in 1983, when liberal lion Justice William Brennan announced that there was a "federal policy favoring arbitration," despite no real history supporting that claim. A trio of cases in the 1980s followed, establishing that arbitration could be used for all different kinds of statutory claims between companies. The court quickly transformed a modest act, designed for resolving business disputes between equals—the FAA—and turned it into a quasi-constitutional statute.

The definitive victory came in May 1991. Jose Canseco was dating Madonna, George H. W. Bush was president, and the Soviet Union started allowing citizens to travel abroad. The radical consolidation of corporate power had been ten years in the making, but the politics of the moment were anything but populist. The pivotal case this time: an older, white, upper-middle-class man was bringing a suit for being fired by an investor firm, a narrative much easier for a conservative court to make bad law out of. The man, Robert Gilmer, had signed an arbitration agreement with his employer but wanted to go to the public, open courts and bring a lawsuit under the Age Discrimination in Employment Act. A divided Supreme Court rejected Gilmer's concern that the arbiter might be biased, and made quick work of his argument. The case held that because Gilmer had signed a contract to arbitrate all statutory claims, the contract would be enforced absent clear indications in the statutes that those rights could not be arbitrated. The fact that arbitration was not even in the minds of Congress when it passed civil rights laws was not addressed.

Justice Antonin Scalia wrote the majority opinion. He dismissed any suggestion that the company held "overwhelming economic power"—after all, the plaintiff was an "experienced businessman."[14] While he didn't explicitly overturn *Alexander*, he waved away all the concerns about the capacity of the arbiter to determine public rights, and the danger that critical civil rights would not be vindicated. Essentially, he treated federal courts and arbitration as two equally valid forums.

The decision in *Gilmer v. Interstate Johnson/Lane Corp.* was all that CPR and the biggest companies in the country needed. After *Gilmer*, they knew that unless there was very explicit language in the statute forbidding arbitration, an employer could ask an employee to waive the right to bring any statutory claim to a public court. A merchant could ask any customer to do the same.

The *Gilmer* case was one of the last cases considered by Supreme Court Justice Thurgood Marshall. Marshall joined the dissent and retired from the Court a few weeks later. Since then, the arbitration strategy has only won more victories. At the beginning of this decade, the Supreme Court upheld contracts that banned consumer class actions. And, in 2018, the Court held that people could waive their rights to class actions in employment cases. A few years after *Gilmer*, the number of civil rights and consumer rights cases started declining, and has been declining ever since.[15]

All the 1980s cases had included a caveat that in cases where "overwhelming economic power" faced a powerless plaintiff, the courts might not enforce a waiver of basic legal rights.[16] Scalia left to another day the question of whether the court should consider market structure and the real choices facing an employee, or consumer, when faced with an arbitration clause.

That "another day" has never come; no court has found an "overwhelming economic power" exception to *Gilmer*.

THE FANTASY OF CHOICE

At the heart of the Scalia logic in the *Gilmer* case, and the entire series of cases involving arbitration agreements, is a fantasy of choice—a fantasy that relies on a nonexistent power dynamic and a set of unavailable non-arbitration options. In the Scalia logic, the choice one makes when signing a contract with AT&T is similar to the choice one makes when swiping Tinder; you're free, and more options are just a few clicks away. If the options aren't there and consumers want more choice, the invisible hand of the market will make those options magically appear.

Scalia's contract logic reflects neoliberalism, a powerful ideology in American legal thought. Neoliberalism is defined by a deep skepticism of democratic institutions, which it treats as corrupt and unreliable, and a mirror-image faith in market institutions, which it treats as responsive and reliable. For most of Anglo-American history, a whole series of principles shaped contract enforcement. Corrupt contracts weren't enforced, and contracts with a real power imbalance were not enforced. The neoliberal view is that freedom of contract should be presumed and contracts almost always enforced. The neoliberal view relies on a fairly radical view of choice, like that expressed in the *Gilmer* case. Neoliberals treat choice as a binary; either you have it or you don't. Neoliberal thinkers do not look under the hood at the various pressures and realities of a particular contract situation. If you sign a contract, the presumption is that you signed it freely, and freedom is treated as a formal matter, not a contextual one. Many neoliberals are drawn to this world view because its simplicity is satisfying. Things get messy, they correctly point out, as soon as we start making judgments about real-world power relations. Was Scalia cynically serving big business or naively imagining a world that didn't exist? Was he a con artist or a dupe? Neither one, except to the extent that power makes fools of us all: people, including judges, who reliably serve powerful interests are often promoted. You don't need to be a cynic to prefer the kind of thinking—and writing—that leads to status.

Corporate lawyers may not personally hold neoliberal views—many do, many don't—but they don't need to. They only need to see the advantages of arbitration, if you happen to be a big company dealing with consumers or workers; and those are obvious. The bigger the company, the easier it is to avoid meaningful negotiations or lawsuits by having an arbitration clause. In other words, arbitration and monopolization reinforce each other, as arbitration strengthens the hand of the big corporation, relocating power from the public to a private, protected court where the monopoly can't be challenged.

Research by Cornell law professor Alexander Colvin shows that the big companies, those involved in repeat arbitration, are the most likely to benefit from the shift from courts to arbitration. And when an arbiter works again and again with the same employer, the employer is more likely to win.[17] The arbiters are paid by the employer, so they consciously or unconsciously favor the employer over the employee on average, although bias may be impossible to detect in any particular case. As Lina Khan and Deepak Gupta argued in a 2017 essay that described arbitration contracts as a form of wealth transfer, "Concentration at the firm level has handed a relatively small number of companies outsized influence over the contractual terms that govern most transactions."[18]

It took a few years for wholesale adoption of the arbitration option that *Gilmer* offered. In 1991, 2% of employment contracts had mandatory arbitration clauses. Now, over half of non-union private-sector employers have mandatory arbitration agreements covering all legal violations, and nearly two-thirds of all big companies (companies with more than 1,000 employees) have these clauses.[19] Such agreements are more common in low-wage workplaces, and in industries with high numbers of women and African American workers.[20]

Almost every major consumer product is sold by only a few companies, and radical consolidation in the workplace makes meaningful choice between contracts almost impossible to imagine. Class action waivers are in close to 100% of major companies' consumer contracts, so people have no choice, when they sign up to use Amazon, or buy a car—or, in the cases that are the most likely to disappear—sign up for a loan with a bank, get a credit card, sign up for cell phone service, or go to a hospital. Five out of eight cable companies and three out of four national banks use similar arbitration clauses. Uber, Seamless, and other tech companies have been outdoing each other in writing the most draconian arbitration clauses. There is now a competition to develop the most unlaw-like fora and the most structural disincentives to bring claims.

Professor Colvin, one of America's experts on arbitration, begins his classes by asking his students to look up Verizon's arbitration contract. Then they look up T-Mobile's. Then on to Sprint. In real terms, the choice a consumer has is between arbitration defined by Verizon and arbitration defined by Sprint, and the definitions tend to be almost identical. Or try opening a bank account with any major bank. Wells Fargo, Bank of America, Chase, and Citibank have virtually identical arbitration contracts. When it comes to credit cards, the contracts are also all the same. So the idea that you can *choose* not to waive jury and class action rights is risible.

When Wells Fargo engaged in a scheme to defraud consumers by opening new accounts in a customer's name without the customer's permission, the people who were hurt could have made a real case if they could have banded together. But they were barred from bringing a class action suit against Wells Fargo because of an arbitration clause in a consumer contract they had signed with the bank.[21]

In employment, the idea that a waiver represents an autonomous, negotiated choice is a cruel joke. Poor and working-class people looking for work are not likely to turn a job down because of fine-print language about potential future lawsuits. Instead, employees almost always sign a waiver, and when they are hurt, they are shut out of court. When Charmaine Anderson sued Waffle House for sexual discrimination, she could not bring her case and her story to court because of an arbitration clause.[22] When Kevin Schiller was hit in the head by a falling mannequin, leading to severe head injuries that left him disabled, he sued Macy's for workers' compensation. Macy's sent doctors who decided he was lying, and he was not allowed to appeal his decision because of an arbitration clause.[23] And when a woman (name undisclosed) was not adequately compensated for the work she did cleaning homes for users of the Handy app, she couldn't go to court and couldn't recover her lost wages.[24]

Two law professors looked at nearly 3,000 cases of arbitration in 2015 and found that large-scale employers—the repeat players—win more often in arbitration than when they are taken to court, and incur lower damages. They called it the "employer-arbiter pair effect"; arbiters tended to favor the big companies that they had worked with more than once.[25] This is exactly the kind of bias the public selection of judges was designed to protect against.

The private court system is becoming increasingly uniform, with big companies converging on a set of practices that shape monopoly courts. The early arbitration agreements tended to come from large employers who had the money for lawyers to draft the terms, and to plan for big litigation. They were more likely to be bespoke. Now, arbitration is more likely to be off the rack, and while it changes, it doesn't change in the public way that court practices change. Instead, it is a race for law suppression. If one company figures out a better way to shut down complaints, the other firms quickly follow suit. At tech companies, labor and employment lawyers compete to outdo each other in ways to keep all disputes out of court and out of the public eye. The clauses continue to develop as power-protectors. The new innovation in arbitration clauses is "loser pays," which specifies that if you bring a claim in arbitration and lose, the costs of the arbitration fall on you, including the other side's legal fees. Essentially, as Stone describes it, this is the ultimate poison pill. No one who is poor will bring a suit if they know they will have to pay all the fees if they lose. The risk is too great. Most of the time, the people who sign the Handy, Wells Fargo, Macy's, or Waffle House contracts simply don't go to court at all.

Stone calls it "litigation suppression." "An arbitration clause may require that you travel to Idaho to have your case heard," she says.[26] A person overcharged on a phone contract in Florida can't afford that and won't take the economic risk of $2,000 to make back the $2,000 they believe they are owed—even when the lost $2,000 can mean insecurity for a year. The win rates are low, the recovery rates are low, and lawyers who might once have brought a class action suit will decline individual cases with capped recoveries. Yale Law Professor Judith Resnik explains that "although hundreds of millions of consumers and employers are obliged to use arbitration as their remedy, almost none do so—rendering arbitration . . . an unconstitutional evisceration of statutory and common law rights." As

Judge Richard Posner, hardly a liberal icon, has written, "The realistic alternative to a class action is not 17 million individual suits, but zero individual suits, as only a lunatic or a fanatic sues for $30."[27]

Lawyers know that employees in arbitration win barely over a fifth of the time, compared to the likelihood of winning about a third of the time in litigation, and that they tend to get much smaller rewards. Because of these low rewards, and the class action ban, arbitration agreements have destroyed a key tool that might help us get out of this monopoly mess: private litigation around antitrust. Given the behavior of Amazon, Tyson, and others, one might expect that sellers and farmers would be actively pursuing antitrust violations of big ag and big tech in courts. But class action–denying arbitration clauses like those between Amazon and Amazon sellers, or Visa and small businesses, mean that Amazon sellers cannot band together to bring a public lawsuit against various kinds of antitrust violations.

The Supreme Court addressed this problem in 2013, and held that small restaurants that were getting squeezed by American Express fees could not band together to bring a class action lawsuit, because of contractual arbitration binding them to one-on-one arbitration. The contract was hardly optional for a restaurant; accepting American Express is necessary for a business to survive. And Amex would clearly not bend its rules.

The dissent was written by Justice Elena Kagan, who explained the Kafkaesque situation that small businesses find themselves in, where monopolization has led to forced arbitration, and then made lawsuits against monopolization impossible: "So if the arbitration clause is enforceable, Amex has insulated itself from antitrust liability—even if it has in fact violated the law. . . . The monopolist gets to use its monopoly power to insist on a contract effectively depriving its victims of all legal recourse."[28]

Shaoul Sussman, a litigator and Amazon expert (and former law student of mine) is convinced that Amazon is likely violating existing antitrust laws against predatory practices. He believes that arbitration clauses are the biggest barrier to meaningful litigation. He said that the allegations he hears regularly from small-business owners who depend on Amazon's platform would be sufficient to sue—or at least to explore a suit—but because of arbitration, they are barred from court.[29] Given the high costs of serious arbitration, the inability to band together, and the caps on how much can be recovered, it isn't worth it to them.

THE LOSS OF CIVIL RIGHTS

In the 1960s and 1970s, Congress passed sweeping legislation to protect workers and consumers. The Fair Labor Standards Act, which governs minimum wage and rules for overtime, was expanded to cover all big companies in 1961. In 1963, the Equal Pay Act, addressing gender bias, passed, and three years later the Civil Rights Act of 1964 outlawed racial discrimination in employment. In 1967, Congress banned age discrimination in employment with the Age Discrimination in Employment Act. Congress also passed critical consumer protections in the sixties and seventies, including laws to prevent people from getting ripped off by banks or other big companies, such as the 1968 Truth in Lending Act and the 1978 Fair Debt Collection Practices Act.

The laws worked. Workers were bringing cases—hundreds of thousands of them—alleging racial, age, and gender discrimination and wage theft. Consumers were bringing fraud claims. These laws bothered big companies in many ways: they were irritating, they cost money, and they exposed stories about the companies' inner workings that they wanted kept private. Unseemly press accompanies a poor worker confronting an abusive boss—trials are dramatic, the kind of thing a tabloid can follow. The old-fashioned democratic way to deal with laws one doesn't like is to advocate that they be overturned, but even in the political climate that produced Ronald Reagan, the idea of loudly denouncing the Civil Rights Act or the Equal Pay Act seemed like a non-starter. So companies instead tried to enforce arbitration clauses against workers and purchasers, attempts the Supreme Court initially rejected.

Law professor Charlotte Garden, an expert in arbitration law, explained that she doesn't like the phrase "forced arbitration" because it makes it sound like the big companies are forced to arbitrate. In reality, these forced arbitration clauses and class action waivers mean something different: they mean that the cases are never brought in any forum at all. Violations of the Civil Rights Act of 1964, the Americans with Disabilities Act, the Family and Medical Leave Act, the Fair Labor Standards Act, and all state human rights and non-discrimination laws—they are not scuttled away into the privately controlled courts; instead, they are vanished.[30]

One trial lawyer described the new regime this way: "What we lose is law. When people go to trial and those trials are appealed and appellate courts write opinions, law develops and law changes and law evolves. When all of that happens in an arbitration context, nothing happens."[31] When the disputes are shut out of courts, the stories of what happens inside the walled fortresses of Google, Monsanto, Spectrum, and Amazon leave public life. We don't know the details of the cases that aren't brought. What we do know, as Cardozo law professor Myriam Gilles describes, is that "whole categories of legal claims are disappearing from the docket—private claims sounding in abusive debt collection, predatory lending, consumer scams, illegal foreclosures, unfair or unpaid wages, and employment discrimination . . . the types of legal issues that economically vulnerable populations are very likely to encounter."[32]

Arbitration has not been the sole tool for this juridical disenfranchisement. It is part of a larger project of dispossessing people of the right to be free of arbitrary power. Other elements of this project of rights stripping include higher pleading standards, which make it harder to bring a claim; easier summary judgment, which makes it easier for claims to get ejected from court; and the restriction of punitive damages, which makes it foolish to bring lawsuits, even if they are successful, because the reward is unlikely to be greater than the cost of litigation. This has been a central goal of arbitration, and is arguably the most insolent.

The scope of the catastrophe will always be unknown—in this case, by design. As one workplace organizer, Tanuja Gupta, explained to me, "The people we are trying to tell these stories about are looking for a job. They are in a terrible catch-22."[33] If they tell their story publicly they will get no damages—because they are bound by arbitration—and they are likely to be seen as high-risk candidates for future employers. The group she works with has an internal saying to describe how big companies use arbitration to control people: "divide, silence, and conquer."

She represents a spate of new energy and activism around this crisis. In 2018, a group of Harvard Law students, angry about the way the largest law firm in the world used forced arbitration in their employment contracts, encouraged students seeking summer employment to boycott Kirkland & Ellis. The boycott worked, and Kirkland announced a few months later that associates and summer associates would not be asked to sign mandatory arbitration agreements.[34] Harvard Law students seeking summer jobs may be the only people who truly represent the vision of choice and autonomy that Scalia's case law reflects. They have hundreds of law firms to choose from, and they are not scared.

Having said that, these students—along with a cohort of tech workers—are playing a critical role in a new movement to address forced arbitration. Growing public pressure led Congress to pass a law that would ban forced arbitration (the Senate has not taken up the bill). And after growing evidence of sexual harassment and lack of diversity at Google, 20,000 Google workers, led by Gupta—who is a Google employee— and others, walked out because of the forced arbitration clause in Google's contract. It is scary to go up against Google, Gupta told me. Workers feel like they are in a huge power imbalance. Gupta hears workers say, "We need a salary. We need healthcare. It is incredibly scary, they are huge, they can withstand walkouts."[35] When she and her colleagues looked at other tech companies, they all had the same clauses. The idea that workers have a choice in signing these waiver clauses is fantastical, she said; forced arbitration is baked into the tech industry.

In March 2019, Google workers won a major victory. Google announced it was getting rid of all forced arbitration waivers for all direct Google employees. The change still doesn't apply to the temps and contract workers, or food and other service workers, who work with Google, and they make up close to half of the people that Google, in one way or another, pays. If you work at Bon Appétit on the Google campus, you don't get the protections Google just offered, and that isn't right, according to the activists. That creates different classes of law for different classes of workers. While Google met the walkout demands, it also allegedly retaliated against two of the organizers—one organizer, who later quit, said her manager gave work to other people and asked her to go on medical leave, although she was not sick. The other says she was reassigned.[36]

But the Google workers, and the Harvard students, aren't giving up: as Gupta puts it, arbitration is the "gateway" problem, and all Google's efforts to do good in the world don't matter if the company doesn't respect the importance of fair open procedures. She knows her job at Google might be jeopardized by her activism, and she suspects her supervisor was talked to about her protest work—but she is willing to continue, because "if we are going to deny basic civil rights, forget about the rest."[37]

5

The Body Snatchers

Monopoly crushed the laborer and made him vote
with it.

—Chicago mayor Carter Harrison[1]

I ran for Congress in 2016 in a swing district. After winning a
spirited, issues-based primary, I turned to the general election,
and faced a surreal experience. On paper, I was running against
Republican John Faso, but in terms of who held the power
to make strategic decisions, I found myself running against a
few wealthy billionaires. While Mr. Faso himself spent under
$3 million, super PACs spent over $6.3 million, $1.2 million
of which came from just three men.[2] As a result, voters in my
district were *more* likely to hear messages from super PACs than
from my opponent. When the super PAC donors wanted the
race to be about the Iran deal, the race was about the Iran deal.
Faso showed up in debates and local news coverage, but since
few people watched debates, and local news coverage is dwin-
dling, he played a secondary role in his own race. The ads voters
saw on television and on YouTube and Spotify and Facebook
came from super PACs. The opposition research came from
super PACs. A super PAC paid for a staffer to follow me and
videotape me at every public event. I challenged the super PAC
donors to a debate.[3] They did not respond to press questions:
unlike candidates, they do not face the exposure of the trail. In
one of those super PAC ads, they hired a body double, a woman

with my haircut, clothing style, and posture, to misrepresent my agenda. If I wanted to complain about the assertions in the ad—or the use of a body double—I had to appeal to the super PAC, not the candidate. A super PAC puppeteer using a body double may make for a good parable, but it also made me angry, and disoriented.

Such democratic disorientation is spreading. There is a natural, existential uncertainty that many of us experience, the occasional *Body Snatchers* fear that one's spouse, house, or life has been replaced with a dummy. In American democracy, that fear is increasingly prevalent, and increasingly justified. As I discussed in the last chapter, courts are being replaced by court look-alikes. Other democratic institutions are undergoing more complicated, but equally troubling, transformations as they are reshaped to serve the new powers: as my experience illustrates, super PACs (corporate entities that can spend unlimited money in candidate races) have taken over as the primary source of advocacy for candidates in close elections. Political parties are being replaced by corporate-run institutions. Big corporations, which consider political strategy essential to their overall strategy, increasingly use the tools of authoritarianism—centralized regimes, opposition suppression, forced public displays of alignment—to hold on to their power, and they do so in the name of political speech. A persistent paranoia has naturally slipped into politics as these institutions are corroded, and this has led millions to flee politics as quickly and quietly as possible, and millions of others to embrace the nihilism of Donald Trump and Fox News.

We lack a political language to talk about the depth of the problem because the look-alike institutions—private political parties, campaign ads about candidates, trade associations—share some of the familiar features of democracy, but they are made of something altogether different.[4]

Corporate money is everywhere in politics, as Jane Mayer showed in her blockbuster book *Dark Money*. In this chapter I explore just a few concrete examples of the body snatcher problem: corporate institutions replacing democratic institutions by burrowing inside them and using their language and forms. I explore how corporate money is taking over parties as essential organizing institutions, and how monopolies use trade associations to hide their ambitions behind the language of small business. Finally, I look at the future that is fast overtaking us: a new kind of political system, in which big companies directly become the primary political institution in many workers' lives. This is company-town politics on a national scale, which has quickly grown out of the leeway given by *Citizens United*.

TO LIVE TOGETHER IN THE WORLD

Democracy requires that people, acting freely, come together and decide what to do: Shall we build a bridge or hire a cop, or both? Shall we go to war or refrain? Shall we hold pharmaceutical companies liable for opioid deaths, shall we tax sugar drinks, shall we ban fracking? How shall we pay for schools? While we hear a great deal about poll numbers, polls, operated from above, questioning us each as individuals, cannot do the work of bringing people together. Mass democracy, to retain its democratic features, requires real mediating institutions, community organizations and associations and political parties that enable meaningful conversation and debate. The political philosopher Hannah Arendt, who sought to understand totalitarianism and how it could arise from a democratic society, argued that conversation and deliberation were essential to make it possible for people "to live together in the world." There must be a world or worlds held in common, a public realm, which operates like "a table located between

those who sit around it; the world, like every in-between, relates and separates men at the same time." The public realm,
she argued, "gathers us together and yet prevents our falling
over each other, so to speak." Mass society makes that common
table experience much harder; we are not forced together by
circumstance, and can feel disoriented by the disconnect between the abstract fact (we live under a shared regime) and the
felt experience (we are not together).[5] In order to have the freedom to develop independent perspectives and act on them, we
need institutions that enable discussion, and institutions that
enable collective action. Grassroots political parties are essential
in mass society, therefore, because they provide some means of
coming together to fight, talk, share, plan, and be connected
to power.[6]

REPLACING POLITICAL PARTIES

Grassroots political parties in America have played an essential
role in binding people together, not just as partisans, but as
communities that connect people to the levers of power. The
political party at its best is not merely a shorthand for policy or
identity, but enables people with little power, via engagement
in that political party, to play a part in shaping a platform that
in turn shapes their lives. In the early years of the country, two
elite networks, each of which owned newspapers around the
country, battled each other in the press with little meaningful grassroots and popular involvement. This "First Party System," as it is sometimes called, was replaced in the 1830s with
the Jacksonian parties. From the 1830s until the 1880s, parties
became the driving force behind campaigns. They engaged
in mass leafletting, held big events, and developed grassroots
organizational structures.

These parties were funded by the spoils system; active campaigners for a candidate were assured a job in government if their candidate won. Once in government, they were expected to give a cut of their salary to fund the party that had put them there. This led to high degrees of engagement, and high degrees of incompetent officeholders. Parties set priorities, groomed and picked candidates, fundraised, held events, and organized job seekers. When the spoils system was outlawed at the end of the nineteenth century, big business rushed in to fill the void of candidate financing, but the essential elements of the party structures stayed; in some cases, like Tammany Hall, politicians still promised jobs or contracts in return for votes. In others, the promises were for job programs, social security, or education policies.

For the next 80 years, parties remained the essential mechanism of connecting people to politics. They were far from ideal; parties were racist and engaged in ballot stuffing and violence and big and small forms of corruption. But they served an essential purpose of linking public opinion with policy making. They were deeply grounded in people who identified as members of the party and who in some way contributed or engaged with it.

After a series of scandals involving big money and foreign money, and spurred to final action by Watergate, Congress tried to pass legislation to limit how much money could be spent in campaigns, but the Supreme Court struck down that legislation in *Buckley v. Valeo*, a 1976 case that removed limits on campaign spending by campaigns, candidates, parties, and individuals. In *Buckley*, the Court said that money spent on campaign ads should be treated as speech, and given the highest level of First Amendment protections.

Starting in the 1980s, in part as a result of *Buckley*, the connection between grassroots and leadership began to fray. Unlimited spending led to unlimited time fundraising. As television advertising became expensive, parties turned aggressively to corporations and big donors for funding. The shift was the most noticeable in the Democratic Party, where the funding turned quickly from the old model (a blend of union funding and a few wealthy contributors) to a new model, in which campaigns were underwritten almost entirely by wealthy donors with ties to Wall Street. Arguably because of the temptations of the new funding system, Bill Clinton led the charge in stripping the Democratic Party of its historic antagonism toward Wall Street and big business. Corporations funded "soft money" ads (ads ostensibly about issues, not about candidates), and corporate leadership developed close ties with party leadership.

Corporations could give money through a mechanism called a PAC (political action committee), where employees contributed to a fund that was in turn donated to preferred candidates and parties. They could fund ads that clearly helped candidates but were ostensibly only about issues that they cared about (for example, the American Insurance Association funded an ad in Republican Nancy Johnson's district, saying, "Join Nancy Johnson in the fight for real tax reform").[7] Despite these huge loopholes, the American Insurance Association could not directly fund ads supporting Nancy Johnson's re-election, and in order to influence the platform of political parties, they tended to work through, instead of around, party leadership. The route to influence—big donations—was effective, but nonetheless mediated. Party leaders might want a major donation from Comcast for the convention, and that desire might influence their position on industry regulation, but at least they would have to justify their position to members of the party. They'd have to explain, in public, why they voted the way they did.

And so, flawed and corrupted as they were, political parties maintained many functions of their past. Responsiveness in both parties persisted. Local party committees had enormous sway over local races, and if a lowly party operative complained, there were mechanisms for that operative to be heard. Although big money had a lot of power, the laws still limited the amount that any corporation could inject into any one race. Parties retained their core feedback mechanism: an angry grassroots could push the party to the left or right, as the case may be, by appealing to party organizations through primaries.

Ten years ago, one case changed the balance of power. In 2010, the Supreme Court decided *Citizens United v. Federal Election Commission* and tore off all limits on corporate political spending. Since then, the relationship between parties and big money has been changing rapidly. In *Citizens United*, the Court struck down a law that banned direct spending by corporations in elections. A majority of the justices held that the law violated the First Amendment of the Constitution, resting its determination on four arguments. First, that people had a right to listen to all speech, regardless of the source. Second, that corporations were "associations of people" whose rights to speak should not be limited. Third, that a contrary ruling would allow Congress to create times when books and newspapers and other corporate-created information could be shut down. Finally, that the law limiting corporate spending didn't serve any anti-corruption purpose, because outside corporate spending isn't corrupting.

In *Citizens United*, the Supreme Court sent a strong message to corporate America. Justice Anthony Kennedy wrote that the long-standing rule against corporate electoral spending shut out "some of the most important voices" in our country. He treated corporate politics as desirable, not worrisome.

After *Citizens United*, there is only one thing corporations can't do: directly coordinate with candidates or parties and make plans about what messages to share and what strategies to use. Everything else is fair game.

In the decade since the decision, the relationship between big money and political parties has transformed in three significant stages. The first stage lasted from 2010 to 2014, when big money dipped its toe into politics: during these years, super PACs tended to be general cheerleaders for existing candidates, amplifying the arguments made by party leaders and those seeking office.

The second stage, from 2014 to 2018, involved super PACs taking the reins from candidates and parties. Instead of candidates or parties deciding how to differentiate themselves on healthcare or education, the super PACs took over that role. With extensive polling research and billionaire funding, they could lead the way, and political parties increasingly followed. In twenty-two close congressional races in 2018, there was more super PAC money spent than candidate money.[8] Sometimes, a lot more. Kansas Republican Steve Watkins spent a little over $1 million, while super PACs supporting him spent $3.6 million. The same was true in seven Senate races. Indiana Democrat Joe Donnelly was outspent by super PACs supporting him by $1 million, and Republican Josh Hawley spent less than half of what super PACs spent in his Missouri Senate race.[9]

Super PACs shifted from amplifying candidate messages to getting the candidates and parties to amplify theirs. In a West Virginia Senate race, a Joe Manchin–aligned super PAC accused Republican Patrick Morrissey of being a carpetbagger, and a

Morissey-aligned super PAC said Manchin "endorsed Hillary 100 percent and Joe Manchin voted no on the tax cuts." The $28 million spent by the super PACs combined was far greater than the combined $14 million spent by the candidates. The ads were put together without Manchin or Morrissey in the room: in terms of strategy, the candidates were increasingly becoming spectators in their own races.[10] As a result, these candidates and the party leaderships now take cues from multimillionaire donors and big corporations about the strategies they should be using.

The third stage is beginning right now, as corporations and billionaires start creating their own political parties and infrastructure. When Donald Trump and the Republicans in Congress pushed through their 2017 tax law, they were supported by something that looked and acted like a political party, or really, like a political movement, but it was really corporate cash. The group, Americans for Prosperity (AFP), spends its own money on ads, pursues its own platform in domestic and foreign and environmental policy, and pays a deep bench of organizers to go door to door and engage with voters. The president of AFP calls the program a "permanent grass-roots infrastructure," and it's working to build the same kind of voter database that a political party would traditionally build.[11] During the fight over the tax bill, AFP mobilized to punish, and later to defeat, Democratic senators who jeopardized the bill. AFP replicated all the functions of a political party except responsiveness: the one thing that would give it democratic value. AFP is an organization paid for and controlled by the Koch family.[12] In this third stage, super PACs like AFP do not just do the work of campaigns, but all the work that parties once did. And the political departments of big corporations are starting to hire the men and women who would have gone to work for the Democratic Party a decade ago.

A WHALE INSIDE THE FISH TANK

Meanwhile, big corporations are also taking over another democratic institution: trade associations. If you walk through the streets of Washington, DC, large, nameless buildings cluster around the Capitol. The National Communications and Telecommunications Industry announces itself with only the number of the building—*25*—outside. The National Federation of Independent Business has no sign on its building. The National Retail Federation is housed above a Starbucks, in the old Fireman's Insurance Company building, with no sign out front. These are the modern trade associations. Out of these buildings shuffle men and women who claim to represent the small-business owners of America but who are paid by some of the biggest corporations in world history.

Americans have always been famous for what the French writer and political observer Alexis de Tocqueville called the "art of association."[13] When Tocqueville toured the country in the 1830s he found clubs—religious, industrial, commercial, small, large, futile, and serious—everywhere he looked. For him, they represented a kind of national genius, a capacity and tendency to deal with sorrows and joys in an egalitarian, collective way; he saw associations as a central part of American society. In the late nineteenth century, the trade association took on a special role, and during President Woodrow Wilson's tenure, that role was enshrined in the federal tax code: trade associations are quasi-public institutions, meant to foster connections among members of the same trade and give them a voice in the outside world. For most of the last century, trade associations were an essential part of American business:

they connected small- and medium-sized businesses with each other, held trade shows and published newsletters, funded technological developments, and upheld industry standards. In the 1950s, tens of thousands of orange growers congregated once a year in California for the orange growers trade show, a meeting bigger than the current Consumer Electronics Show, where they shared stories and strategies.

Above all, they shared information and community. This was the key to the art of association: they created a constant flow of information among competitors, and this information stimulated innovation. What's more, they created transparency with the outside world: association newsletters were essential source reading for national and local reporters.

We still have trade associations, and their role in American politics would seem to be greater than ever. They are certainly spending more than they ever have. In 2004, the total trade group political spending was $107 million; eight years later, *one* group spent that much alone. However, of the over 60,000 trade associations in the country, the vast majority are shadow associations—vestiges without a real function. The majority, 65%, have budgets under $100,000 and just collect a few dues and send out small newsletters.[14] persists as a front for one or two businesses that want to do minimal lobbying. For thousands, the trade group is a single part-time staffer, called a "president," who provides certification.

Only a few whales are left. The Tocquevillian mess of thousands of trade associations has been replaced by 100 politically important giants, trade associations with lobbying budgets of $1 million or more. Think the American Apparel and Footwear Association, the National Retail Federation, and the Internet Association. Their agendas are set by the big companies that fund their activities. Cargill, Tyson Foods, JBS, and National Beef Packing, which together control 85% of the meatpacking business, also control the National Cattlemen's Beef Association (NCBA). "It's pay to play," says author and political scientist Lee Drutman. The trade groups are run by the "companies that pay the most money to be members."[15]

The trouble is, these big companies often have interests that are directly opposed to what a genuine membership organization would want. The National Retail Federation (NRF), for example, is heavily funded by Amazon—a company relentless in its quest to destroy or control all other retailers, not just in America, but on the planet. This is an obvious case of the wolf guarding the sheep. (Naturally, when the NRF goes to lobby Congress, it's represented by Dave Ratner, an eccentric pet store owner from Agawam, Massachusetts, not Jeff Bezos.) Amazon pays to keep the lights on at the NRF, and the NRF gives a democratic veneer to Amazon's policy objectives. The same story is repeated in one trade association after another. In 2013, Comcast spent $18 million on lobbying in its own name; it also supported the National Cable and Television Association, which spent $19 million on lobbying, and the National Association of Broadcasters, which spent $14 million.[16] The NCBA purports to speak for small-scale ranchers, but Cargill's interest is often diametrically opposed to the men and women it claims to represent. The Internet Association was created by Google, Facebook, Apple, and Amazon to make it seem like their interests align with those of the internet more broadly.

Trade associations are used to advocate for the politically unpopular work that a company wants. One survey showed that 77% of Global 500 companies used trade associations to lobby on climate policy, against new climate rules.[17] They mask simple needs. Tech has been proliferating trade associations recently. Google, Lyft, Uber, and Ford are happier to speak through the Self-Driving Coalition for Safer Streets.[18] The Partnership on AI, led by Facebook, Google, Amazon, and

Microsoft, among others, claims to "provide a regular, structured platform for AI researchers and key stakeholders to communicate directly and openly with each other about relevant issues." They describe what they do as "independent reflection and analysis."[19]

In other words, industry lobbying has become a charade, using small-business owners and anodyne names to hide corporate power on Capitol Hill. Politicians are comfortably half-fooled; they would genuinely rather listen to the National Association of Broadcasters than to Comcast, and when they consider a bill on the sales tax or minimum wage, they'd rather say they are listening to Dave Ratner than Jeff Bezos. The trade associations give them political cover, so that they seem responsive to small businesses when in fact they are in the pockets of monopolies—the biggest threat small businesses face.

THE COMING THREAT

Given these examples of body-snatcher politics, it's all too clear what is coming next: corporate direction of employee speech and activism.

Non-unionized private-sector workers do not have free speech rights in relation to their employers. Anyone can be fired for sharing a political opinion, but before *Citizens United*, companies had to be careful about anything that looked like corporate electioneering, which was banned. Now, the dam has broken.

If Google wanted to, it could fire (or quietly demote) all employees and subcontractors who shared Bernie Sanders memes. Facebook could give bonuses dependent on the frequency of employees contacting their congressmember to advocate for a Facebook-friendly tax policy. Tyson, or Uber, could regularly amass political reports on all the farmers or drivers who use their distribution centers and provide different prices or fares based on politics.

In a startling recent book, *Politics at Work*, Columbia University political scientist Alexander Hertel-Fernandez surveyed workers and bosses about corporate-directed politics and found that nearly half of companies share political information with employees and that 16% of American workers reported that political retaliation occurred at their job. As of today, *one in eight* American workers believes that "someone at their job was treated unfairly, missed out on a promotion, or was fired as a result of political views or actions."[20]

As Hertel-Fernandez shows, technology-enabled political surveillance of employees, at work and out of work, is becoming ubiquitous, especially in larger companies. While it used to be hard to know what a line cook might be saying about a president or a climate deal, now it's easy to record what she says to her coworkers on the job, and to see what she's posting online when she gets home. There are now off-the-shelf tools designed for big companies to target political conversations, to monitor who is opening emails of a political nature, and to see who follows a link to a political website. A 2018 survey of IT professionals working for big companies asked them how much they spied on employees: 98% said they tracked employee digital behavior. Employers used to find prying inconvenient, but now it is routine: 87% tracked employee email, and 70% grabbed web browser history. Nearly half of all companies listened to voicemails. A third of companies tracked social media behavior.[21] Just last year, Walmart was awarded a patent for a tool that would allow the company to eavesdrop on the conversations of its baggers.[22]

Surveillance means power. So does consolidation. It weakens the hand of workers and makes job loss that much more of a threat. In a deeper sense, it has changed what it means to be a big corporation. With scale and market share, the job of the corporation becomes political in a profound, intertwined, embedded way; *business becomes politics*—politics in lobbying, politics in campaign contributions, politics in self-surveillance. When there are only a few big players in any market, any worker in that market is going to pay attention to the political ramifications of speaking out. Companies with enough market share don't just chill their own workers' speech, but that of workers more generally: a worker at Popeyes isn't going to speak out in favor of Democratic Socialism if he worries that could blacklist him at all Yum! Brands–owned fast-food restaurants (KFC, Taco Bell, Pizza Hut) *and* at McDonald's. As Hertel-Fernandez's research has shown, the bigger a company is, the likelier it is to engage in political surveillance of employees, and to reward or punish employees based on their activities. If we continue on this path, these companies are well placed to replace political parties as the key institutional nodes of organizing activity.

In 2010, Harrah's told supervisors to ask employees whether they had voted in a tight congressional election. In 2012, a coal mining company told employees they had to show up at a Mitt Romney rally, without pay. In January 2019, facing fierce opposition to its proposal to locate a new headquarters in Queens, Amazon sent an email suggesting its New York employees attend a public hearing. These actions will come to seem quaint if we don't break up monopoly power. They might be palatable in a decentralized economic environment—if your boss loves Mitt Romney so much she'll fire you over it, you can get a new boss—but when economic power is held by a handful of men, we find ourselves on the path toward authoritarianism.[23] The main reason we have secret voting in this country is that the money power in the Gilded Age punished workers who voted the wrong way and rewarded those who voted in the companies' interest. Now, people's ballots may be private, but with surveillance and concentration, very little else about their political activity is. The growing control of a few companies makes this behavior uniquely pernicious and has the effect of spreading seeds of fear and anxiety into the exercise of basic political rights. For democracy to work, we need people to feel free to vote for whom they prefer, and to speak up about it, and to explain why.

The companies that increasingly run our country do not hesitate to ask for favors, to speak for the public, and to get involved not only in policy but in decisions. When the banks crashed the economy, we treated it as natural that they should design their own bailout. Lobbyist-written laws are no longer seen as scandalous, but as routine. When Amazon scrapped its plans to move to New York—because the state refused to cede control over the personnel decisions to an obscure state authority, the Public Authorities Control Board—this demand for political power was treated as a normal part of doing business.

Amazon recently spent \$1.5 million in Seattle's city council races.[24] It is giving some warehouse employees special status to tweet positive things about how great it is to work at Amazon. (Including tweets about free cupcakes, safety consciousness, and how easy it is to get time off.) What if Amazon charged different fees for sellers depending on their public statements about a candidate? What if Amazon required tweets from the workers of those sellers?

These rewards and punishments can be tied to the larger political operations of these companies. Fear of losing a job is a powerful motivator: as fear creeps into all aspects of society, people may not even need to be punished or rewarded in order to fall in line with corporate politics.

An agenda to beat back the body snatchers has to be ambitious: we must work on not just overturning *Citizens United*—a clear and urgent necessity—but on overturning a much longer line of cases, going back to the 1976 Supreme Court decision *Buckley v. Valeo*, which, as noted, struck down any absolute political spending limits. We need publicly financed elections at all levels of government so that candidates no longer need corporate support for their voices to be heard. But all this is only half the battle. *Campaign finance rules, even at their best,* are not sufficient to achieve democracy without changing the role of concentrated power. Break them up *and* cap the spending, and we'll have a fighting chance.

6

Race and Monopoly Power

> After the war, triumphant industry in the North
> coupled with privilege and monopoly led an orgy
> of death that engulfed the nation.
>
> —W. E. B. Du Bois,
> *Black Reconstruction*

The American political economy, since its first founding in
1787, and its second founding after the Civil War, has worked
to benefit people of European descent and oppress and shut out
African Americans and other communities of color. Monopoly has frequently been a powerful tool of this oppression. At
times, monopoly is an instrument of white power; at other
times, owners of monopolies leverage racial anxiety and racism
to increase their own power.

As W. E. B. DuBois lays out in his masterful *Black Recon-
struction*, the meta-politics of the 1870s was about the creation
of a new bargain between northern financial power and southern conservatives, and the development of an informal dictator-
ship of northern banking power and northern monopoly over
industry that made a mockery of the formal democracy. Consider, for example, the credit monopolies of the post–Civil
War era. After the Civil War, ex-slaves had nothing to sell but
their labor. Their right to vote was formally recognized, along
with the legal right to own property and to sell their own labor and skills, but after 240 years of torture, abuse, theft, and

murder, freed slaves were not given any money or land with
which to exercise their rights. Nonetheless, for a brief period,
black Americans were politically active and elected to office
at record levels. Sixteen African Americans served in the U.S.
Congress, over 600 were elected to the state legislatures, and
blacks worked together with whites building new state constitutions. Some of the many devices that stopped this democra-
tization in its tracks were land and credit monopolies.

Here's how it worked: Former plantation owners rented
land to farmers in exchange for a 50% share in everything they
sold. As part of the land contract, the landlords would specify
the means of cultivation and the tools to be used, and provide
the seeds. The farmers then had to take out loans to fulfill their
obligations. In most parts of the South, there was only one
source of credit within geographical reach of a local farmer:
a general-store owner, whose credit, in turn, was dependent
on northern banking interests. Because a farmer could not
live without credit, these general-store credit monopolies had
near-absolute power over every choice a farmer made. Owners
would refuse credit to anyone who did not shop at their store,
and they forced farmers to cultivate cotton and not food crops
because they feared self-sufficiency. Essentially, the sharecroppers were governed by three coexisting forms of government:
the state, their landlord, and their creditor. Any one of these
could punish a farmer who dared to exercise political rights:
the landlords could cancel the land contract, and the merchant/
creditor could withhold credit. This system only dissolved
when transportation and communication made northern em-
igration more feasible, and the boll weevil destroyed cotton
crops. But for 40 years, ex-slaves were governed by the states
and the national government in conjunction with corrupt
credit monopolists.

Jump forward 130 years, and we find a centralized financial

system in which black businesspeople's difficulty in accessing capital markets continues and the redlining faced by black homeowners has played an ongoing and central role in our political economic system. The cost of the 2008 financial crash to black communities was especially catastrophic, and the discrimination in lending and the predatory loans targeting minority communities fueled the crisis, with snowballing, disparate impacts. Over half, or 53%, of total black wealth was destroyed in the financial crisis in 2008.[1] In her 2017 book *The Color of Money*, Mehrsa Baradaran chronicles the long history of concentrated white financial systems that have kept black Americans at a deep disadvantage, with the result that blacks now own less than 2% of the wealth of the country, up from 0.5% in 1863, the year the Emancipation Proclamation was signed.[2] The financial sector provides just one of many mechanisms through which concentrated economic power interacts with race and racial politics. In this chapter, I look at three other ways in which modern monopoly power serves to crush the political power of people of color: how greater concentration means less black ownership; how corporate monopolies cut deals with white politicians to suppress the vote; and how big tech companies' monopoly business models thrive on discrimination.

This chapter is primarily about racism against black people, although in a few places I touch on the interactions between monopoly and racism against other communities of color. We need to do a lot more work to fully understand and expose the ways that monopoly power creates and sustains systemic racism, exclusion, and extraction as it relates to unique communities.

THE BLEACHING OF AMERICAN BUSINESS

In the spring of 1960, in Biloxi, Mississippi, black activists walked single-file on the beach, wearing business suits and bathing suits, carrying no weapons, protesting segregated beaches with a "wade-in." They were confronted by young white men armed with clubs, brass knuckles, and bricks. The mob attacked, and the police left them alone, instead arresting the 69 black protesters. A huge cheer erupted from the crowd of 200 white people watching. White gangs roamed the streets that night, beating people up. The incident became known as Bloody Sunday.

The wade-in was the first major instance of civil disobedience in Mississippi and a critical moment in the civil rights movement. Many of the wade-in protesters were teenagers and women; the men were worried they would lose their jobs if they joined. It was led by drugstore owner Gilbert R. Mason. Mason wrote in his autobiography that his particular status as an independent business owner gave him freedom to protest in such an oppressive and terrifying regime.[3] The civil rights movement relied on "an economically independent class of black businessmen" who were "difficult for the white establishment to control." More than a few black business owners in that era were liberal Republicans who prided themselves on independence from anyone, especially the Democrats.[4]

Black-owned businesses appear everywhere in the history of the civil rights movement. In the Montgomery bus boycott of 1965, protesters risking everything relied on black-owned taxis and a black-owned pharmacy to coordinate alternative transportation to get to work.[5] A private black-owned bus fleet in Birmingham carried activists to the March on Washington when no white-owned company was willing to charter buses to transport black protesters.[6]

The wade-in and related activism highlight how politically important it can be to have a system that allows for the proliferation of black-owned businesses, and how vital commercial nodes of power have been in American democratic movements.

Black-owned businesses have been central spaces for gathering, conversation, dissent, protest, and planning. Take, for instance, the funeral home industry. Tiffany Stanley explained in a 2016 *Atlantic* article how "from their earliest incarnations, black funerals were political, subversive—a talking back to the powers that be."[7] Slaves who were allowed to conduct their own funerals used those moments "to plan for their freedom, spiritually and physically." Nat Turner was rumored to have made plans at a funeral. The funeral of an enslaved black child became the planning ground for an insurrection in Virginia. Funeral home owners played a vital role in the civil rights movement and were often political leaders.

What happens to black-owned businesses in a white, monopolized economy? In *Washington Monthly*, author Brian Feldman chronicles the "wholesale collapse of black-owned independent businesses and financial institutions" and lays out a persuasive case that black businesses have been routed by bad antitrust policy.[8] Key centers of black economic power have been wiped out: black publishing has been bought out by white-owned businesses, while black pharmacies, black funeral homes, and black banks have merged into white-controlled companies.

For instance, Feldman reports a decline in the number of black-owned insurance companies, from 50 in the 1980s to 2 today. Black Americans, he shows, are less likely to own their own businesses now than in the 1990s. Between 1997 and 2014, the number of black employers per capita went down 12%.

If the boycott, the wade-in, or the March on Washington happened in today's top-heavy economy, who would support them? Today, while the funeral industry booms, black power declines: black-owned funeral homes have been gobbled up by big chains like Service Corporation International (SCI), which has dominated by buying up 1,500 funeral homes and 400 cemeteries. In 2013 it bought the second-largest death care company in the country; the Federal Trade Commission (FTC) was worried enough to whimper but allowed the merger with a few conditions. SCI is no civil rights icon. The SCI PAC spent hundreds of thousands of dollars in 2018, dividing donations evenly between Republicans and Democrats. It is impossible to imagine the CEO of SCI leading, let alone supporting, dangerous civil disobedience. The funeral home owners, and similarly situated business owners, either were bought out or pushed out by companies like SCI, but they frequently had no choice; if they did not take the cash, they would not be able to compete against the new goliaths.[9]

Antitrust is, therefore, important for black economic power because the distribution of power in small- and medium-sized businesses is different from that in large corporations: small- and medium-sized businesses are much more diverse. Nearly one-fifth of all American businesses are run by black men and women, compared to just 4% of the Fortune 500.[10] Think about that: a *non*–Fortune 500 company is nearly 6 times more likely to be run by an African American than a Fortune 500 company. Financial ownership of corporate America is even more homogeneous. A 2017 study showed that firms owned by minorities and women manage only 1.1% of the $71.4 trillion in asset management.[11]

And as corporate power gets more and more concentrated, Fortune 500 companies control a larger and larger swath of our economy—when 96% of Fortune 500 CEOs are white, that means that the white vise grip on power has grown, because the white men at the top govern more of our lives than they did 30 years ago.[12] The higher up you go in a corporate structure, the more who you know matters, and the clubbiness increases, excluding those who are not from the same background, the same schools, or don't have the same way of talking, or the same ancestry. There *has* been a rise of a small but very wealthy business class in black America that moves across racial lines, and is sometimes given authority to speak for "the black community," but it often shows a relative disdain for progressive politics, and that rise has coincided with the decline in the number of middle-class black business owners.

Instead, the more a society concentrates power, the more that institutional power reflects the legacy power-holders in it.[13] The combination of systemic racism, financial concentration, and corporate monopolization has led to power being wielded predominantly by white people, and this is justified by a corporate system designed to appear neutral and to foster indifference to social consequences.

Even where black and brown business owners are thriving on paper, their economic—and political—power is vastly diminished. In chapter 1, I explained how chickenized industries work: a single, centralized hub maintains a high degree of control over small-business owners, who bear the risk of failure. The modern franchise model works that way, in which a central company, like McDonald's, gives local "business owners" the right to use the McDonald's name, and dictates most aspects of how the business is run, all the while washing its hands of liability.

African Americans, along with Hispanics and Asians, are overrepresented as franchisees, and there are more black and brown owners of franchised businesses than of non-franchised businesses.[14] This franchise model, when it works, provides a path into business for people who would otherwise be cut out. But far too often, the reality of the franchisor/franchisee contract creates a structurally abusive relationship, where the franchisee is liable for lawsuits and responsible for problems, yet lacks the freedom to hire people at a decent salary. The franchisor has a high degree of visibility into the businesses and margins, and makes sure that any extra margin goes into fees, which go to executives and investors. When they enter into a franchise agreement, they often give the franchisee a 500- to 1,000-page document to sign, and the franchisor uses its huge power advantage to maximize its flexibility and minimize its liability if something goes wrong.

These business owners, unlike Warren Buffett and Mark Zuckerberg, do not have extra cash that then gets plowed into politics; they barely have enough margin to survive on. And to add insult to injury, when protesters object to the low wages paid at fast-food restaurants and other franchise arrangements, the franchisor points the finger at the franchisee—often a person of color—and says they are to blame. Big corporations are well aware of the potency of the connection between race and monopoly and routinely try to build connections with leaders in communities of color to neutralize criticism.[15] Walmart, for instance, contributed millions to national civil rights groups, including the NAACP, after which the NAACP supported Walmart in its bid to enter New York City.[16]

WHY IS AT&T SUPPRESSING THE VOTE?

The loss of black business power is not happening in an economic vacuum, but coincides with white owners of big business and *their* financial owners taking more political power. This is how it works: the financial gains of monopoly power are used to fund political efforts that use the media to divide low-income black and white voters to gain political power, and then deploy that power to gain tax benefits and further coalesce their own power.

Take the suppression of voting rights, which we tend to see through the lens of partisanship or racism. Here's how the standard story goes: in the 1990s, a Democratic North

Carolina legislature passed laws making it substantially easier to vote—allowing same-day registration, early voting, and pre-registration for 16- and 17-year-olds. It was a major success story in a state with a long history of voter suppression. Voter turnout rose quickly, with the biggest increase in African American turnout. Then a Republican wave took over the legislature, and in 2013, after 20 years of Democratic governors, Republican governor Pat McCrory took office.

The new legislative-gubernatorial combination set about immediately changing the rules of the game. On August 12, 2013, McCrory signed a law that added some of the most extensive hurdles to voting in the country. It shortened the early voting period from 17 days to 10 days. It ended pre-registration for 16- and 17-year-olds who would be 18 by Election Day. It eliminated same-day voter registration. It required all voters to present government-issued identification at the polls. It loosened the rules by which poll watchers could challenge a voter's eligibility. It classified college IDs as inadequate proof of eligibility for voting.

When civil rights groups sued to block the law, the evidence that emerged in trial showed just how carefully this law had been designed to suppress the black and Hispanic vote. While writing the law, one Republican staffer asked for "a breakdown of the 2008 voter turnout, by race (white and black) and type of vote (early and Election Day)." Another lawmaker asked for data showing the Hispanic vote. A key adviser to the Republican House Speaker asked for "a breakdown, by race," of "registered voters in your database that do not have a driver's license number."[17]

Those passing the bill were certainly very happy to use dog-whistle racial politics to hold on to their newfound power in the legislature. The Republicans, realizing that demographics were against them, had been willing to do everything they could against fair and open voting in order to protect Republican power. In this story, the 2013 law was a direct result of Republicans and racist leaders in North Carolina trying to hold on to power by leveraging racial fear. North Carolina county precinct GOP chair Don Yelton famously told *The Daily Show* in 2013 that if the state's new voter ID restriction "hurts a bunch of lazy blacks who just want the government to give them everything, so be it."[18] He had to resign for saying that.

A federal court struck down the law with an extensive decision, calling it "the most restrictive voting law North Carolina has seen since the era of Jim Crow," and concluding that it had been designed to suppress the African American vote with "almost surgical precision."[19]

Everything in this story I just told is true, but it is missing the most important player: ALEC (the American Legislative Exchange Council), which has become a way for big corporations to get their legislation passed by Republican lawmakers. Don Yelton was not the leader. He didn't write the voter ID law: ALEC, paid by companies like AT&T, did the writing. It would never have been introduced, or passed, without big money and the support of big corporate actors, including some of the most neutral-seeming companies in the country. As Ari Berman reported in his book on the history of voting rights and new voter suppression efforts, *Give Us the Ballot*, the voter suppression law "didn't come from nowhere."[20]

ALEC makes it easy for lawmakers by writing legislation that is essentially ready to go. It holds conferences on its preferred policies and gives awards to local elected officials who push through its agenda.[21] It provides lawmakers with free family vacations to ALEC events.

ALEC began actively pushing model voter ID legislation in 2009. The model voter ID law was initially called the "Taxpayer and Citizen Protection Act." This model swept the country. As the Brennan Center for Justice reported, the ALEC laws "fall most heavily on young, minority and low-income voters, as well as on voters with disabilities."[22] And unsurprisingly, the best way to get these laws passed is to help elect big business–friendly legislators, and the best way to do that is to engage in dog-whistle politics.

In 2009 through 2013, when the model voter identification laws were being written, ALEC was supported by monopolies across several sectors: Exxon, Pfizer, Microsoft, Google, Amazon, Coca-Cola, GlaxoSmithKline, and Walmart. If you had a wireless phone in 2010, part of your phone bill was probably going to fund voter suppression. ALEC was funded by all three of the big wireless providers: AT&T, Verizon, and T-Mobile, which collectively dominate 85% of the market for mobile phones. What was AT&T doing funding ALEC, and why did it share a funding recipient with its purported competitors? While they technically compete, they share many interests, including, for instance, blocking municipalities from offering broadband. They cared a lot about North Carolina, because ALEC was pushing a bill to make it illegal for towns or cities to create their own broadband networks.

In 2011 in New Orleans, Thom Tillis, the Speaker of the North Carolina House, was honored as 1 of 11 "legislators of the year" by ALEC. As Rob Schofield of a local North Carolina watchdog group quipped at the time, the award might best be described as "Outstanding Performance in the Use of a Copier."[23] ALEC pumped out over 800 "model" bills, and the North Carolina leader used many of them, either word for word or very close in intent and structure.

From the time the Republicans took over, Tillis pushed and carried the voter suppression bill. Now, backed by a major Koch-funded network, he is the junior U.S. senator from

North Carolina. ALEC cultivated him from his early days in power—Tillis was a target because of his extraordinary platform as the lawmaker with the most leverage in North Carolina. ALEC, in other words, was the institutional dealmaker who facilitated the bargain between Tillis, Yelton, and some of the wealthiest corporations in the world.

What should we make of Pfizer funding voter suppression? There's no reason to think that Amazon, or Microsoft, or Walmart, or any one of the many pharmaceutical companies who funded ALEC was particularly interested in the voter suppression part of ALEC's work at the time. As Mary Bottari, former press secretary to Russ Feingold and award-winning investigator, explains it, corporations tend to support ALEC to provide *particular* services—they are interested in blocking municipal broadband, or pushing aspects of tax policy or specific kinds of deregulation, or pushing tort reform. They tend to fund particular pockets of ALEC's work, but their involvement helps legitimate the entity as representing a broad cross-section of corporate America.[24] Does it matter whether Thomas Rutledge, the head of Charter Communications—which has never severed ties with ALEC—is ideologically racist? Does it matter what he held in his heart, given the collateral damage? At best, he is extremely indifferent to the serious harms caused by inflaming racial hatred, preferring to put Charter's bottom line above those human costs.

One of the state's legal defenses at the trial of the North Carolina law was that it wasn't racist, it was just politics: fewer African American voters meant fewer Democratic voters. The Republicans who pushed it were just protecting incumbency (under current Supreme Court jurisprudence, laws designed to protect political power are expected and fully allowed). The Reverend William J. Barber II, prominent minister, political activist, and leader of the Poor People's campaign, had this to say about that defense: "You can't expect racists to come right out and sound like racists. They've substituted the word 'racial' with the word 'political.'"[25] Likewise, you can't expect the head of Google to come out and say he is racist. But if he is supporting laws that predictably lead to voter suppression, then he has just substituted the word "racial" with the words "corporate bottom line." As long as big businesses have excess profits to fund organizations whose goals align with the enhancement of corporate power, monopolies will have incentives to suppress the vote, to gerrymander, and to crowd out dissenting voices.

Bucknell University economist Marcellus Andrews argues that we should understand that corporate monopolies aren't just indifferent, but making a bargain with a segment of white society. He wrote, "Monopoly is a form of politics, a concentration of private power whose leaders then use all sorts of mechanisms to achieve their ends, including cutting a deal with a segment of society—whites—to abuse others in exchange for certain privileges and guarantees in pursuing business interests."[26] The result is terrible for people of color, and it doesn't work well for poor and working-class white people either; the three winners are big corporations, political entrepreneurs, and the people who work for organizations like ALEC. According to Andrews, Google, ALEC, Walmart, midlevel operational entrepreneurs, fear, and white supremacy in "democratic" (elected) form "all enmesh to establish a stable and enduring complex by virtue of mutually supporting strategies that land heavily on the disfavored."[27] Voter suppression is a tool for keeping out black voters, but also for elevating racial narratives. Racial stories make the unearned seem earned—the privilege of membership in a superior collective is a perceived virtue. Non-racial stories demand much more of people as citizens—civic virtue must be earned. Racist stories, therefore, are incredibly useful in creating alliances between powerful and weak interests against racial minorities.

Andrews argues that we ignore monopoly problems at our peril:

> The plutocrats use racial identity as a wedge and then grant whites the right to use state power—on loan from the plutocrats—to pursue their dreams of racial power vis-à-vis nonwhite citizens, but only on the condition that white working- and middle-class people grant big business free rein in managerial affairs.

To be fair, the relationship between race and anti-monopolism is not always straightforward, and anti-monopolism, too, can be used as a tool of exclusion. Senator John Sherman (the author of the Sherman Act) as well as Woodrow Wilson (the most anti-monopolist of our presidents except Franklin Roosevelt) were both rabid segregationists, and their anti-monopolism was designed to protect a certain class of white small-business owners against both big business and non-whites. As historian Gerald Berk wrote recently, "anti-monopoly's . . . ideology can look down as readily as up to identify adversaries. When it does, immigrants, African Americans, and women are coded as nonproducers alongside bankers and monopolists, equally worthy of vilification, regulation, and exclusion."[28]

The moral of the story is not that anti-monopoly is a panacea for deeply embedded racism, or that anti-monopolists have always been right. It is that race and corporate power are totally intertwined, and while fighting the local fights against voter suppression and similar issues is vital, we cannot ignore the corporate structures behind them. We play into the monopolists' game if we attack local racist politicians but fail to strike at the root of their funders' power.

BIG WHITE TECH

The cutting edge of monopoly racism is, as with so much else, in big tech companies, where a toxic combination of power and opaque bias is repackaged and defended as neutral algorithms. Machine learning tends to exaggerate existing inequalities. When doing web searches, poor people are shown worse jobs and apartments, while elites with purchasing power get access to real estate deals and better employment opportunities. Machine learning is also remarkably prone to error, but since the error lies in an algorithm, not a person, there is no person to shame for failure when people of color are persistently discriminated against.

We miss the big picture if we think of machine learning algorithms in the abstract, and not as devices used to make money and coalesce power by particular dominant companies. Google, Facebook, Amazon, and Apple pose unique race bias dangers in two ways. First, they are among the few companies with the resources to extract and exploit publicly available datasets in combination with their own data, creating data monopolies. Second, their choices about what data they use to serve what content have uniquely powerful impacts on everybody in society. When Google bakes bias into results, everyone is impacted. Finally, they don't just passively allow bias, they make money off it.

In her engrossing book *Algorithms of Oppression*, UCLA professor Safiya Noble shows how Google's business model is designed to prioritize the needs of advertisers for wealthy, white potential purchasers.[29] For instance, when you searched for the word "girl" in America in 2018, 46 of the first 50 images were white girls.[30] After publication of Noble's book, Google changed these particular search results. When researchers pointed out racist autocompletes for "black women are," Google simply removed the autocompletes altogether. It became a game of algorithmic whack-a-mole, with Google responding to individual incidents, but not revealing how they came to be: the underlying business model, which thrives on exaggerating existing social stereotypes, remains unchanged.

Noble persuasively argues that human-created algorithms necessarily reflect the biases of the humans who create them, reproducing discrimination in a computer code while deflecting responsibility for this discrimination by blaming the code for its operations. The leadership of big tech companies is notorious for the absence of African Americans—barely 1% of Google's full-time workforce are black women. And employees at Facebook have spoken up about a workplace in which racism, discrimination, and bias are built into the company culture. One employee posted a blog about the "small actions that mount up over time and build into a culture where we are only meant to be seen as quotas."[31]

Yet the problems with algorithms can't be resolved without addressing the underlying power dynamic. Noble argues that there are deep democratic and race problems with "one monopolistic platform controlling the information landscape."[32] Google's algorithms are secret, and because they serve up different information at different times to the same people—and to different people—it is extremely difficult to investigate their bias.

Google is not alone: a damning ProPublica report showed how Facebook allowed advertisers to select audiences based on "ethnic affinities." Landlords and employers could use Facebook tools to advertise by zip code (a traditional method of redlining), and include or exclude categories such as "non-American-born," "non-Christian," or "interested in Hispanic culture." In response to a lawsuit by the National Fair Housing Alliance and charges by the Department of Housing and Urban Development, Facebook no longer allows housing advertisers to target by zip code and has removed ethnic affinity groups, gender, and age as options for targeted Facebook ads.

It's a step, but it doesn't solve the problem of paid bias. The Facebook "Lookalike Audience" tool allows advertisers to target a community that resembles their current community, matching country of origin, other demographics, and common interests. If the existing community of tenants is white, the Lookalike Audience will doubtless be overwhelmingly white; the landlord never has to use proxies, but the look-alike nature of the beast will work to exaggerate existing segregation. In settling a lawsuit this summer, Facebook agreed that the Lookalike Audience tool cannot be used for credit, housing, or employment ads.[33]

However, Lookalike can be used for checking and savings accounts, car sales, event announcements, and every other kind of consumer product sold. "When you take systems like that and apply them to a society that is built on discrimination, the data inputs from the society feeding into the algorithm have the taint of historical biases built into them," said David Brody, counsel at the Lawyers' Committee for Civil Rights Under Law. "The advertising and technology companies are stumbling through the dark and afraid to turn on the lights to see how many cockroaches there are."[34]

The nature of Facebook's tools makes it hard to avoid discriminatory advertising, because the business model of Facebook *is* discriminatory advertising.[35] Even where the advertiser selects no proxies for race, age, or gender, Facebook is serving ads differently to different races, ages, and genders, because it is designed to share ads with people most likely to click on them, and if (when) there is a racial, age, or gender skew to those categories, ad segregation results.[36]

Because of the extreme risks that systematic informational bias poses to society, University of Maryland Law School professor Frank Pasquale proposed—a decade ago—that the FTC use its power to monitor and investigate claims of bias[37]—a traditional role of a competition authority, but one that has not (yet) been taken up. Instead, we have to take big tech's word for it that they don't want bias. I proposed in chapters 2 and 3 that we get rid of targeted ads for big platforms because of the dangers they pose to journalism and democracy. These examples provide a third reason.

When the relationship between white power and monopoly power is spoken out loud, the political results can be electrifying. Today, we are in the midst of a battle for a free internet—the battle for network neutrality, the principle that internet service providers (ISPs) must treat all internet communications equally, and not discriminate or charge differently based on the user, the content, the website, or the method of communication. As the coiner of the term, Columbia University law professor Tim Wu, explained, it represents a classic anti-monopoly principle: no big company should be able to abuse a chokepoint role. The ISPs should remain neutral to allow the full flourishing of diverse ideas, debate, and discussion, and not replace an open internet with a pay-to-play internet.

The network neutrality debate changed when grassroots civil rights groups got involved in the early 2010s, transforming it from an academic fight to one about the power of marginalized communities to be heard in a modern political ecosystem. One activist argued that, without net neutrality, Comcast, AT&T, and Verizon would be given too much power to censor speech and crush movements for racial justice. Steven Renderos, an organizing director with the Center for Media Justice, pointed out that "in a media environment where communities of color own less than 3 percent of TV stations, the internet allows us to bypass racial discrimination to speak for ourselves."[38] The online pressure group Color of Change, which led the charge, argued that "*Net neutrality* is essential to protecting our free and open Internet, which has been crucial to today's *fights* for civil rights and equality."[39]

Their message clearly resonated: working with other groups, they helped organize one of the largest online protests in recent history, on July 12, 2017. Yet the Trump administration repealed the 2015 network neutrality ruling of the Federal Communications Commission (FCC), and the fight is ongoing. A long-term victory for network neutrality can happen either with a new administration and new FCC, or with a new Congress. Moving forward, all progressive voters who care about racial equity must insist that their candidates support net neutrality.

More importantly, we need to understand how race and monopoly are both forms of illegitimate power, and each amplifies the other. The Massachusetts abolitionist Charles Sumner understood that when in 1866 he proposed legislation that would ban all systems of racial discrimination, class, and monopoly:

> There shall be no Oligarchy, Aristocracy, Caste, or Monopoly invested with peculiar privileges and powers, and there shall be no denial of rights, civil or political, on account of color or race anywhere within the limits of the United States or the jurisdiction thereof; but all persons therein shall be equal before the law.[40]

It didn't pass, but that's the kind of aspiration we need more of today.

7

The Wage Mystery

The wealth inequality in our country is obscene. In response, many people are drawn to a handful of familiar policies, including raising the minimum wage and taxing the wealthy and redistributing the money through public services. I support these policies, but they do not go far enough in changing the power dynamic. Instead of merely focusing on after-the-fact redistribution of *wealth*, we should put a lot more progressive energy into before-the-fact redistribution of *power*.

In the 1950s, CEOs made 20 times the salary of the average worker. Now, S&P 500 CEOs are paid *361 times* the average salary of their employees.[1] From 1940 to 1980, the value produced by workers, adjusted for inflation, increased by 98%, and the average pay rose nearly 95%. And then, despite gains in productivity, people's wages simply stopped growing. Wage growth slowed in the 1980s as a percentage of overall income and then took a nosedive in the early 2000s. Between 1980 and 2019, productivity rose over 75%, but average pay rose only 5%. Executive pay shot up nearly 1,000%, while the share of income going to workers fell precipitously. Wages have stayed frozen—marching evenly with inflation, but not outpacing it—even as unemployment levels have dropped dramatically.

The divergence has been called the "wage puzzle" and a "mystery" that "no one" understands.[2] Unemployment is at the lowest level in decades, and you would expect that wages would be quickly rising. Mainline economists have long been promising strong wages and better benefits with a tightening labor market. Moreover, the labor force is more educated than it used to be, which traditional theory says should mean increasing pay.

So why aren't wages rising? The economic columnist for the *Washington Post*, Robert Samuelson, acknowledged: "By standard economic theory, the strong demand for labor should be pushing up wages. But that isn't happening."[3] He trotted out a series of possible explanations, none of which he found satisfying.[4] It can't, for instance, be explained by the surplus value being passed along to the consumer through lower prices. A paper published last year showed that companies were charging substantially more over their marginal costs than in 1980.[5] In other words, consumers are paying more *and* workers are getting paid less—even though there is a labor shortage.

Paul Krugman described the wage puzzle this way: "The unemployment rate is now very low by historical standards. In fact, it's back down to 2000 levels; those were the days when employment was so full that people used to joke about the 'mirror test' for employment: if your breath would fog a mirror, that is, if you were alive, you could get hired. (Sorry, zombies.) Yet wage growth remains restrained, well below pre-crisis levels."[6]

In 2018, on the IMF blog, a senior economist for the IMF shared a "wage puzzle" chart, arguing that since the rate of productivity growth was declining, workers were naturally making less. "Wages in the US have grown slowly in recent years, even as the unemployment rate has fallen to the lowest levels in decades. This is puzzling. Economic theory and common sense suggest that companies competing for a shrinking pool of available workers would have to raise wages as the labor market tightens."[7] The economist explained the stagnant wage growth with a chart showing "slower growth in labor productivity, the amount of goods or services produced in an hour of work—and a decline in the share of income that goes to workers."[8] These trends, he argued, have held wages down. This answer just relocates the question, and doesn't really answer it—yes, a smaller share of income goes to workers, but why?

Failure to predict and understand this is a major black eye for most mainline economists, who also failed to predict the crash of 2008. In fact, when economists noticed the decline in the "labor percent"—the amount of money going to workers—they assumed that less money and benefits to workers meant more money to capital investments. Companies must be buying land, machinery, manufacturing plants, right? This was true from 1940 to 1980, when the 100 largest firms put, on average, 13% of their revenue into capital investment. But as economist Simcha Barkai showed in a recent blockbuster paper, both labor and capital investors are losing. Instead, the value created by workers has been going into big companies buying their own stock to inflate the price. In the 1970s, stock buybacks didn't exist (they were illegal until 1982).[9] By 2005, the 100 largest firms were spending more money on stock buybacks than on capital investments. In other words, economists thought that companies would compete to provide better products, but they are simply paying their shareholders more.

Now we understand the root cause of the puzzle: monopolization. In the last two years, there has been an explosion of literature showing how market power explains the wage puzzle.[10] In the economics literature it is called "monopsony."[11] When companies have too much power, they suppress wages, reduce benefits, and defy supply-and-demand models, because they are more like lords than participants in an open, competitive economy.[12] Economist Barkai estimates that excess market power has caused corporations to spend $14,000 less a year per worker on compensation, training, benefits, and so forth.[13] That's a lot of lost income. In a major paper published in 2018, four economists found that in most areas, people don't have many choices for a job within their industry due to consolidation, and that the local concentration has a significant impact on the posted wages for job openings.[14] These findings, in turn, have sparked more research, all confirming the monopsony thesis. As Marshall Steinbaum, one of the economists on the 2018 study, explained to me, "New research on employer power in labor markets shows that it is systemic, in contrast with economists' historical assumption that labor markets are competitive and workers are, in general, paid what they are worth. Instead, we now know that employers dictate pay and benefits, decide for themselves what sort of workplace to provide, and can pick and choose who works there. Permitting consolidation and vertical integration and control in supply chains has made labor markets less competitive and worsened outcomes for workers, which is in direct contradiction to the (untested) economic assumptions that motivated the Chicago School's antitrust takeover in the first place." Paul Krugman has recently adopted this argument as well, crediting growing evidence that too many employers in concentrated industries don't experience pressure to raise wages.[15] Monopoly turns out to be a major driver of inequality.

With the massive collapse of an economy into sectors that are each dominated by corporate monopolies, workers may be in great demand, but they are not in a good position to bargain for a fair portion of the value they create. Teresa Ghilarducci, an economist at The New School, explains that if we see wages as representing a power struggle between capital and labor, the wage decline *does make* sense. In simple terms, "Capital won. Labor lost."[16] Labor unions lost power, trade policy favored big companies, and, in a critical development that the economists who have governed the world of economic ideas for the last 40 years do not take seriously, big companies became so large and powerful that they no longer needed to participate in markets, but instead began to govern them.

Here's how it works. In an open, competitive economy, companies do everything they can to find the best workers and retain them, because if they lose them, the quality of their product or service will go down. But when a few companies dominate a market, they can set—and suppress—wages without having to check in with workers. Big companies that dominate labor markets don't have to send each other notes on how low they plan to keep wages—they just have to understand that raising wages hurts both them and their competitors, and they have no need to do it.

Imagine a town with a KFC, Pizza Hut, Taco Bell, McDonald's, Popeyes, Subway, Burger King, Walmart, and Starbucks. Five companies own all these brands, and all of them pay poverty wages. The tiny number of owners makes it easy to stay in line with each other's poor treatment.[17] Can you imagine a 24-year-old line cook going to her manager at Taco Bell—who himself has no authority—and saying that she wants to be paid $11 instead of $10 an hour? Perhaps. But you can also imagine the manager's dismissive answer. And she can't threaten to leave, as no other place pays any better. Traditional economists would say that wages should rise as companies compete, but for that to happen, the companies would have to have an incentive to compete for wages, which they do not—with a tiny club, they can collude without colluding. Sometimes, they pull off the façade and make clear what is going on: Burger King, Carl's Jr., Pizza Hut, and McDonald's had agreements that prohibited franchisees from hiring workers away from one another.[18]

Look at what has happened to employees of big-box stores. In the 1980s and 1990s, the same story played out across America. Walmart would enter a town and wipe out the myriad competing local grocers, initially offering lower prices on a few staples. After a few years, the workers in town would be left with one choice: work at Walmart or not at all. Even now, with unemployment at 4%, Walmart, Kmart, and Target don't really use higher wages to compete for workers. They tend to own particular territories, and they have no interest in a wage war or a benefits war. They can trust that, unlike independent small-business owners, monopolies are not going to poach one another's workers by providing decent wages and benefits. As a result, Walmart workers, underpaid and poorly treated, are among the largest recipients of food stamp subsidies.[19]

We got here because of too much deference to professional economists, who tend to favor abstraction, models, and a bizarre faith in private systems of power being superior to public systems of power.[20] According to the theory taught in most economics courses, the threat of a single company newly entering a market should keep wages high. For example, if Walmart thinks Target *might* enter, it acts preemptively. By doing this, Walmart hopes to avoid a wage war and prevent Target from entering its market. Otherwise, Target would see that Walmart workers were getting underpaid, and it would provide better wages to steal employees. However, it doesn't work out that way, because power doesn't work like that, and there are all kinds of quiet ways to avoid a price war in a concentrated market.

Research from drug pricing shows that prices can stay artificially high—above what real competition would predict—even when there are three competitors. To get to a reasonable, non-monopolistic price, you need several competitors that aren't aligned in their interests. When a market is controlled by a small number of companies, strategic non-competition happens all the time; Walmart and Target don't have to talk to each other to realize that both benefit if they suppress wages. When they aren't competing against 40 other local retail outlets, they can wink-and-nod collude without speaking.

While you might think that skilled industries would be immune, the industries in which higher skills are required tend to be even more concentrated. Take nursing. Hospitals have been on a merger spree for two decades, and regional hospital monopolies are now the norm; CEO wages are rising, while nurses' ability to negotiate is regionally constrained. As a result, nursing wages have stopped growing, and nurses are losing the ability to bargain for fair wages. Recent research shows that pharmacists and nurses working in hospitals in heavily concentrated markets have lower wages than their counterparts in non-concentrated markets.[21]

None of this happens in a vacuum. Instead, powerlessness reinforces itself much as power reinforces itself. Poverty—and attendant debt—and monopoly are mutually reinforcing. Low wages and unstable work contribute heavily to family debt, and credit struggles in turn work to further erode the power of workers to demand decent treatment. When people have no personal savings, their ability to capitalize on a work-shortage advantage is severely weakened.

According to one study, 50% of 24-year-olds have $0 in savings.[22] Those 24-year-olds cannot afford to take off a week. That week may be worth $270 in pay. Imagine that they could make even a whole dollar more an hour by switching from their current job to Burger King, but it would take a week to do the switch. It would take nearly two months for the lost week to be made up, and if the salary change was $0.25 an hour, something more likely, then it would take eight months for that lost week to be made up. Given the risk that the week off could become two weeks, the 24-year-old will not leave one job for another. If he had savings of even $300, the calculus would change, but most employers have workers with radical dependency, no savings, and access to only very expensive credit.[23]

Along with debt, surveillance decreases power. We often talk about surveillance capitalism through the lens of companies collecting information about consumers, but the other part of modern surveillance capitalism is the central role surveillance plays in spying on workers. Uber—placing itself between drivers and riders—monitors driving speed, watches acceleration patterns, and keeps close tabs on customer ratings. Freelancer.com uses software that keeps track of the keystrokes of users and takes random screenshots; the software is easy to justify but horrifying to contemplate. Lonely, isolated workers have to work under the constant scrutiny of a ruthless piece of software.[24]

Consolidation and surveillance come together, as I showed in chapter 5. Both make political retaliation more likely. Both weaken the power of workers and strengthen the capacity of employers to threaten job loss. They strip political autonomy from people, and transform citizens into things from which value can be extracted.[25]

In chapter 1 I described how middle-class America is getting chickenized. It is even worse for wage laborers. For example, one McDonald's worker has alleged that when she slipped on a greasy floor and caught her arm on a hot grill, her manager told her to put mustard on the burned arm and not seek treatment. She said almost her entire forearm was burned, and the nerves in her wrist were damaged.[26] Every month, on average, someone working at a Tyson Foods processing plant amputates a finger or limb.[27] Tyson employees' breaks are so short that, according to a 2016 Oxfam report, the poultry processing workers "urinate and defecate while standing on the line; they wear diapers to work; they restrict intake of liquids and fluids to dangerous degrees."[28]

If power makes people selfish and rude (as I argued in the introduction), powerlessness also changes us, and transforms our experience of the world. A recent social science experiment showed that boxes actually feel heavier if you feel powerless.[29] When workers lack meaningful choices among companies, their bargaining power changes in economic terms, but their entire human relationship to the world they live in changes as well. Workers come to see themselves not as free men and women choosing to sell their skills, but as men and women being humiliated. Being out of power is an economic fact and a political one; it infects the whole person and transforms her relationship to the world, her role in the democracy, her role in the community. In other words, it takes away people's freedom and humanity.

All of this means that although workers may be in high demand on paper, in practice they are fearful and insecure, and companies are not competing to offer them security. People are increasingly working temporary or contract jobs, without any promise of continuity, let alone good benefits. Somewhere between one-third and one-half of the American workforce is contingent, as companies are quickly replacing employees with temporary workers and independent contractors. Google has more temporary and contract workers (121,000) than full-time employees.[30] Most companies intend to increase the percentage of their workforce that is contingent.[31]

WHAT ABOUT THE UNIONS?

Monopolization and corporate concentration are in many ways the unionization of capital, and as with unions, they increase companies' power over those with whom they are negotiating—namely, you and me. But let's talk about unions of workers, which are a very important part of how we as citizens can come together to establish our rights. The main route to better wages and working conditions is traditionally a union. The dream of wage negotiation is no fantasy when you have a union; workers can come together and demand, en masse, better wages and benefits. But union power diminishes with the consolidation of corporate power. When a union can't use choice between companies as leverage, companies can shut out union workers from all negotiation.

For this reason, monopolies have baked anti-unionism into their DNA. Walmart has a dedicated hotline for managers to call whenever they suspect union organizing. These managers have special "Delta teams" to stop labor organizing. Lockheed Martin contracted the creation of a web tool to spy on workers, including their social media accounts, analyzing behavior that might lead to "organized movements."[32] Google—which often gets cast as progressive—successfully fought to overturn a 2014 National Labor Relations Board (NLRB) decision that held that companies could not punish employees for using their workplace email to circulate petitions, organize walkouts, or attempt to form a union. In 2018, a leaked 45-minute video showed how Amazon was training managers to bust unions and stop organizing.[33] In other words, these big companies know that power structure matters, and actively work to maintain the status quo.

One might expect that labor unions would vocally fight back, that they'd be on the front lines of merger protests, representing the wage laborer. Mergers are bad for workers, bad for wages, and bad for union membership. Unions have a strong hand to play against mergers: during a merger, they get deep access to the companies' financial status; they have a unique platform from which to protest; and if workers speak out, they can gum up the works substantially.[34] But even a quick glance at recent history tells you that labor unions have made clear that they do not see market consolidation as their fight. Let us visit one recent labor resistance to a merger.

It was late February 2018, and employees from regional hospitals in California took to the streets to protest the merger of Dignity Health and Colorado-based Catholic Health Initiatives. They marched around a city block for three hours, chanting down the merger. Jermene Ebanks, an employee at Mercy Hospital Southwest, explained to the press that it's common for mega-corporations to "squeeze employees and harm patients" in a merger.[35] The protest by the fifty-odd hospital employees lasted a total of just two days.[36]

One might think, given Ebanks' unassailable assertion, that the protests would have pressed on with urgency, but a week later the union canceled future planned actions. The union got what it had really wanted—terms in a new five-year contract. The protests were just a tactic in ongoing negotiations. In February 2019, the merger was finalized, creating a new entity, CommonSpirit Health, an octopus Catholic regime that spans 142 hospitals and employs 150,000 people.[37] Five years from now, CommonSpirit Health will have enormous negotiating power to strip benefits, but for now, the union will live another day. (CommonSpirit, by the way, is also part of a growing consolidation of Catholic hospitals, leaving patients seeking treatment disfavored by the church stuck.)[38]

The protest is notable nonetheless, just because it happened at all. The public objection to Dignity joining Catholic Health Initiatives was one of the bigger in-person, in-the-street expressions of labor opposition to a merger in the last few years. I have scoured newspapers for other examples, and they are hard to find.

Consider what is happening *today* in downtown New York City, the most union of union towns. Charter Communications workers have been on strike for over 1,000 days as of December 2019. The strike began after the merger between Charter's Spectrum and Time Warner. That merger made Charter the second-biggest cable operator in the United States subscriber-wise and the third-largest provider of paid TV.[39] It has not worked well for customers. Post-merger cable service has been so bad that the state has threatened to unwind the merger, and the company agreed to pay $174.2 million to settle a case against it for defrauding internet subscribers.[40] During the merger, the companies agreed to expand broadband service to at least 145,000 unserved or underserved residential units over four years, with a minimum of 36,250 new units per year. An audit found that Charter falsely claimed 14,000 addresses already served by the company as "new" deployments.[41]

It has been even worse for workers. Charter has refused to negotiate and has been dictating terms. Before I called a former Spectrum technician to talk, I had to give him my number via email, because he got so many calls from bill collectors that he had to carefully screen them.[42] He started working for Spectrum at $9 an hour, and worked his way up to $37 an hour before the strike. Now, he has been out of regular work since the strike began and has been doing delivery for his wife's title insurance company, paying for his own tolls, scraping together money for his kids, who are in sixth and eleventh grade.

Prior to the merger, Spectrum and Time Warner would at least come to the table to negotiate, but now, as Charter Communications, they simply ignore the strike, because they face no competition; their skilled workers have no competitor to go to. To add insult to injury, the strike is subject to a virtual media blackout. When Charter bought Time Warner Cable, it also bought a stable of regional news stations, including the most important news channel for New York City politics. Not surprisingly, the channel has not covered one of the longest strikes in city history.

The International Brotherhood of Electrical Workers (IBEW), which organized the strike, did not make protesting the merger part of their bargaining strategy. Instead, IBEW president Lonnie Stephenson said that the merger would be a "boon to good jobs in the cable and telecommunication industry."[43] They did not storm the statehouse or hold signs outside the Public Service Commission—the state authority that could have blocked the merger on state grounds. A major coalition of groups against the merger, called the Stop Mega Comcast Coalition, included no unions in opposition.

IBEW's lack of interest in stopping that merger reflects how unions have treated the concentration crisis for decades. Unions tend to publicly treat mergers with indifference, or, occasionally, to support them when the union gets something else in exchange. On November 14, 2017, the Communications Workers of America (CWA), one of the most outspoken unions and a supporter of Bernie Sanders' 2016 campaign, came out with a strong statement in favor of the proposed merger between AT&T and Time Warner Entertainment. The statement said that "CWA supports mergers when the partners are fully committed to creating good jobs."[44] AT&T promised that employees from acquired firms would be able to join the union. The AT&T merger was approved. Two years later, AT&T appears to have reneged on its side of the deal. The union expected 22,000 former Time Warner Entertainment workers to be covered by the agreement, but AT&T claims only 82 are covered.[45]

In a similar vein, in September 2016, union leaders from Dow Chemical and DuPont came together for a four-day meeting in Kentucky to talk about the prospect of the Dow-DuPont merger.[46] They talked about collective bargaining and shared problems they faced, the issues of pensions, benefits, insurance, and workplace safety. Represented at the meeting were local steelworkers; the International Union of Operating Engineers; the metal trades; the United Food and Commercial Workers; the National Conference of Firemen & Oilers; the Ampthill Rayon Workers; and union representatives from the United Kingdom, Switzerland, the European Union, Germany, and Argentina. While they raised a few concerns about the merger, none of the unions spoke out against it. At best, they issued small notes of concern. There were no protests in the street.

To be fair, labor unions in America are in a difficult position right now: they are both the most powerful institutional forces for working men and women and much weaker than they used to be. They have a unique leverage point in mergers, but they have typically used it, as the Service Employees International Union did with the hospitals, to gain leverage over contract negotiations, not to try to block mergers altogether.

Some of this is due to short-termism, some of it is because of culture, some of it is about already feeling disempowered. Perhaps labor leaders, like many on the left, have been intimidated by antitrust law and finance.

Effective unions generally use their power to obtain better wages, healthcare, and working conditions for their members than non-union workers garner, proving to their membership that their dues are paying off, rather than agitating for broad gains for the working class. Although this approach may seem like a winning strategy, it can lead to short-term gains but long-term devastation. In his recent book *Beaten Down, Worked Up*, longtime *New York Times* labor reporter Steven Greenhouse showed how some of the most effective union organizing has aimed at deep, long-term structural change. Some unions believe mergers aren't going to serve their members, but think mergers are above their pay grade. They don't want to interfere in the market; they have so deeply internalized the neoliberal story that the market is a fact of nature, not policy, that they treat mergers like weather, for good or ill. Instead of seeing the structural threat that mergers pose to workers, they tend to look at whether a particular merger will lead to job reductions, and unions have typically asked for written assurance that it will not. They've also looked for assurance that terms and conditions of employment won't be negatively changed post-transaction.

And some unions also have a pro-merger preference, because for a long time larger companies were perceived to be easier to organize; mergers in the past have meant a greater unionized workforce. In terms of labor union organizer hours, it doesn't cost much more to organize 800 workers than to organize 200, and therefore, unions have preferred more dense and concentrated industries.

Moreover, for several decades, big firms—though not nearly as big as today's—were seen as essential institutions in mediating worker salaries and ensuring that workers got the value they produced. Workers at large firms tended to have higher wages than those at small firms, as a well-established literature reveals.[47]

To some degree this is still true, but it is more a feature of the culture of legacy firms than size itself; the large-firm pay premium has significantly declined, and in some industries—such as retail—it has reversed, becoming a large-firm pay *penalty*, as a few big, low-paying, bad-benefit firms have taken so much market share.[48] But labor history and tradition ensure that the big-firm pay benefit assumption remains.

Another reason unions are skeptical of antitrust efforts may be a residual effect of workers' long and negative relationship with antitrust authorities. Antitrust has been used as a heavy

cudgel *against* labor for over a hundred years. Antitrust was the
tool used to stop secondary strikes, a key tool in organized labor, as early as 1908, and has never been seen as a workers' tool.

When I spoke to labor leaders involved in different mergers, some were most concerned about the spin-offs that mergers created, because it meant working with new leadership and
establishing new terms. While a union and the new company
may have an agreement that new benefits need to be "substantially equivalent" to the older ones, negotiations will be more
fraught than negotiations with companies whose leadership the
union knows. When I asked one labor leader why his union
didn't think of speaking up, knowing that the merger might
hurt its leverage, his response was a shrug.

Part of the challenge, according to one farmworker activist
I talked to, may be cognitive. If I start talking about breaking
up Tyson, or breaking up Driscoll's, the automatic response is
very practical: "Where would I work?" It is a real concern, and
an understandable one, but one that is rooted in the lack of a
vision for another kind of economy, a reality that is possible.
As the farmworker activist said, you can break any monolith up
into smaller companies and still have jobs.

When we recognize that anti-monopolization and union
power are two sides of the same coin, we can start taking back
power—instead of begging for five-year contracts, one at a
time, gradually trading away power for scraps.

In 2013, workers created one of the first agricultural
unions in the country, in Sakuma, Washington, after a blue-
berry picker was fired for asking for a wage increase. The other
pickers decided to walk off the job in solidarity. They created
Familias Unidas por La Justicia and organized work stoppages
when there were extreme abuses. The grower, Sakuma Brothers
Farms, promised $10 an hour, but only for those who could
pick an unrealistic amount of fruit per hour.[49] The company

was also the landlord for many pickers, and not a good landlord. The company rented workers homes with toilets that
backed up and appliances that didn't work.[50]

Looking for leverage, the farmworkers realized that the big
farm they worked for was part of the Driscoll empire. They
reached out to students, and then to activists around the country, asking people to boycott Driscoll's—and they kept walking off the job and adding members to the union. In 2017, they
won some concessions.[51]

The farmworkers are now setting up a worker-owned berry
farming co-op, which Jose Oliva, who at the time I spoke to
him was the co-director of the Food Chain Workers Alliance,
sees as a vision for the future. But he is under no illusions that
the co-op model can survive without changes in laws and without breaking up companies like Driscoll's. Right now, berry
farmers "need to go through Driscoll's," he says. They can't
compete with Driscoll's, because "they will edge you out of the
market." Driscoll's has close ties to the big chain stores, so you
can't compete by going to those stores; Driscoll's will undercut prices to make sure you can't get in. And if your strategy
is to start in some local place, it will block you there. "If your
strategy is to start with Seattle, they will lower their prices in
that market and make sure you go bankrupt."[52] Unlike a co-op,
Driscoll's can take a hit in profits to ward off competition that
threatens its control.

The extraordinary—if modest—success of Familias was
possible because of a joint strategy that combined worker actions and consumer actions. And incredible bravery and per-
sistence. But as Oliva recognizes, people seeking a more equal
society need a double strategy: strengthening the power of
unions *and* weakening the power of the monopolists. When
every farm in an area is part of Driscoll's supply chain, walkouts
are precarious, because workers can be left with nowhere to go.

If we step back, we see that the real failure of the economists who were stumped by low wages is that they grounded
too much of their thinking in the idea that consumers, not
the public, should govern markets. It is a trick of our current
way of thinking to separate workers from "consumers." Many
economists point to "consumer welfare" as an economic goal.
But thinking in this way has damaged our ability to see the
harm to people. The consumers who are buying cheap toothpaste on Amazon are also the workers at a company controlled
by Amazon, who is in the position to push down wages by
pushing up seller fees on its site. The consumer welfare framework blinds us to all the ways in which our money and power
can be siphoned away by monopolists, and has made us think
that so long as prices are low, the law is doing its job in regulating monopolies.

But we are never *just* consumers.

8

The Money Power

The Money Power is more despotic than Monarchy, more insolent than Aristocracy, more selfish than Bureaucracy. It accumulates by conscious fraud more money than it can use. It denounces as public enemies all who question its methods or throw a light upon its crimes. It can only be overthrown by the awakened conscience of the Nation.

—William Jennings Bryan, 1906[1]

While mainline economists may have missed the boat on monopoly power, as I describe in the last chapter, the men and women who make up the other half of the wage mystery—the inexplicably wealthy—understand it well. The 26 richest people in the world own $1.4 trillion in wealth, the same amount as the total wealth of the 3.8 billion poorest people.[2] Most of them are Americans. Most are men. Most are white. Most of them made their money off monopolies: owning the market, not competing in it, is the best strategy for extracting wealth from workers, purchasers, and business partners alike.[3]

Look, for instance, at Bill Gates, Jeff Bezos, Mark Zuckerberg, Larry Ellison, Michael Bloomberg, Bernard Arnault, and Carlos Slim.[4] Bill Gates' Microsoft money derives directly from the company's extraordinary profits from the 1980s to the

1990s. In a rare exception to decades of non-enforcement, Microsoft was found guilty of monopolization, in violation of the Sherman Antitrust Act. By then, Gates already had his wealth. If Microsoft's scheme had been stopped decades earlier, Bill Gates would not have been able to amass such wealth, build a foundation, and be in the position he is now, controlling much of philanthropy and shaping education policy.

As I explained in chapter 2, Jeff Bezos' Amazon wealth is a direct result of bad anti-monopoly enforcement and bad anti-monopoly theory; his much-vaunted genius at shipping good products is probably better understood as a genius for reading the weaknesses of antitrust law.[5] Mark Zuckerberg earns monopoly profits in digital advertising because he has been able to buy up competitors—like WhatsApp—before they could challenge him. Oracle co-founder Larry Ellison made his money through acquisitions and dominance in high-end software applications, using mergers and contract law to lock in huge fees. Carlos Slim, with a net worth of $60 billion, got rich through a telephone company and cell tower monopoly in Mexico. Bernard Arnault, worth $100 billion, shares a duopoly in the luxury goods market, where his company owns, among other brands, Louis Vuitton, Sephora, Dior, Givenchy, Fendi, Bulgari, Hublot, Rimowa, and Veuve Clicquot. Michael Bloomberg became rich by developing the financial terminal, but he became a grotesquely wealthy billionaire because of weak antitrust enforcement, which allowed him to create a sprawling conglomerate and protect his position as a duopolist in financial information terminals and financial service messaging.[6]

In the populist era, the late nineteenth and early twentieth centuries, the collective power represented by the fat cats was sometimes called "the Money Power." The modern money power includes not only the above-mentioned men, but also men in finance: private equity managers, hedge fund managers, venture capitalists, and the CEOs of big banks.

One way to think about the financial markets is that they are the governing power behind the governing power of the monopolists, a central force that co-rules, relating to the biggest companies like the American federal government relates to the states, and relating to smaller companies as direct overlords. The seven men I listed above are unique even among big CEOs, because of the outsized power they have or had in directing their companies. At many companies, however, investors have the loudest voice, and effectively control those companies from their seats behind the money.

MORE CAPITAL

Wall Street has been a driving force behind the gutting of antitrust laws, because when it is allowed, monopoly power is a means of taking a big chunk of money and multiplying it, without adding any value. Access to seed capital, combined with bad antitrust policy, meant big unearned profits. This is not a new or brilliant insight. In Charles Dickens' *Great Expectations*, Mr. Pumblechook bored young Pip with the same observation, noting there was "an opportunity for a great amalgamation and monopoly of the corn and seed trade on those premises, if enlarged, such as had never occurred before." All that was needed to create a "vast fortune," he argued, was "more capital."[7] The vast and unearned fortunes of Wall Street come via the same principle: sufficient dominance in one market to either charge monopoly prices, lower wages, or force down the costs paid to suppliers.

Berkshire Hathaway chairman and CEO Warren Buffett, one of the richest men in the world, has made his money by investing in already-monopolized industries. He said as much in a call with investors: "If you've got the power to raise prices without losing business to a competitor, you've got a very good business. . . . If you've got a good enough business, if you have a monopoly newspaper or if you have a network television station," Buffett said, "your idiot nephew could run it."[8] He invests in closed markets, monopolies, and oligopolies. He prefers businesses with substantial "moats," or, as a friend of his called it, "unregulated toll bridges."[9] When asked what his ideal business was at an annual meeting, he described it as one with "high pricing power, a monopoly."[10]

In their book *The Myth of Capitalism,* Jonathan Tepper and Denise Hearn describe Buffett's strategy this way: "If you're investing in a business with competition, you're doing it wrong." Digging into Buffett's investments, they chronicle some of the bigger investments he has made:

> Buffett was one of the biggest shareholders in Moody's Corporation, a ratings agency that shares an effective duopoly with Standard & Poor's. (You might remember they rated the toxic subprime junk bonds that blew up the economy as AAA gold.) He and his lieutenants bought shares in DaVita, which has a price-gouging duopoly in the kidney dialysis business. (They have paid hundreds of millions to resolve allegations of illegal kickbacks.) He's owned shares in Visa and MasterCard, which are a duopoly in credit card payments. He also owns Wells Fargo and Bank of America, which dominate banking in many states. (Wells Fargo recently created millions of fraudulent savings and checking accounts in order to charge more fees to depositors.) In 2010, he fully acquired railroad Burlington Northern Santa Fe, which is a local monopoly at this stage. He has owned Republic Services Group, a company that

bought its largest competitor to have a duopoly in waste management. He has owned UPS, which has a duopoly with FedEx in domestic shipping. He bought all four major airline stocks after they merged and turned into an oligopoly. Lately he's been buying utility companies that are local monopolies. He really doesn't like competition.[11]

Tepper and Hearn explain how the midwestern Buffett appears to be the temperamental opposite of Peter Thiel, the Silicon Valley libertarian billionaire, but in fact shares Thiel's anti-competition values. Thiel doesn't believe in competition because he thinks it undermines innovation. He has made his money through investing in Facebook, LinkedIn, and Google, reaping massive profits.

Monopolization as the key to excess profits is something of an open secret. On the TV show *Shark Tank*, the greatest factor leading to investment is whether a company can tell a story of how it will own a market, via shelf space or a patent, not how it will compete in that market. Goldman Sachs recommends to clients that they buy oligopolies. In Goldman's view, oligopolies are attractive because of "lower competitive intensity, greater stickiness, and pricing power with customers due to reduced choice, scale cost benefits including stronger leverage over suppliers, and higher barriers to new entrants all at once."[12] While Goldman's "Buy Oligopolies!" white paper made headlines when it was issued in 2014—perhaps because of its brazenness—it is a strategy that has been baked into Wall Street thinking for 40 years.

In business schools, a key part of the curriculum is based on how to create choke points in markets. In a highly influential book, *Competitive Strategy: Techniques for Analyzing Industries and Competitors*, published in 1980, Harvard Business School professor Michael Porter identified five forces that have shaped every industry.[13] Those five forces have now been taught at business schools for 40 years, and investors have trained themselves by using them to determine the attractiveness of an investment. The five forces are:

1. **Competition in the industry**—The more competitors, the weaker the power of the company, and the less attractive the investment.
2. **Potential of new entrants into the industry**—An industry with strong barriers to entry is good for investments, because it allows for charging higher prices and negotiating better terms with suppliers.
3. **Power of suppliers**—An industry with many suppliers is a more attractive investment, because with few suppliers those suppliers can drive up the costs.
4. **Power of customers**—A company with large, disconnected customers will have an easier time charging higher prices.
5. **Threat of substitute products**—Where there are no close substitutes, the company's power to drive up prices and drive down the cost of inputs is greater.

In other words, business school students learn to invest in the areas where antitrust fails. Antitrust is supposed to—and can again—police excess power, so that there are always enough competitors to ensure competition, barriers to entry are not too high, and suppliers, customers, and producers are all of sufficient number that no one part of the supply chain can sit in a choke point to squeeze out the value.

Porter's five forces have given way to other techniques, and variants. The more modern framework, one often used by venture capitalists in Silicon Valley, is the network effects framework. The simple form of network effects is the idea that the more users you get, the larger your user base becomes, and the more appealing you become for new users. This alone can create market power and start a self-reinforcing competitive advantage—one that is good for investors. One successful venture capital firm argues that network effects have accounted for up to 70% of the financial value created in tech firms since 1994.[14] The methods of gauging network effects are in turn ways of gauging degrees of monopoly control.

Tepper and Hearn uncovered this great advice from the book *Monopoly Rules: How to Find, Capture, and Control the Most Lucrative Markets in Any Business*: earmark part of your profits "for top-flight anti-trust attorneys." All the big tech companies have been doing just that.[15]

THE META-MONOPOLISTS

Increasingly, the investors behind different oligopolies are the same people or institutions creating a behind-the-scenes merger of ownership across an entire industry. This phenomenon is known as "common ownership" when the companies are direct competitors, and "horizontal ownership" more broadly. In the last few years, scholars have produced a flurry of evidence that horizontal ownership leads to anticompetitive behavior. Harvard Law professor Einer Elhauge has called common ownership the "greatest anticompetitive threat of our time."[16] Research shows that the behind-the-scenes owners of multiple companies are driving corporations away from investments in their businesses and toward high returns for investors, which in turn drives inequality.[17] Horizontal shareholding also ends up being a possible reason why executive pay is above where competition suggests it should be: common owners don't necessarily want to punish managers for failing to compete, because they make more money if their portfolio doesn't compete against itself.[18] It also helps to explain why companies delay entry into pharmaceutical markets and why common ownership of banks was correlated with the amount the banks charged in account fees[19]—banks give larger loans and better interest rates to firms with a common owner.

One of the most obvious examples of how this works comes from airlines. The same investors are big players in all the big airline companies (Delta, American Airlines, United, and Southwest).[20] T. Rowe Price, PRIMECAP, Vanguard, BlackRock, State Street Corporation, Fidelity, BNY Mellon Asset Management, JPMorgan Asset Management, and PAR Capital Management all own significant stakes in *all* of these companies. Recent blockbuster research showed that these airline companies hold back from fierce competition among themselves. As a result of common ownership, airlines have "increased prices and reduced seat capacity."[21] Professor of finance Martin Schmalz, one of the economists behind that research, explained in the *Harvard Business Review* that there are ample channels of influence if they don't want different companies in their portfolio to compete. For instance, because of their significant stakes, the managers of BlackRock and Vanguard have a direct line to leadership within every airline.[22] They know direct and indirect ways to discourage United from engaging in a price war with Southwest, a war that would decrease the share prices of both airlines. Although investors deny their ability to control pricing or production decisions,[23] the mechanisms of control needn't be overt. Schmalz writes that it is

> absurd to expect that a common owner of multiple firms in the industry similarly encourages each one of them to steal market share from the other firms in the investor's portfolio. So even if Warren Buffett promises to remain a quiet ("passive") investor, basic economic theory and existing empirical results indicate that his involvement in the

industry is likely to help lessen competition between airlines and further improve their profitability.[24]

At a commercial level, the tragedy is that suppliers and fli-
ers lose out, and the airline investors win. At a democratic level,
this means a new form of regulatory power is being amassed,
as a handful of investors have built mechanisms to become private banking regulators, and to take over from the FAA as the
regulators of the nation's airways.

The money club and money power is everywhere. If you
pull on the Uber string, you find major investment by the Jap-
anese firm SoftBank, which led to Uber's huge valuation. And
here's the rub: SoftBank is also investing in several of Uber's
rivals around the world and has flirted with investing in Lyft.
Observers praise SoftBank for its savvy—if there are mergers
it will have a major stake, and in the absence of mergers, the
funder behind several crowns can shape policy.

ANTI-MONOPOLY RULES AS A
COMPLEMENT TO FINANCIAL
REGULATIONS

A traditional job of antitrust was to make sure that monopolization wasn't possible, either through common ownership, or
through market power. From the New Deal until Reagan, the
way federal antitrust enforcers achieved this goal was by making
sure that industries were competitive. The Department of Justice had a clear set of rules prohibiting concentration in markets.
In practice, this meant that investors couldn't do what they do
today by seeking out pockets of monopolization. I'll use just
one example: predatory pricing. If we actively enforced predatory pricing rules, private equity managers wouldn't be able to
make so much money.

You are likely familiar with one kind of predation: predatory lending. Wall Street bankers essentially steal money from unsophisticated borrowers, ignoring or taking advantage of the borrowers' inability to repay the loans.[25] In the run-up to the financial crisis, bankers targeted minorities, the poor and elderly, less-educated borrowers, and people who needed cash for emergency medical bills—bills that were too high because of monopolized hospitals and drug companies. Predation in home mortgages, payday loans, and car loans has led to ruined credit, debt, homelessness, and despair for borrowers; lenders get high rates of return, can charge high and undeserved fees, and sometimes benefit from foreclosure.

Like predatory lending, predatory pricing takes advantage of power imbalances. A company engaging in predatory pricing offers a product for less than it costs to make it just in order to force its competitor out of business. Antitrust laws against predatory pricing are designed to make sure companies compete on fair grounds: improving quality, providing good service, creating innovations. As antitrust expert Lina Khan explains, "Through the mid-twentieth century, Congress repeatedly enacted legislation targeting predatory pricing. Congress, as well as state legislatures, viewed predatory pricing as a tactic used by highly capitalized firms to bankrupt rivals and destroy competition—in other words, as a tool to concentrate control. Laws prohibiting predatory pricing were part of a larger arrangement of pricing laws that sought to distribute power and opportunity."[26] Companies, lawmakers thought, should not be able to use Wall Street capital to push out competitors just by throwing excess cash at an industry, allowing the companies to sell below cost and making it impossible for anyone producing products at cost to compete.

A classic example would be Company A dropping the price of its products below the cost of production. Its competitor,

Company B, can't produce at that price and still survive, so it goes out of business. Company A, having gained monopoly status, raises prices, and makes back the loss from selling below cost. A slightly more complicated case involves Company A raising the amount it pays for an essential component. Company B can't match the amount paid for the essential component, so it goes out of business. Company A lowers the amount it pays for the component, and makes back its lost value.

In 1967, the Chicago School of Economics launched an all-out war against American predation rules.[27] Ward Bowman, an economist at Yale Law School, argued that the predatory pricing laws were based on a bad premise, because companies would find it nearly impossible to gain monopoly profits big enough to justify predation.[28] At first, the attack was sidelined and ridiculed, but in the 1980s, after President Reagan installed new judges, and economics departments were flooded with Chicago School scholars, the new theory won. The new court decisions did not get rid of predatory pricing laws as a concept, but they made it so difficult to prove a predatory pricing claim that in practice any lawsuit became nearly a dead letter.[29]

In essence, the new rules did two things that made it very hard to prove predation. First, the rules were far more anxious about "false positives" than "false negatives," and so when a case was close, judges would always assume that any price cuts were made to benefit the consumer, and not to push out a competitor.[30] Second, the rules required that whoever challenged a price cut had to prove that his competitor had a clear plan to make back the money lost because of the price cut. Ever since this new, very difficult-to-meet standard was introduced, the number of predatory pricing cases has plummeted.[31]

Predation has become illegal in theory but easy to skirt in practice, because of this new standard, and because of the structure of finance. Investors are willing to allow businesses to lose money for years, or to regularly lose money in particular sectors, so long as they continue to grow. The investors are confident that the growth will lead to recouped profits.

Moreover, when you consider companies like Amazon, Walmart, Facebook, Google, and Bayer, all of which have many different areas of business that can cross-subsidize, opaque accounting, and huge pools of loose Wall Street cash, they don't fit into the abstract predation model built by judges. They can cross-subsidize huge losses from different ventures.[32]

According to a growing number of scholars, Amazon would not exist as it does today without Wall Street seeing, and taking advantage of, the gutting of predatory pricing rules.[33] As Lina Khan has persuasively argued, investors have given Bezos an extraordinarily long leash to shift money around in different ways so that he can serially dominate different markets, leverage domination in one market to gain domination in a related one, then leverage the extra cash made to gain domination in yet other markets.[34]

The same is true at Uber. In chapter 2, I wrote about how once the Uber business model took over the cab industry, the company made money off the drivers in the newly monopolized industry by ensuring that any surplus over the cost of the drive would go to Uber. For the Uber model to work, it needed cash to keep itself alive during the years when it was underpricing competitors. That cash came from Wall Street.

While predatory pricing regulation has been gutted in the United States, the rules still exist in international law, suggesting an alternative way forward. International law allows a country to impose an "anti-dumping duty," a tariff assessed on imported goods that are set at "unfairly lower" rates than the prices for the same products sold in that country.[35] We recognize that dumping hurts the economy, because the foreign seller can drive the domestic sellers out of business, and then, after having taken over the market, raise prices or lower the quality of the product. For instance, if China subsidizes the production of steel so that Chinese steel producers can sell steel in the United States below the cost of production, that would be an example of dumping, and the United States could impose a tariff to allow for fair competition. Without such a tariff, the Chinese government, which is deeply involved in Chinese industry, could decide to take over huge swaths of the American marketplace, creating market dependencies that would shape political dependencies.

PREDATORY SUBSIDIES

Predation isn't merely a pricing and wage practice; it is also a political practice: one of its most powerful tools is local or state subsidies. In 2018, when Amazon was offered $3 billion in state subsidies to locate a new facility in New York City, the owner of the Strand, the legendary Union Square bookstore, wasn't having it. She told the *New York Times*, "The richest man in America, who's a direct competitor, has just been handed $3 billion in subsidies."[36] The basic insight in her complaint is essential: any subsidy that goes to a particular firm necessarily hurts its competitors.

In fact, the economic function of most subsidies is not to improve a local economy, but to make competition harder for small- and medium-sized businesses. One study showed that even when a retailer brings the promised value of a subsidy to a locale, "as much as 90 percent of the apparent direct benefits of tax incentives are offset by losses among the subsidized retailer's local competitors."[37] In other words, when states give subsidies to any individual company, they risk hurting other companies within their borders, a loss that won't typically be offset by whatever number of jobs the subsidy may bring. Job growth that one community treats as new is often simply taken from another community—with a wealth transfer to the company that receives the subsidy, and a transfer from lots of smaller companies and the economy at large to the larger corporation.

Unsurprisingly, concentration and subsidies have a dynamic and mutually reinforcing relationship. States want companies to locate within their borders and create packages to incentivize that. Firms that get the subsidies are likely to be big, because few politicians will crow about a relatively unknown company coming, whereas they can brag about Boeing, Google, and their ilk. Professor Nathan Jensen of the University of Texas–Austin has built an impressive body of work that shows how little people benefit from subsidies, but how much politicians like boasting about them.[38] Those big, supported companies can then use their leverage to push out other firms. Meanwhile, both the politicians and the firms have no incentive for serious follow up, so the development projects' impacts lack transparency.[39] Big, hard-to-track projects go to big companies, and help make them bigger. A recent study of 13,000 firms in Belgium, where there are relatively high rates of state subsidies (for a European country), showed that industries with greater subsidization were more likely to be concentrated. More subsidies, in short, means weaker competition.[40] Incentives tend to benefit the big, established firms, making it harder for their competition and for competition itself. Another study of incentives in 14 states by the nonprofit subsidy tracker Good Jobs First shows that most incentives go to the big firms.[41]

These big firms—like the big banks—often become too big to fail, and therefore are able to use their leverage to squeeze even more in subsidies from the government, reinforcing the monopoly-subsidy cycle. Once a firm is big enough—either in relative size to the economy or total size—it can demand bailouts, and the loan market knows it can demand bailouts, so it becomes cheaper for the firm to borrow, giving it another leg up against competitors. Chrysler was bailed out during the recession; Lockheed is so insulated from market failures by public support that it can easily borrow cheaply. They are also both among the biggest receivers of local subsidies in the country.

The monopoly-predation-subsidy-capital cycle goes like this:

1. The promise of monopoly power attracts excess capital investment;
2. with that investment, the company can engage in predatory pricing to push out competitors and win subsidies;
3. only the biggest companies win individual company subsidies, which they use to push out remaining competitors and reinvest in politics;
4. they then use the investment in politics to block antitrust and influence the tax code;
5. without being subject to antitrust and having to pay taxes, they can promise more monopolistic behavior and attract more capital investment.

Subsidies may seem like a sideshow, because they aren't where the action of market competition exists. But in a way, that's the point: more and more of the action of wealth accumulation is not happening through a victorious quality competition, but through a victorious competition for access to power—a competition that most small-business owners will never be able to enter.

Fears of the financial sector taking over the real economy and the institutions of democratic power go back to the founding of this country.[42] The essential role of antitrust principles is perhaps nowhere more obvious than in banking itself, where the gross political size and reach of the big banks has made significant financial reform impossible. After we bailed out the big banks, they took a big chunk of government money and invested it in lobbying to undo the legislation that was passed after the financial crisis. They successfully gutted a critical part of the Dodd-Frank Act, which limited the government's bailouts of bad bets, and then ramped up new investments in risky products, confident they would be bailed out if they failed again. And while they benefit from concentration in their own realm, they also feed the concentration crisis in other industries. Loans to small- and medium-sized companies have fallen in the last decade, from 30% of all loans in 2007 to 18% today. Moreover, these banks make billions in mergers, so they have an incentive to pitch mergers between companies, the bigger the merger, the better.

But as I've argued in this chapter, it isn't just the big banks that need to be broken up, and reforming the financial sector doesn't stop with reinstating the restraints of the Glass-Steagall Act of 1933, which separated commercial banks from investment banks. One of the most important ways to reform Wall Street isn't through direct Wall Street reforms at all, but by making certain ways of making money illegal. The Buffett/Pumblechook strategy has led to an enormous amount of unearned modern wealth and inequality, which is why making that strategy illegal, as good antitrust policy will do, is so essential.

The power amassed by these investors does not sit caged and tame, to be used only for diamonds and yachts, but always bleeds into politics, until Wall Street investors have such immense economic and political power that their tentacles are everywhere. In the 2017–2018 cycle, lobbyists representing the financial sector spent the equivalent of over $2 million a day.[43]

Anti-monopoly laws used to make it impossible for any company to take over more than a small part of an industry, and in doing so created barriers to temptation. Why engage in predation when the market will always be competitive? When predation is possible, it proves irresistible; when it is impossible, pursuing greatness in other areas becomes far more attractive. If corporate owners cannot imagine making huge profits by taking over an industry, they might start using their imagination to build better products, instead.

9

✦

No, You Don't Have to Quit Facebook

When people hear about some bad corporate practice, their first reaction is often to consider cutting ties to the company. If there is a story about Heinz treating workers badly, for instance, they might think about boycotting Heinz. And so it is not surprising that each time I spend an hour talking about the democratic dangers of Facebook or Amazon or Google or Monsanto, the first reactions I hear are about personal consumer choice. Instead of being about policy (antitrust, data rules, outlawing arbitration), the conversation veers quickly into pride or guilt. One woman worries that she can't leave Facebook without leaving her social life. One man sheepishly says he quit Facebook for a few weeks and crept back when he missed his friends. At the heart of this kind of conversation is a thesis: using a service is an endorsement of its business model. Or, more pointedly: if someone is not strong enough to boycott, she lacks standing to object to the behavior of lawmakers and to petition them for change.

This belief is wrong, bad strategy, and dangerous for democracy. It is based in a confused idea of our obligations as consumers. This belief does not lead to more boycotts, but radically dampens activism: guilt gets in the way of protest, and complicated chains of self-justification take the place of simple chains of democratic demand.

This consumer model is most problematic when it comes to the biggest monopolies. Most people can't boycott them precisely because they are governmental and provide infrastructure services. We don't ask people to boycott libraries in order to change library rules; we don't ask people to boycott highways to ask for them to be safer; we don't demand that you buy only bottled water while protesting water utility governance. A strategic, organized, well-thought-through boycott with political goals can be transformational. And there is nothing wrong with people personally quitting products when they can. However, ethical consumerism has taken too central a role in progressive thinking, and we shouldn't require people to boycott essential communications infrastructure like Facebook and Google in order to demand that they be broken up. The railroads were regulated by anti-monopoly protesters who depended on the railroads, and the same can be true for the next generation of trust-busters. In this chapter I explain how we got confused about boycotts, how they can play a really important role in political change, and why they should not be used as a test of integrity.

FROM SUGAR TO NESTLÉ

In 1791, the first major bill in Parliament to ban slavery in the British Empire failed by a vote of 163 to 88.[1] British abolitionists, in furious response, started a mass effort to get people to stop eating slave-produced sugar, hoping to cripple the slave trade. They convinced about 400,000 people—out of a population of 8 million—to give up slave sugar. Some boycotters went without sugar altogether, while others bought it from what they called "free labor" India because of the absence of

African slaves. Women, responsible for home purchases, were at the heart of the boycott.

Total sugar sales dropped by a third, while sugar sales from India increased 1,000%. Abolitionist ceramists made tea sets with anti-slavery slogans. A pamphlet titled *An Address to the People of Great Britain on the Utility of Refraining from the Use of West India Sugar and Rum*, beseeching people to stop buying sugar, was read by millions. All of us are connected to torture and slavery, the author argued, laying out the math of murder. A family that abstains from sugar for 21 months will stop one enslavement or murder. "So connected are our consumption of the commodity, and the misery resulting from it, that every pound of sugar used, we may be considered as consuming two ounces of human flesh."[2]

The boycott didn't lead to commercial collapse, but it nonetheless lit a fire of awareness, forcing conversations about slavery into one of the most intimate spaces in a society—tea at home—and creating a powerful social community of abolitionists. That in turn helped cement the passage of the 1807 law that banned buying and selling slaves in the British Empire—but not slavery itself—and the 1833 Slave Abolition Act.[3] The boycott was built on the consumer's link to torture, and created a way to break people's complicity in the ownership of human beings. Half a million people who might not march in the streets were doing at least one small thing. They were refusing to buy sugar, and in so doing, cutting at least part of a tie between themselves and violence.

The British sugar boycott is among the most important consumer boycotts in modern history, and it is worth noting that the leading abolitionists in England never took their primary focus off the central target: Parliament. The boycott was always supplemental, never primary, never intended to stand alone to destroy the slave trade. It was a tactic in a fundamentally political, electoral strategy designed to create public support to alter the structures of formal power.

Likewise, the famous bus boycotts of the civil rights movement were always conducted hand in hand with a sustained effort to change laws. Unlike the sugar boycotts, which required abstinence from a luxury, the bus boycotts were among the most difficult and demanding in boycott history, because they asked people to quit using something necessary for work; they were not entered into lightly. And the boycotts were part of a strategy designed to change laws, not private behavior.

The successful grape boycott of the 1960s, led by union organizer Cesar Chavez, was undertaken in conjunction with militant strikes, and was also supplemental to a larger goal. Striking farmworkers used the boycott to augment their strike and gain public attention, and eventually won their desired collective bargaining agreement. Like the sugar boycott, the 1963 grape boycott was well organized, with farmworkers traveling in caravans around the country to protest outside supermarkets.

Then, a new way of thinking started to take hold, and to shape the way we thought about markets, and consumers, and boycotts. In the mid-1960s, a small group of thinkers from the University of Chicago started advocating a new ideology, one that replaced the citizen with the consumer as the central actor in their vision of a fair society. The hugely influential economist Milton Friedman argued that markets did a better job of social welfare than politics, and that "[w]hen you vote daily in the supermarket, you get precisely what you voted for, and so does everyone else. The ballot box produces conformity without unanimity; the marketplace, unanimity without conformity. That is why it is desirable to use the ballot box, so far as possible, only for those decisions where conformity is essential."[4] A new kind of boycott, influenced by this pivot to consumerism, arose. It was not collective, but individual, and designed not to change laws, but business practices.

Friedman's language elided the roles of citizen and consumer, by arguing that they *do* the same thing. In this worldview, "voting," as he called it, by shopping (or not shopping) is the more satisfying, and more meaningful, option because each person will win his personal daily election and have a direct, daily impact. Unlike the old tradition of boycotts, which were enmeshed in public politics, the new vision of boycotts grew out of an anti-political, neoliberal vision of consumer and market supremacy.

The word *consumer* became popular not just on the right, but on the left, where ethical consumerism joined with the boycott tradition. Progressive ethical consumerism called on the histories of the sugar, bus, and grape boycotts, but redirected more energy toward the companies, and away from legislative action. This change played a role in the rise of corporate social responsibility (CSR), a movement that responded to the growing power of corporations and to the concomitant impulse to pressure them, as well as to boards' desires to give integrity to corporate endeavors, by trying to change them from within.

Successful consumer-led movements in the 1970s, 1980s, and 1990s suggested that this merger of right-wing market ideology with left-wing ethical consumerism might provide a powerful path forward. A late-1970s exposé of Nestlé's pushing of breast-milk substitutes led to a boycott and real business practice changes. The 1990s anti–sweatshop labor movement made Gap synonymous with sweatshops, forcing the company to change its labor practices. Some efforts—like the South Africa apartheid boycotts—were directed at politics, but many were increasingly directed solely at companies.

In this modern boycott/ethical consumer model, the Gandhi/King/Chavez activist history was merged—and in some cases submerged—into neoliberal consumer supremacy. Taken to its extreme, this vision of activism replaces tension in the political sphere with tension in the private sphere. A boycott creates tension that is typically resolved by the firm either doing nothing or changing its behavior, but it locates the central axis of tension as being between the firm and the activists. *Will they or won't they?* As such, it can lead to community benefits agreements that are not in line with the initial purpose of the boycott. As one critic recently argued, "When consumers and environmental NGOs channel their desire for environmental justice through the firm, their desires get absorbed into business strategies for growth and expansion."[5]

The popular *Vox* columnist Matthew Yglesias has endorsed this view, writing: "Consumer brands are a leverage point for progressive politics because there's no gerrymandering & marketers care more about young people. Consumer marketing is almost the exact opposite of voting and a younger, more urbanized, and more female demographic carries more weight."[6]

Yglesias' logic may lead to a short-term sense of empowerment, but to longer-term disempowerment—the more progressives lean into their consumer power as the key point of leverage, the less they focus on exercising their political power, the less long-term collective power they will amass. The "vote with your feet" model has a lot of appeal, in that it allows people to import virtuousness into their lives without the struggle of organizing and building a coalition.

Consumer politics has the appeal of feeling cleaner and less complicated than direct action or appeals to those in power, and is certainly less complicated than actually wielding power. University of North Carolina sociology professor Zeynep Tufekci argues that people "want to stay out of politics because they fear corruption and co-optation. They have a point. Modern representative democracies are being strangled in many countries by powerful interests." But, she points out, the long-term impact of dropping out of politics may be to make individuals cleaner and the system dirtier. "Operating this way makes it hard for them to sustain over the long term and exert leverage over the system, which leads to frustrated protesters dropping out, and even more corrupt politics."[7]

The success of a handful of boycotts leads to a constantly renewed sense of hope around them. Today, there are hundreds of boycotts every year, and most do not have an impact. "Very few boycotts have led to changes," says University of Pennsylvania professor Maurice Schweitzer. "Most accomplish very little. People lose interest, don't maintain a public presence around a boycott, and the number of people involved is typically too small to make a market difference; what difference is made typically revolves around media attention, not the loss of income."[8]

The Chick-fil-A boycott, one of the largest in recent memory, came about when the Chick-fil-A CEO made anti–gay marriage comments. Organizers staged kiss-ins, and mayors said Chick-fil-A was not welcome in their towns. But Chick-fil-A ignored the protests, people forgot the comments after a few years, and nothing changed. As one commentator put it, "It is hard to stay mad at a ubiquitous and powerful brand."[9] While in theory people committed to stop eating at Chick-fil-A *until it* changed its posture on marriage equality, the company outlasted the protest; it still rates a zero on the Human Rights Campaign's Buyers Guide, and LGBTQ people are not included in its non-discrimination policy.

Three grape boycotts tell a similar story of early success and later failure. The 1963 table-grape boycott achieved its aim;

a targeted 1977 grape boycott also led to changed laws in California; but a 1984 grape boycott lasted 16 years and was quietly called off after it lost energy and support.[10]

TOO BIG TO BOYCOTT

Ethical consumerism—and its close relatives corporate accountability and corporate social responsibility—is especially poorly suited to monopolized economies, and a tragic misfit for disciplining companies that play a quasi-governmental role. By accepting big corporations as partners, and not challenging their legitimacy as our rulers, the consumer boycott model allows for short-term victories that appear to be progressive, while the partner corporation is building sufficient power to become boycott-proof.

If Chick-fil-A was hard to boycott, think about what it would mean to boycott Google. First, imagine a one-person boycott, someone angry about, say, Google-enabled job discrimination. He would have to get rid of his Android phone and switch from Gmail. He'd have to stop using Google Search and Google Maps. He'd have to refuse to watch anything on YouTube. He'd have to get rid of Nest. If he owned a business, he'd have to avoid Google ads, which he may rely on to reach customers. He'd have to refuse to use municipal Wi-Fi in cities where Google is behind "free" Wi-Fi. He'd have to avoid the waterfront in Toronto, where Google runs the infrastructure. If he had children, he would have to tell them to refuse to use the technology required to interact with their teachers.

And even if he succeeds in doing all these things, Google will not boycott *him*. If he uses the internet, he will necessarily see Google-served ads, and his responses and non-responses to those ads will feed into Google's databank. Google will still collect information about him when he walks by a LinkNYC kiosk. Google will still collect his tax dollars in subsidies. You can join the "Do Not Call" registry, banning companies from calling you at home with sales pitches, but you cannot ban Google from tracking your behavior.

Now try imagining an *effective* organized boycott of Google, large enough to actually dent the company's profits. There are over five billion Google searches a day. Can we really imagine enough people switching to an alternate search engine or going without asking their question? Google will not stop collecting information on those people regardless, and Search is just one part of the Google behemoth. And as if that weren't daunting enough, imagine a sector-based boycott of the data-collection practices of all the big tech companies, boycotting Facebook *and* Google *and* Amazon for their shared behaviors.

Sure, the search engine DuckDuckGo is an alternative to Google. At one point it might have been a threat; at some point in the future it may be a threat again. It is not supported by targeted ads, and has better privacy rules. But it doesn't really hurt Google: its presence allows Google to pretend it has competition, in much the same way that the existence of opposition parties in Russia allows Vladimir Putin to pretend that there are open elections in his country.

In a comic *New York Times* article, one reporter chronicled the social media accounts that pushed boycotts using products from the companies they were boycotting. "Dear @apple," wrote one activist protesting Apple's National Rifle Association Television (NRATV) connections from his iPhone. "Your silence is deafening. #Boycottapple."[11] A quarter of the people who tweeted #boycottGoogle (a campaign organized to protest Google's firing of engineer James Damore) did so from Android phones. And people boycotting Amazon kept shopping at Amazon-owned Whole Foods. Cher protested Facebook's role in the Cambridge Analytica scandal by leaving Facebook for Facebook-owned Instagram. "I don't know if I can get out of the ecosystem," said one activist. "Where am I supposed to go?" said another. "I wish there was something else."[12]

In early 2019, the city of Richmond, California, ended its contract with Vigilant Solutions, a data analytics company that does business with Immigration and Customs Enforcement (ICE). The city of Berkeley, following suit, debated boycotting all products that provided services to ICE and Customs and Border Protection, including Amazon, because these federal agencies rely on Amazon Web Services. The Berkeley city manager, Dee Williams-Ridley, argued against boycotting Amazon because it "would have a huge negative impact to the citywide operations." Amazon helps to manage city documents, and hosts housing and mental health programs, and Amazon servers host many other tech companies that provide services to the city.[13] People unwittingly using the thing they are supposedly boycotting to advertise their boycott can seem funny. But the lack of choice facing all boycotters actually represents a serious narrowing of the window of moral political behavior.

The challenge of boycotting continues as you move down the food chain to the minor lords of the new monopoly moment. Monsanto isn't quite infrastructure, but it is ubiquitous. To boycott Monsanto would mean boycotting all food grown by any Monsanto farmer, as well as bread at grocery stores, soy milk, aspirin, and local beef that was raised on Monsanto corn.

In banking, there is something more like an oligopoly than a duopoly, so it is conceivable to imagine a mass boycott of Chase, leading to people switching to Bank of America. For such a boycott to work, of course, it would have to be possible to pit the companies against each other, which is difficult when their pathological behavior is industry-wide.

Even if you could stay mad, as the Google example shows, your voice is weaker because of monopolization. Concentration weakens boycott power even over the consumer goods that seem the most vulnerable to boycott, like sneakers and makeup and cereal. In a market with 30 shoemakers, and no shoemaker with more than 5% of the market, a petition to force one shoemaker to change its rubber sourcing can change its position—in a market with four shoemakers, the market power of the consumer is very weak. As a result, because of monopolization, boycotts are harder now. To effectively boycott Gap, you would now also have to boycott Banana Republic and Old Navy.

After the gun massacre at Marjory Stoneman Douglas High School, online outrage coalesced into a national effort to get companies to stop streaming NRATV. Despite petitions and ongoing public pressure, Amazon Fire TV, Google Chromecast, and Apple TV continue to stream NRA programming. Activist efforts to engage with Amazon were met with a shrug. The companies were so ubiquitous and essential they weren't threatened by a boycott and could ignore the activists.

Nothing better illustrates the limits of the consumer model of change in the face of monopolized markets than the extraordinary success of the local, slow-food, organic agriculture movement and its simultaneous failure to make a meaningful dent in the way that food is created. The farm-to-table, slow-food, sustainable-food, healthy-food movement has reached unimaginable heights. About 75% of all Americans try to eat local, organic food, and one survey showed that nearly 90% of people want locally grown food at the grocery store and would consider that as part of their shopping decision.[14] As Stacy Mitchell, who runs the Institute for Local Self-Reliance, points out: "The local food movement has gone further than any other [consumer] movement in terms of widespread adoption."[15] We have craft breweries, co-op slaughterhouses, farmers' markets. There is a deep emotional attachment to the provenance of food. Local food is celebrated on *The View* and by Michelle Obama.

Despite the health food movement's unmitigated success, and the fact that food is where people have the peak amount of leverage—they can buy or not buy, or "vote with their pocket-book," three times a day—only 5% of all farms are organic, and only 0.3% of total farm sales are direct-to-consumer sales.[16] Monsanto may be widely reviled, yet Monsanto's power keeps rising. Consumer choice simply cannot get us to a world where most farmers and farmworkers are treated better.

Driscoll's, for instance, does not mind at all if a worker-owned berry co-op sells 5% of the berries in Seattle. In fact, the existence of a few worker-owned co-ops in the berry market, like the existence of a small seed company that isn't Monsanto, is a major public relations boon for the monopolist, because it creates a perception that Driscoll's isn't a monop-oly. But everyone knows that the co-ops exist by the grace of Driscoll's, not despite Driscoll's. If Driscoll's wanted to wipe out a worker-owned co-op, it would simply demand that the grocery stores that sell Driscoll's berries don't buy from the co-op. The berry co-op could limp along, but it wouldn't be able to grow.

The change in effectiveness can be confusing for people who remember the successful boycotts in the 1980s and 1990s of such companies as Nike. Companies have reorganized their supply chains in a way that insulates them from liability and protest. Garment manufacturers no longer have direct rela-tionships with big companies, and build systems of deliberate ignorance into their purchasing.[17] As Michael Hobbes details in his riveting story "The Myth of the Ethical Shopper," after the deadly fire in the Tazreen garment manufacturing facility in Bangladesh, we learned that Walmart had banned suppliers from using Tazreen. But 60% of the goods at Tazreen were still going to Walmart. How? It hired a supplier, who hired another supplier, who subcontracted to make garments. Moreover, suppliers have learned to answer the right questions when inspectors come by. Professor Richard Locke studied ten years of Nike inspections and found that on paper, Nike working conditions were improving, but in reality, 80% of its root suppliers were either the same as or worse than before. Most importantly, every part of Nike's supply chain is monopolized, with just a few major players, so boycotters have nowhere to go, and a serious boycott would involve buying *no* foreign-manufactured garments, not targeting particular companies.[18]

Growing consolidation of power interacts with the rise of social media, leading to more boycotts that are less effective and shorter-lasting. As Zeynep Tufekci has argued, these actions tend to the ephemeral and episodic, instead of the effective and persistent:[19] "Digital infrastructure allows movements to carry out protests with the same size and energy as past protests but without similar organizational capacity. While this appears a shortcut for protests, it also engenders weaknesses, as these protests do not signal the same level of capacity as previous protests, and do not necessarily pose the same threat to governments and power."[20]

The result is a combination of hyperactivity online and decreased power. Boycotts gin up social media presence on an almost daily basis. Companies know exactly who is actually boycotting and the disconnect between the actual boycott and the public-facing one. Unlike a demand for legislative action—where inaction by a lawmaker grows in meaning over time—the longer that a company does not change in the face of protests, the more powerful it gets. When a lawmaker does not change, she is often weakened, but when a company does not change, it is often strengthened. The lawmaker becomes vulnerable to a primary challenger; the company has proven that it is strong.

And too many times, the very companies we are protesting are working to leverage feel-good leftism for profit and power. Coca-Cola knows what it is doing with Odwalla, and Colgate knows what it is doing with Tom's of Maine. Perdue is happy to advertise with pictures of happy chickens. These are old tricks of big corporations, but Google, Facebook, and Amazon take it a step further: Google uses its home page daily doodle to reinforce a liberal feel for the company; Facebook steps in when there is a disaster to enable humanitarian relief; and both companies give money to journalism and support education. Amazon often stops customers with a pop-up question of whether they want to make a charitable contribution, and offers "Amazon Smile," a program that directs 0.5% of each sale to charities of the purchaser's choice.

There is also a strong class and social element to boycotting something like Facebook. It may not be essential for an upper-middle-class man living in New York, with an existing strong network of friends who appreciate his eccentricities, to use Facebook or Instagram, but for a young person looking for work, let alone friendship, it can be hard to check out of Facebook, Instagram, WhatsApp, and all the Facebook-owned properties, because they are so central to social life, let alone the web of job connections. Facebook is the place where events are planned, the place where humor is shared. The human cost of social isolation is enormous, and while some people may have sturdy offline social networks, many people do not. I met one anti-monopoly activist who guiltily confessed that she stayed on Facebook because she wanted to check on her grandmother's health.

Yet, we have somehow inculcated a belief that if someone fails to boycott a company, such as Facebook, she lacks standing to object to political behavior or to petition Congress for change. People feel guilty about not boycotting, and that guilt gets in the way of full-throated political protest. In law, there is a doctrine called "exhaustion of remedies." It prevents a litigant from seeking a remedy in a new court or jurisdiction until all claims or remedies have been pursued as fully as possible—exhausted—in the original one. In politics, consumer supremacy has led to a kind of exhaustion of remedies thinking, through which people adopt a hierarchy of modes of resistance, and feel they must *first* boycott, and only *then* ask lawmakers for change. It places consumer obligations over civic ones, when instead we need to understand that we should *first* ask lawmakers for change, and *then*, if possible, use our other powers to augment our actions in the marketplace.

∗

In 1963, Martin Luther King Jr. wrote his famous "Letter from Birmingham Jail" after he was arrested and imprisoned for defying a state court's injunction and leading a march of black protesters to call for an Easter boycott of white-owned stores.[21] In his letter, King speaks from a place of profound morality, profound love, and profound desire to create a tension that will then create the possibility for power. For King, the goal was to exercise power and create change, and boycotts were a tactical option in service of that larger goal.

Although he had studied and learned from Henry David Thoreau, who was also a boycotter, King did not exactly echo the apolitical, even anti-political, Thoreau. For Thoreau, as he explained in *Civil Disobedience*, disobedience and protest were less about achieving a goal than goals in and of themselves, a way to live consistently with oneself. Thoreau's civil disobedience began and ended with his discomfort with the fact of government and the fact of law itself. Although he said he was not one of those who called themselves "no government men" (radical libertarians of the time), he was close, endorsing the motto, "That government is best which governs least."

At his most powerful, Thoreau excoriates the enablers of slavery, the "hundred thousand merchants and farmers here, who are more interested in commerce and agriculture than they are in humanity." These merchants and farmers, he felt, should remove themselves from commerce. But then he asks himself why he does not want to engage in changing laws and the electoral system, and answers himself that it is too exhausting. "As far as the ways the state has provided me for remedying the evil, I know of no such ways. They take too much time, and a man's life will be gone."[22] He reveals an aesthetic and personal distaste for politics, accompanied by a sense of private moral obligation.

King's form and tradition of protest is profoundly *political*, in that it creates tension, it is collective, and its goal is change; Thoreau's form—and I say this with great admiration for him— has more to do with himself and who he is and whether or not he can live with himself. King starts with law, and then uses boycott—and civil disobedience—to change the law, whereas Thoreau rejects politics, and uses boycott to serve his belief in moral consistency.

As such, King and Thoreau represent two strains in the modern boycott sensibility: boycotts that are personal, isolated, and designed to achieve a narrow end, and boycotts that are designed to be political and part of a larger strategy to change the structures of power. The goal of the Thoreau model is to preserve one's own integrity. The goal of the King model is to preserve the integrity of society, and to create tension that can only be resolved through politics. While the Thoreau model does no harm, it is rarely transformative, and can be twisted into a form of personal consumerist politics that actually undermines public politics.

As I write, we are starting to recover the King model, after decades of being swindled by a more consumerist approach. While corporate accountability campaigns have been at the heart of much organizing for the last few decades, more groups are running corporate illegitimacy campaigns, questioning the corporations' right to exist at all, and demanding that companies get broken up.

In 2018, labor and community groups came together to protest Amazon getting billions in subsidies to build a headquarters in Queens, New York. Amazon and its allies assumed that this was another routine corporate benefits campaign; activists would complain, but their goal was to get a few community benefits, not to block the deal. They were surprised by the seriousness of the protesters, who succeeded against huge odds. In the wake of that success, a national organization of labor and community groups was created to stand up against Amazon: Athena.[24] Unlike in other corporate accountability campaigns, the continued existence of Amazon in its current form is not taken for granted. In fact, the terms of the coalition required every group to agree that it wants Amazon broken up.

We will see whether targeted strategic boycotts become part of the Athena campaign; if they do, I will join them. And I like supporting local retail for shopping whenever possible. But I will not shame people for buying from Amazon the magic markers they use to write, "Break up Bezos' power" on a big poster they parade outside their state attorney general's office, and I don't believe that anyone has to quit Facebook to demand that the FTC dismantle it. There is more than enough transformative *political* work to be done, as I show in the next chapter.

10

We Have the Tools

It is better for people to own the monopolies than
for the monopolies to own the people.
                                   —*The Labor Annual*, 1898[1]

People's hearts are breaking. People power is blossoming. We
are rapidly losing essential democratic institutions. We are living amid the greatest democratic awakening in history. We
have been here before, and we have never seen anything like it.
The sleeping giant of American progressive populism is waking up after decades of slumber and we are facing a threat of
technologically enabled authoritarianism unlike any we have
ever known. The American left is both more energetic than in
generations past and more confused, fighting important battles
and winning some, but, as I argue in this book, not seriously
engaged in one of the most central arenas of the war.

Today's progressive populism traces back to September
2008, when the banks crashed the world economy and were
bailed out. All the major institutions—Congress, statehouses,
universities, think tanks—acted like nothing major had
changed and went on talking about policy and arguing about
solutions just as they had during the prior generation. Greedy,
arrogant bankers who destroyed people's lives were showered
with government money, which they used to get richer and
more powerful, and to fund fossil fuel exploration. It was a dis-
heartening but clarifying moment. The complete inability of

mainline institutions to deal with the crash in a serious, honest, and equitable way gave rise to new institutions, new ideas, new, unafraid communities—the Occupy movement, Black Lives Matter, the Sunrise Movement, the Bernie Sanders 2016 campaign. Out of those movements, ideas that were once considered ludicrous began to be taken seriously: the Green New Deal, Democratic Socialism, universal healthcare, the student debt jubilee, reparations, universal voting.

This fierce new activism has enjoyed some startling successes. Climate organizers and indigenous leaders in North Dakota stood waist-deep in frozen water to stop a major fracked gas pipeline, and the Obama administration halted its construction. Low-wage workers, organizing early-morning rallies, won victory after victory in the fight for a $15-an-hour minimum wage. Fracking was banned in New York. Wells Fargo stopped funding private prisons after years of consumer protest. Voting rights activists marched on the state capitol in North Carolina every week, and its corporate funders walked away from backing the American Legislative Exchange Council, the group pushing model voter suppression laws discussed in chapter 6. Parents refusing to let their children take standardized tests changed national policy on high-stakes testing. In the 2018 midterms, half of eligible voters turned out, the highest rate in 50 years. A progressive 28-year-old activist with a preternatural ability to communicate, Alexandria Ocasio-Cortez, beat a longtime mainline incumbent in an improbable congressional upset. Florida easily passed a progressive ballot measure that gave former felons the right to vote. Teachers across the country walked out in the thousands and won major concessions after decades of austerity education politics.

There were a few other notable moments, including a brief burst of powerful activity demanding bank breakups after the crash of 2008. I co-founded a group that held over a hundred rallies around the country asking for bank breakups, with the awkwardly wonky rallying cry of "Nationalize, Reorganize, Decentralize!"—you don't remember us because we never expanded beyond the thousands. Occupy Wall Street, which transformed America, represented a powerful anti-financial-sector moment.

However, when it comes to divestiture (the technical term for breaking up a company), there has not been one single, notable, in-the-street protest targeted at fracturing one of the giants. Students go days without sleep to pressure Harvard to divest from fossil fuels but—except for the occasional tweet—don't crowd outside Senator Chuck Schumer's office, demanding that he break up Charter, Unilever, CVS, Lockheed Martin, or Walmart.

To figure out what that antimonopoly activism might look like, let's go back 130 years.

THE FIRST ANTITRUST MOVEMENT

In February 1900, a blizzard descended on Chicago, and snow towers appeared on frozen piles of manure in the city streets, making it difficult for a crowd of angry people to get from their boardinghouses to the convention hall. They were mad because, despite decades of soaring economic growth, prosperity had been wrested from middle- and working-class Americans by a small club of millionaires. Inequality in America was at an all-time high. The wealthiest 2% of Americans owned a third of the country's wealth, and the bottom 40% had no wealth at all. The richest 1% owned over half the property, and the bottom 44% owned barely over 1%. Those gathered were at one of the biggest antitrust conferences of the decade, demanding antitrust action.

In the convention hall, the mayor of Chicago, Carter

Harrison Jr., welcomed farmers, small-business owners, and manufacturers from around the Midwest, groups that had often been at odds with each other. They had come together in shared anger at the gargantuan companies that were abusing all of them. Harrison roused the crowd to action by raging at the dissolution of democracy across states and industries. Big steel and oil trusts were threatening "the integrity of the nation," he shouted. The Senate "has been reduced to a small convention of the owners and representatives of the trusts," and, he argued, the judiciary could fall next, becoming a mere tool of corporate power. The goal of this conference, which was covered on the front page of the *New York Times*, was to force national politicians to start some serious trust-busting.[2]

These furious citizens and workers, their liberty and livelihoods crushed by big companies, didn't want concessions, or for the big companies to act in a kinder way, to merely agree to pay higher wages, or to voluntarily provide better information on the rates they charged. This protest was not about what we might now call corporate accountability, or good corporate citizenship; the activists wanted the current structure of corporate power to be abolished, either through nationalization or decentralization. As Harrison boomed to the cold Chicago crowd, it was time for the "uprooting of the whole trust system!" This wasn't a particularly radical or rare example of labor activism; this was the tone and stance of much of the country, and not just in 1900—from the 1860s through the New Deal.

Against incredible odds, the antitrust movement worked, although not all at once. Within a decade, Standard Oil and the Beef Trust were dissolved, and, 35 years later, FDR restructured the American economy.

We used to see power problems with big corporations, hold massive rallies that would force Congress to fix them, and expect that lawmakers would take concentrated power seriously.

We used to understand that concentration was neither inevitable nor an essential part of having private markets to sell consumer goods. We used to fight to change laws so that co-ops could thrive, instead of trying to build tiny co-ops in infertile soil. And we are starting to do these things again.

In this chapter I lay out the key elements of a new antitrust movement. First, I briefly summarize the long history of antitrust laws and activism, if only to allow people to know that their current fight has deep roots and many successes. Many of those hard-fought laws are still on the books. Antitrust law today is a room filled with drawers of old, rusty tools that have not been used for decades, but that can, with a little effort and a lot of political will, be cleaned up, sharpened, and taken to battle. Next, I explain how we can push statehouses and Congress to overturn bad case law, and pass new laws addressing the particular democratic threats posed by technology.

OUR ANTI-MONOPOLY HISTORY

Opposition to corporate governmental power runs deep in the American sensibility. The Tea Party protest in Boston was an anti-monopoly riot, an uprising against excessive corporate and political power exercised by the British East India Company monopoly. Thomas Jefferson argued that an anti-monopoly clause should be added to the Constitution in the same letter he argued for the First Amendment. From the 1860s to the 1940s, one of the most persistent demands of workers and activists was the insistence that government break up, regulate, and rein in highly concentrated corporate power.

In 1865, Charles Sumner, the famous abolitionist from Massachusetts, assailed "confederate corporations," which had amassed so much power that they rivaled the U.S. government. Corporations that could govern, and humiliate, were not, he argued, legitimate institutions. Sumner treated monopoly government and white nationalism as enabling two interrelated forms of illegitimate power. He called New Jersey the Valley of Humiliation "through which all travelers north and south must pass, and the monopoly, like Apollyon, claims them all as 'subjects,' saying 'for all that country is mine, and I am the prince and god of it.'"[3] The problem with the men who built the railroads wasn't just that they were racist, which they were, and wasn't just that they were unfair to farmers, which they were; it was that they were actually trying to be kings, usurping the legitimate exercise of self-government.

In the 1870s, one in ten farmers was a Granger. The Grange movement demanded an economy built on supporting farmer cooperatives and breaking up big agricultural trusts. Grangers warned that monopolists were ripping people off, stripping them of human dignity, and destroying democracy. The Grange movement slogan was "Down with the Monopolies!" In 1881, the muckraking journalist Henry Demarest Lloyd wrote a story about Standard Oil titled "The Story of a Great Monopoly." It was so popular that *Atlantic Monthly* had to reprint the issue six times. In 1884, presidential candidate Ben Butler, the nominee of the Greenback and Anti-Monopoly Parties, railed against the sewing machine monopoly, the railroads, and Standard Oil. The people's movement that grew out of the Grange was anti-monopoly and anti-racist: the Populist Party called for a united front of black and white farmers and sharecroppers against the Money Power.[4] The populist Farmers' Alliance of the 1880s and 1890s was a truly cross-race populist movement that understood itself as laying bare false divisions (race against race) and exposing the true divisions (the monopolist against the people).

In the late 1800s, most businesses were not corporations, and people understood the corporation as a state construct—

and a threat to democratic power—rather than as a fact of nature. A corporation, granted a charter by the state but with no obligation to the public, presented a threat of selfish, untrustworthy, whimsical government if it grew too large (public obligations were therefore written into state charters). In the 1880s, corporations started using the legal device of the trust—in which one entity holds property for the benefit of another—to combine businesses, leading to a whiskey trust, an envelope trust, paving pitch and school slate trusts, and paper bag trusts, among others. "Trust" began to be used interchangeably with "big business," and the hatred of monopolies migrated quickly to a hatred of trusts. The trusts corrupted government by paying lawmakers, drove out competitors by lowering prices, and abused workers. Opponents cried "feudalism" and warned of a "great, unscrupulous, powerful plutocracy."[5]

The Sherman Antitrust Act of 1890 was the first federal effort at trust-busting and remains a pillar of antitrust power. The act was designed to improve economic opportunity, stability, and security; to bring freedom to the marketplace; and to create political liberty.[6] As an advocate explained, it was necessary because: "Enterprises with great capital have deliberately sought not only industrial domination but political supremacy as well."[7] It is a short law, with language so succinct and aspirational that many have compared it to the Constitution. The most important two provisions take up fewer than 80 words:

Section 1: [e]very contract, combination in the form of trust or otherwise, or conspiracy, in restraint of trade or commerce among the several States, or with foreign nations, is declared to be illegal.
Section 2: every person who shall monopolize, or attempt to monopolize, or combine or conspire with any other

person or persons, to monopolize any part of the trade or
commerce among the several States, or with foreign nations, shall be deemed guilty of a felony.

The Sherman Antitrust Act obligated the government to
imprison and fine people for unfair business practices. But two
essential terms—"restraint of trade" and "monopoly"—are
not defined in the law. Thus, it gives enormous power to the
courts—and to the Supreme Court in particular—because the
definitions of these two terms, untethered by congressional direction, decide almost everything about what is legal and what
is not. Weak prosecutors can choose not to engage by redefin-
ing "monopoly," as they did in the early years of the law.

By the time Mayor Harrison spoke in 1900, the Sherman Antitrust Act had been underenforced and gutted by the
Supreme Court, and people were not satisfied. There were
thousands of local antitrust leagues throughout the country,
organized school district by school district. Congressman
William Jennings Bryan spoke for millions of anti-monopoly
populists during his second run for president. That spring,
Congress debated a constitutional amendment to give itself the
power to rein in monopolies—an amendment required because
of a hostile Supreme Court, which treated monopoly regulation as beyond congressional Commerce Clause power.

You couldn't read the *New York Times* without encounter-
ing commentary on the "Trust Problem," the problem of the
"Wire Combination" (concentrated telegraph and telephone
systems), and a huge array of ideas about how to deal with monopolies. A few years later, in response to popular pressure,
Teddy Roosevelt started down the path of breaking up Standard Oil, building the reputation that he still carries today of a
fearless trust-buster.

The period of 1900 to 1916 is one of two major moments

of intense federal legislative action around excessive corporate power, the other being the latter years of the New Deal. Between 1900 and 1916, Roosevelt, Wilson, Taft, and Bryan all treated the "trust problem" as an essential threat to democracy. The Clayton Antitrust Act, passed in 1914, was designed to give more precise shape to the Sherman Antitrust Act by identifying some categories of illegal behavior: price fixing, exclusive dealing, and "tying" (requiring a purchaser to purchase unrelated products). While it continues to provide some direction, the scope of the act, as with the Sherman Antitrust Act, depends on how prosecutors and courts interpret "monopolization." Section 7 of the Clayton Antitrust Act is the primary U.S. law governing mergers. It prohibits one company from acquiring stocks or assets when "the effect of such acquisition may be substantially to lessen competition, or to tend to create a monopoly." Also in 1914, Wilson led the creation of the Federal Trade Commission (FTC), which has jurisdiction over antitrust enforcement.

As Barry Lynn details in his forthcoming book, *Liberty from All Masters*, the anti-monopoly agenda came to a screeching halt when the United States entered the Great War.[8] When we emerged from that conflict, federal policy tended toward Hooverism, a war-inflected belief in the importance and necessity of large corporations, and a faith that they could be trusted to share governmental power with elected officials.

The Franklin Delano Roosevelt administration began with an embrace of the top-down approach, government working hand-in-glove with big corporations to respond to the disaster of the Great Depression. But in his second term, frustrated with big business, worried about the power that corporations could wield, and unimpressed with the results of early top-down efforts, FDR launched a radical antitrust agenda that spread to every part of his administration. The New Deal antitrust enforcers were

led by the committed head of the antitrust division of the Department of Justice, Thurman Arnold, who used the Sherman
and Clayton Antitrust Acts to their full capacity. A belief that
democracy and economic vitality required decentralized power
infused every part of the administration, as FDR worked in
coalition with small businesses, unions, and progressives.

Roosevelt's double approach, nationalize and decentralize,
was the heart of the New Deal. Less than two months after
FDR became president, he announced that the government was
going to transform the business of banking. The government
was "compelled to step in for the protection of depositors"
and the future of the economy.[9] The 1933 Banking Act—
sometimes known as Glass-Steagall—divided banks into two
kinds of businesses: the commercial bank and the investment
bank. Banks that provided a secure place for deposits, and a reliable place for taking out loans, were cleaved from banks that
enabled high-risk trading, akin to gambling. But FDR didn't
just *"break 'em up"*—the Banking Act *also* created an enormous,
centralized, government-run program of federal insurance: the
Federal Insurance Deposit Corporation, or FDIC. It was both
decentralizing and centralizing at the same time; it decentralized the institutions responsible for banking and centralized the
insurance of the banks.

In one blow, an enormously powerful centralized national
program had been created and overly concentrated private
power had been broken apart. The American Bankers Association was vehemently opposed. Deposit insurance—the idea
that the federal government would insure deposits so as to protect a future run on the banks—struck them as excessive governmental meddling, likely to lead to bad business behavior and
an inappropriate distortion of private business. But Roosevelt
welcomed their ire, resisting big business on behalf of poor and
working-class people. This is one of many similar examples.

The golden age of antitrust started by the New Deal lasted from 1940 to 1980. Judges and prosecutors interpreted the Sherman and Clayton Antitrust Acts liberally and used them as prophylactics to prevent excessive power and the abuses that attend such power. For 40 years, the FTC, the Department of Justice, and courts analyzed mergers in terms of power and the potential for abuse: structures that might lead to companies having too much power were blocked. Government organizations treated certain conduct by dominant companies as presumptively illegal. They adopted what is often called a "structuralist" approach to antitrust law: instead of waiting for bad behavior, they enforced a decentralized structure to make such behavior less likely.

For instance, in 1945, Learned Hand, the legendary Second Circuit judge, looked at the personal and civic impacts of concentration and suggested that "unchallenged economic power deadens initiative, discourages thrift, and depresses energy."[10] He concluded that "[i]t is possible, because of its indirect social or moral effect, to prefer a system of small producers, each dependent for his success upon his own skill and character, to one in which the great mass of those engaged must accept the direction of a few."[11] Thirteen years later, in 1958, the Supreme Court described the Sherman Act as serving many purposes, including "providing an environment conducive to the preservation of our democratic political and social institutions."[12]

To serve these ends, prosecutors did not hesitate to act proactively to stop power from being amassed. For instance, in *Brown Shoe Co. v. United States*, in 1962, the Supreme Court approved blocking a merger between Brown, a company that manufactured less than 6% of the nation's shoes, and Kinney, a company that sold 2% of the nation's shoes.[13] Even though each company had only a fraction of the national market, the Court perceived a creeping risk. As the Court said in that decision,

"As a large concern grows through a series of such small acquisitions, its accretions of power are individually so minute as to
make it difficult to use the Sherman Act tests against them."
The "cumulative effect" of many small purchases could be to
transform an industry from an open, decentralized market to
"one in which three or four large concerns produce the entire
supply."

Because the Court used a structural approach, oligopolies
were looked on with suspicion due to their ability to block new
entrants, hike prices, engage in price fixing, and create political
power—and to coordinate in the political arena and further
entrench their market advantage—whether or not there was
proof of any of these particulars. A decentralized market had
civic, generative, creative, and moral attributes that withered
in centralized systems. The Supreme Court understood that
this vision might occasionally lead to higher costs and prices,
"because of costs associated with fragmented industries and
markets." However, Congress "resolved these competing considerations in favor of decentralization."[14]

Another example: In *United States v. Philadelphia National
Bank*, the Supreme Court approved blocking a bank merger
between the second- and third-largest regional banks, a merger
that would have led to one bank controlling 30% of commercial
banking. Despite the lack of evidence that this 30% share
would have negative effects on competition, the Court held that
it need not have "elaborate proof of market structure, market
behavior, or probable anticompetitive effects."[15] Instead, the high
market share alone showed an "inherently anti-competitive
tendency." Federal law barred "anticompetitive mergers, benign
and malignant alike," and in interpreting the statute, the Court
recognized there were concerns about concentration that were
not directly measurable.

The 1968 merger guidelines promulgated by President

Lyndon Johnson's administration reflected the general approach taken during these years. The guidelines laid out specific market percentages at which the Federal Trade Commission and Justice Department would challenge mergers. For instance, in a concentrated market, the government had a default of suing to block any merger between a company that already had 15% of the market and an acquisition target that represented 1% of the market, or any merger between two companies that each already had 4% of the market. Any company with a 20% market share would be blocked from buying another related company in the supply chain.[16]

In 1965, two authors writing on the goals of antitrust for the *Columbia Law Review* summarized it thus: "Another political objective of antitrust is the enlargement of individual liberty. . . . In the absence of strong countervailing considerations, we favor freedom of action and the wide range of choices that freedom implies." The consensus was that antimonopoly policy served freedom, happiness, worker power, and decentralized moral decision-making, as well as low prices.[17]

We may now look back on the 1960s and early 1970s as a time of relative de-concentration, but antitrust activists at the time were nonetheless worried that the existing laws were not strong enough. In 1968, President Johnson's White House Task Force on Antitrust Policy recommended limiting mergers involving companies with more than $500 million in sales, or $250 million in assets. Michigan senator Phil Hart, after whom the Hart Senate Office Building is named, had two passions: civil rights and antitrust law. He was the author of the 1965 Voting Rights Act and went to his deathbed working on antitrust legislation, afraid of corporate power encroaching on individual freedoms. He proposed putting an absolute limit on the size of companies and requiring them to spin off if they got too large.

In 1979, Ted Kennedy proposed a bill that would have prohibited mergers between companies that each had assets or sales exceeding $2 billion—$6 billion in today's dollars.[18]

Then came Ronald Reagan, and the beginning of four decades of a new antitrust vision and weak enforcement. In 1982, he threw out the old rules and percentages. The new theory of the antitrust laws, embodied in new enforcement guidelines, was that the laws had one goal: to ensure low prices. Mergers were blocked only if there was evidence that they would likely lead to higher prices. Conduct that was previously looked on with suspicion was now presumptively pro-competition. Much power could be consolidated, and all kinds of conduct were permissible, *unless* there was strong evidence that they would lead to an increase in consumer prices. Reagan's new guidelines were openly pro-consolidation, stating that "mergers generally play an important role in a free enterprise economy . . . the Department seeks to avoid unnecessary interference with that larger universe of mergers that are either competitively beneficial or neutral."[19]

Reagan's close ally Edwin Meese recruited Bill Baxter to be the head of the Antitrust Division at the Department of Justice, and James Miller to run the Federal Trade Commission. Meese was Reagan's chief policy adviser and eventual chief of staff. He represented a form of white authoritarianism, an urge to reassert authority—especially white authority—in the wake of the successful civil rights movement. The Meese agenda was "to curtail affirmative action, revive the death penalty for federal crimes, ease restrictions on the use of illegally seized evidence, scale back police warnings to suspects, limit prisoners' appeals, curb the right to abortion, reduce challenges to corporate mergers and narrow judicial interpretations of the Bill of Rights."[20]

How do these elements relate? Whether Meese used racial wedges to sell deregulation by offering racial superiority to poor and working-class whites in exchange for an agreement to give big business a license to act freely, or offered big business deregulation in order to get some businesses (which might otherwise have been wary) to support the incarceration agenda, the knot between the agenda for corporate authority and the agenda for white authority was tightly bound.

Within their first two years, Meese and Miller reshaped American economic policy. In 1982, Miller brought only 15 unfair, deceptive, or anticompetitive business practice cases, a more than 75% drop from the number of cases brought under Jimmy Carter per year. At the same time, under Meese's guidance, Reagan appointed judges who reinterpreted the antitrust case law. He appointed three justices to the Supreme Court, including the chief justice, and 47% of all the sitting district and appellate judges (as of 1988).[21]

These new judges—including Justice Antonin Scalia and Judges Frank Easterbrook and Richard Posner, the biggest defenders of big business—overturned decades of case law. They treated all mergers as presumptively positive. They effectively wrote predatory pricing out of the Clayton Antitrust Act, concluding that almost any price-cutting was good for customers—even if the price-cutting was designed to push out competitors and monopolize a market. They reinterpreted antitrust laws as consumer price-protection tools. They rejected a vision that these laws were designed to curb despotism. They rewrote hundreds of years of contract law, excising the power analysis that once accompanied contract interpretation.

You might have thought that Democrats would fight back when they regained power, but Bill Clinton, when he became president, accepted Reagan's transformation and did not revive the 1968 merger guidelines. Nor did Bush or Obama. Instead, Clinton, Bush, and Obama all presided over an ongoing merger wave that would have horrified any 1960s judge. From 1992 to 2016, antitrust was not even in the Democratic Party platform. The post-Reagan years have been defined largely by silence around antitrust and anti-monopoly policy. Almost all the big mergers in recent years were allowed, along with a few settlements—the merging companies have had to make minor changes, provide some funds for the public, spin off a company, and agree not to engage in certain bad behavior.

In sum, from 1980 to today, antitrust was triply depoliticized. First, courts treated the body of antitrust laws as if they were designed only to serve consumer welfare, not growth and abuses of political power in the private realm. Second, practitioners of antitrust—prosecutors, judges, and law professors—depoliticized their own roles, allowing technically trained economists to make the big judgments about what society should look like. They deferred to professional elite economists, whose jargon is complicated and whose claims to special knowledge make it hard for people to feel comfortable challenging them. Giving economists the final say also allowed practitioners to avoid responsibility and to treat decisions as if they were required by abstract laws instead of as hard political decisions that shape power in society. Third, and most bizarrely, these same practitioners treated antitrust as if it were a job for courts, not Congress.

Congress stopped acting as if antitrust were its job. The Sherman and Clayton Antitrust Acts were given a quasi-constitutional deference, as they could not be modified, but it was rare to see new antitrust legislation debated in the House or Senate.

That started changing in 2017.

THE NEW ANTI-MONOPOLY ERA

We are in the early stages of a major battle to reinvigorate the anti-monopoly movement. There are huge toolboxes of existing laws that can be enforced right now; a lot of bad Supreme Court precedents that can be overturned by Congress; and new laws that will need to be passed to address weaknesses in the old laws and new obstacles. The new antitrust era, to meet the crisis of concentration we now face, will require us to do all three.

First, the low-hanging fruit. We can start by demanding that the federal government and states enforce the laws already on the books and demanding executive leadership. Under existing law, past mergers between WhatsApp and Facebook and Instagram, and Bayer and Monsanto, could have and should have been stopped, and can be unwound. The predatory actions and other unfair business practices of Uber and Amazon and Google can be investigated. Some of this is already happening: attorneys general are investigating big tech and opioid manufacturers, and have sued to stop the merger between Sprint and T-Mobile. But we'll need more resources for state attorneys general, and far more action on the federal level.

There are also countless opportunities for federal regulators, and for states whose laws mirror federal law, to pursue those remedies already mentioned and hundreds of other cases. For this to happen, antitrust enforcers must be ready to seek significant structural remedies, instead of simply agreeing to company concessions. But under existing law—and with the political will—the great breakup could begin. A major win against Apple in the Supreme Court last year created a huge opportunity for private antitrust cases.

The Federal Trade Commission—right now—can also play a critical role in changing basic competition rules. As Sandeep Vaheesan argued in a significant article in 2017, the FTC has substantial power to define the scope of federal laws.[22] Congress, anticipating changing business practices and changing methods of unfairness, purposefully gave the FTC the power to define "unfair methods of competition." Executive agencies have enormous discretion to act.[23] As Vaheesan points out, the FTC can and should change merger law by making mergers presumptively illegal in competitive markets, and should lay out very particular clear, bright-line rules—like speed limits —against certain kinds of "vertical" behavior, like when Tyson forces farmers to use the building firms it prefers.

The next president, in particular, will have outsized power when it comes to antitrust; she (or he) can unilaterally promulgate new merger rules, directing the FTC to adopt clear guidelines that declare that it will oppose mergers of a certain size and percentage of the market. The new guidelines for the Department of Justice and the FTC can adopt the posture that policing conduct violations is a top priority. They can strongly signal that they won't stand for a few small changes, but will require structural reorganization. If—when—the next president makes using the full scope of existing law a top priority, it could directly free up millions of Americans currently subject to monopolized regimes.

Even with strong enforcement, we need new laws. Congress should start by overturning all the bad decisions made by the Reagan judges. That alone would serve to sharpen the swords of the laws already on the books. During the golden age of antitrust law, courts treated particular business practices as presumptively bad. As noted, since 1980, they have applied what is called the "rule of reason" to those same business practices and treated these unfair practices as unfair only if they hurt consumer prices. While it sounds sensible, we have all seen the result: judges effectively created an impossible hurdle, a fact-intensive examination of any given conduct that determines only whether that conduct is good or bad for consumer prices. The result is too much discretion in the courts, high and uncertain hurdles to overcome for plaintiffs or prosecutors, and laws that exist in theory but not in practice.

For instance: Congress should pass a law restoring the 1960s approach toward tying contracts, discussed earlier. Congress can likewise pass a law overturning bad precedent on predatory pricing and say that predatory behavior is per se illegal. States aren't bound by congressional action. They can do the same thing: pass state-specific laws that make clear that for New York, California, Massachusetts, or Virginia, stronger laws will apply. You don't have to be an antitrust expert to demand that your lawmakers act: the rallying cry is to restore the antitrust that courts killed.

But if we are honest about the scale of our predicament, we need to do more than get back to 1970s laws and enforcement levels. Mere return to the past is insufficient, for three reasons. First, there were weaknesses in those laws. This time, they should have clearer bright-line rules, and not leave so much discretion to enforcers. Second, the state of the economy now is different from what it was in 1981. It is now so concentrated that more radical action is required than even those laws allowed. Updated anti-merger laws, for instance, won't help us unwind companies that have already merged, and while the old antitrust law was very good on mergers, it didn't have the same strong structural solutions for already-existing monopolies that weren't engaged in obviously illegal conduct. Finally, we didn't face the unique threats of big data and big tech.

To address our current threats, Congress and statehouses should pass new laws banning companies from becoming too large in absolute terms, in terms of their market, and in terms of the economy. We *have* done this before, in particular sectors. No depository institution, for instance, is allowed to be larger than 10% of the market. What if we applied that same rule to all industries: no more than 10% or you're broken up? We could supplement market-share rules with size rules; we could require divestiture—or significantly higher taxes—for any company that grows larger than a certain absolute size or GDP percentage size.

Congress should also pass laws to break up companies by function. Glass-Steagall forced the separation of investment and depository institutions. The 1934 Air Mail Act broke off airlines from aircraft companies. We can apply the logic of the Air Mail Act and Glass-Steagall to other industries. For instance, we can decide that a search company cannot also be an ad company, or a store, or a map provider. A function-like divestiture rule would apply to companies over a certain size or dominance and likely be sector-specific. These new laws would serve as bulwarks against self-dealing and unfair business models, against the temptations that occur when one entity owns two unrelated companies and may want to use power in one area to engage in unfair business practices in another.

Addressing the particular threats of big tech will require reshaping old principles. Even after the behemoths have been broken up into subsidiary parts, some functions of Facebook, Google, and Amazon may be best designated as public utilities and regulated as such. We should require neutrality for all platforms, and ban Amazon, Facebook, Google, and Apple from using the data gleaned from their marketplaces to compete against the companies that use their services. We should ban them from using targeted ads, or at least in the aspects of their business that have become essential to our ability to communicate with each other in the online public sphere. With such a ban, some companies might become state-owned, like the post office or public library. Or they might become fee-based, like other essential infrastructure—water, transportation. Facebook, for instance, and its rivals in social media (which it will have, once it is broken up) could choose to charge $1 a month. They could be funded by non-targeted ads—Google keywords, for instance, do not require surveillance to work, and are more than sufficient to provide Google with a profit. Finally, Section 230 of the Communications Decency Act, as it is currently interpreted, allows big tech companies to avoid liability for everything that is shared on their sites—even the paid content—and it needs a total overhaul.

Taking these steps would mean that Facebook and Google would no longer be competitors against the news organizations they serve, and local news would have an opportunity to recoup the losses of the last decade. Companies dependent on Amazon and Google would have a chance to compete against each other instead of serving Google and Amazon—and democracy would have a fighting chance again.

At the same time, we need to outlaw the arbitration regime discussed in chapter 4 (there is a bill already passed in the House that would do that). We need to block common ownership by Wall Street, discussed in chapter 8, so that a few institutional investors don't control huge swaths of the economy. We must repeal laws that make it hard for workers to organize in solidarity with each other, like the 1947 Taft-Hartley Act, which banned secondary strikes. We need to pass publicly financed elections at all levels of government, either using the New York City model in which each small donation is amplified by public funds, or the Seattle model in which every voter gets a voucher they can use to support candidates for office, or—ideally—a combination of the two. We need to rewrite our corporate laws so that workers have a voice in decision making, and profit doesn't drive everything.

This may seem overwhelming, but the truth is that we are already on our way toward a new anti-monopoly moment, and the biggest hurdle is not identifying solutions, but overcoming passivity. That is already happening. When Democrats took over control of Congress in 2018, the Congressional Antitrust Subcommittee, led by David Cicilline of Rhode Island, started a major investigation and began holding hearings. Those hearings, in turn, seem to have helped spur state attorneys general around the country to begin their own investigations. Within a few months, a once-moribund area was suddenly lively.

Investigations may seem like weak sauce compared with actually breaking a company up, but action builds on itself, and creates its own energy. Federal investigations by Congress can spur the FTC; the FTC can spur states; major hearings can spur outrage; and outrage can lead to laws being changed. The key thing is that people get involved and antitrust returns to the center of politics.

Above all, we must remember a few basic anti-monopoly principles:

1. Open, competitive markets, working together with publicly provided services and neutral infrastructure, are necessary for economic liberty. There is no one-size-fits-all answer to every industry, but unregulated private monopoly poses a unique threat. Private corporations with too much power raise prices for consumers, depress wages for workers, choke off democracy, and regulate all of us.

2. To preserve rough economic and political equality, we should make it easier to organize people and harder to organize capital. It should be as easy to unionize, or to create a cooperative, as it is hard to merge goliaths.

3. It's better to err on the side of decentralized private power. Democratic governance is messy and will lead to mistakes, but corporate government will lead to tyranny.

11

—◆—

Nationalize or Decentralize?
Big Pharma and the Green New Deal

If you wanted to design a way to hurt, bankrupt, and kill as many Americans as possible using monopoly power, you might dream up the American healthcare industry. Or perhaps the global fossil fuel industry, a club of polluters, funded by big finance, that works as a machine to destroy democracy, health, and stability. Powerful solutions are already on the table to address the crises caused by these oligarchs: for example, Medicare for All and the Green New Deal. And so, while you were reading the last chapter about the tools available, you might have found yourself objecting, *Why break things up when we need to nationalize them?* But as I argue in this chapter, this question assumes a false binary: we should be nationalizing *and* decentralizing at the same time. Medicare for All, for instance, will be much more difficult to enact without vigorous anti-monopoly enforcement in the subsidiary health sectors of drugs and hospitals. The Green New Deal proposed by Congresswoman Alexandria Ocasio-Cortez and Senator Edward Markey calls for a national policy, but local, decentralized implementation. The best path forward is frequently, perhaps confoundingly, *both nationalization and decentralization,* not either/or.

HEALTHCARE: NATIONALIZE INSURANCE, DECENTRALIZE DRUGS AND HOSPITALS

"I am not boyfriend material," Shane Patrick Boyle wrote on Twitter. "I don't know what kind of material I am. I think, maybe, I am the material they use to make cheap mobile homes."[1] He was 48, a shaggy, bearded, blondish, ironic, sweet, Gen-X creative. Sly self-deprecation ran throughout his decade of social media posts. He was proud of hitching to New York City to be there for Stonewall's twenty-fifth anniversary in 1994, and of having been part of the creation of an artistic community in Houston. When he was in his twenties he founded Zine Fest Houston, a gathering for people to share obscure zines, and the Houston Area Comics Society. He adored female superheroes and regularly supported unknown female artists on Kickstarter and Indiegogo.

On New Year's Eve 2016, he tweeted, "Watch out 2016, we will be ready for you next time." He was living in his childhood home in Mena, Arizona, in order to take care of his sick mother, after decades in Houston. While in Mena, he amused himself by lining up his mother's dogs in alphabetical order to give them treats. On Facebook, he shared a lovely photo of his mother lying on a hospital bed, wearing a paper crown he had given her. The week she died, he posted a picture of the two of them standing side by side, wearing matching Superman T-shirts, a similarly bemused expression on each of their faces.

In February 2017, during his mother's last months, he also put up a GoFundMe page to raise money for insulin so he could treat his own diabetes. A few people donated, but it never gained traction. He was $50 short of raising what he needed when he died of diabetic ketoacidosis on March 18, less than a week after his mother's death. Mother and son were buried

together. He never got to shake his fist at 2017 as it slipped out
the door.

What kind of world allows something so senseless to happen?
Healthcare has traditionally occupied a separate moral realm in
economies. Every religious tradition treats medicine and heal-
ing as a special category, one in which moral obligations to the
patient must override any desire to make money. The Sanskrit
text *Charaka Saṃhitā*, a compendium of Ayurveda (Indian traditional medicine) written between 400 and 200 BCE, requires
doctors to put patients' welfare above their own financial interests. The ninth-century Muslim text *Adab al-Tabib* ("Morals
of the physician") lays out the ethical requirement to provide
medical care to the poor even if they cannot pay. Doctors in the
United States take a version of the ancient Greek Hippocratic
Oath, promising themselves to their patients in a solemn relationship. The command is even more specific when it comes to
drugs in the Jewish tradition. The *Shulkhan Arukh* (*Yoreh De'ah*
336:3) commands, "One who has medications, and another person is sick and needs them, it is forbidden to raise their prices
beyond what is appropriate." Pricing is a central part of morality. But the *Shulkhan Arukh* has been turned upside down:
the one who has medications now raises the prices above that
which is even imaginable. American and Canadian pharmaceutical companies make $515 billion a year—almost one-eighth
of the total amount of money spent by the federal government
every year. At the same time, the opioid crisis has shown how
pharmaceutical companies will push drugs that cause addiction
in order to create more customers. While drugs are supposed to
provide essential relief from pain, the business model used by
many drug companies leads to addiction and death, is frequently
based on fraud, and causes families unbearable physical and psy-
chic pain. A judge found that opioid seller Johnson & Johnson
built its wealth on false and dangerous marketing campaigns

that "caused exponentially increasing rates of addiction, overdose deaths."[2] Pfizer agreed to pay $2.2 billion to settle federal
charges that it illegally marketed drugs.[3] Eli Lilly paid $1.4 billion
in a settlement of charges that it promoted a drug for Alzhei-
mer's disease that was not yet approved for that use.[4] As large as
these judgments and settlements are, they will barely dent the
profitability of these companies. Meanwhile, it can cost $500 to
$900 a month for a basic supply of insulin, a drug whose un-
derlying structure has not changed significantly in a long time.
Diabetics are starving themselves, rationing themselves against
doctor's orders, and injecting themselves with outdated insulin.
Some people purposely allow themselves to get so sick that they
get a blood condition, which forces them to be taken to the
emergency room, where they can get treatment.

Big pharma claims it needs the profits for research into
lifesaving drugs, but the pretense falls apart on inspection.
Many new drugs on the market are "me too" drugs that add
marginal (if any) improvement over the current medicine on
the market. The costs of research for "me too" drugs are often
not prohibitive—they only have to be tested in clinical trials
against placebos. The companies then make the "me too" drugs
and use advertising and market power to make profits. The real
leader in drug innovation is the government: the National In-
stitutes of Health is leading the way on lifesaving research. One
study found that the NIH had contributed to every one of the
200-plus drugs approved by the Food and Drug Administration from 2010 through 2016.[5] Much of the NIH research was
related to the discovery of fundamental biological mechanisms.
This means that the NIH is doing the groundwork, while drug
companies make the money. Drug companies then plow that
money into politics, funding campaigns and hiring lobbyists.
Last year they spent a record $200 million on lobbying, work-

ing to make sure the government doesn't start regulating prices, blocking their mergers, or reforming patent law.

Unlike most of the monopolies I talk about in this book, built up by acquisition or growth, drug companies get their monopolies directly from the government, in the form of patents. The patent tradition developed when English kings in the fifteenth century started granting an exclusive right to sell something through a "letter patent." These grants became rife with corruption, and in 1624, the Statute of Monopolies was passed to restrict the king's power to grant monopolies. That statute decreed that the exclusive right to sell something could only last for 14 years, and could only be granted if there was something genuinely new created. Article I, Section 8, Clause 8 of the United States Constitution, now known as the Patent and Copyright Clause, grew out of that tradition, and gives Congress authority to: "promote the progress of science and useful arts, by securing for limited times to authors and inventors the exclusive right to their respective writings and discoveries." Modern patent law, developed under this clause, requires the government to give a monopoly, the exclusive right to sell, to companies or individuals who prove that they have created or discovered a new, useful, and nonobvious machine, manufacture, composition of matter, or process.

Just as it was in the early seventeenth century, patent abuse is again rampant. The exclusive right to sell gives the holder of the patent the power to set all the terms of the market, including the exclusive right to set the price. To grab this power, drug companies patent (monopolize) every molecule they can. Once they hold a patent, the companies engage in all kinds of innovative exercises to protect patents from running out. They make slight modifications to old drugs, or declare new inventions in delivery devices, as a way to extend their patent power.

The process is called "evergreening." Pharmaceutical companies will pay companies that produce generics to delay entry, a technique called "pay for delay," giving a potential competitor a cut of the monopolistic prices being charged.

On top of these official, government-granted molecular monopolies, is an unofficial, merger-created drug company cartel. For instance, the insulin market is controlled by a club that keeps prices far above the cost of producing the drug. In the last 20 years, Eli Lilly, Sanofi, and Novo Nordisk kept buying up rivals until they owned 99% of the insulin market.[6] As they came to dominate the market, the cost of insulin almost tripled.[7] Eli Lilly's profit margin is 35%—you aren't supposed to see 35% profit margins in a competitive market. Whether it is an explicit deal keeping prices high, or unspoken winks and nods, something is going on, because Lilly, Novo Nordisk, and Sanofi are not seriously competing on price.[8]

Remember how Mylan Pharmaceuticals raised the price of its EpiPen by 400%? It could do that precisely because it held nearly 90% of the market. EpiPen had a patent, as do Eli Lilly, Novo Nordisk, and Sanofi, but market concentration is a problem with pharma even where government-granted monopolies don't exist. Between 2010 and 2015, almost one in five generic drugs "saw at least one price increase of 100 percent or more, and some saw increases of 1,000 percent or more."[9]

Monopolization is compounded by the unique role of drugs. In the best of circumstances, the drug market is never going to operate like the market for sneakers or beer; people are always in crisis when seeking medical care, and as far back as 1979 the FTC recognized that competition does not work well when the user does not choose and the prescriber does not pay.[10]

Breaking up big pharma, therefore, requires anti-monopolism squared: major patent reform and breaking up the producers of key drugs. Both would lead to vastly increased competition. Every study that has been done tells us that competition has a huge impact on the prices of medical products and services. When a generic drug enters the market, the price drops significantly. It still doesn't drop to zero, because the generic company wants to make money, too, and generics are increasingly consolidating as well. If only one generic enters the market, the price drops a little—and if three generics enter it, the price drops much more.[11] Two-way competition isn't nearly as price-impactful as four-way competition.

It should be harder to get patents, evergreening should be illegal, and we need to enforce laws against pay-for-delay tactics, using maximum penalties instead of agreeing to settlements that essentially become the cost of doing business. And we needn't stop there: the government can provide competition directly, a "public option" for drugs. Senator Elizabeth Warren, for instance, has proposed a plan under which the federal government would produce cheap generic drugs to compete in key markets. To stop the wink-and-nod price-gouging among alleged drug competitors, we should force divestiture so that there are always many competitors in a market. We should also stop vertical integration and related deals between companies, so that drug companies and drugstores don't conspire against purchasers to raise prices.

But wait—what about single payer healthcare? Wouldn't that solve a significant part of this problem, without patent reform and antitrust? Sometimes known as Medicare for All, single payer means the government doesn't provide healthcare, but rather pays bills submitted by private healthcare providers. It would ensure that diabetics like Shane would have their medical bills paid for by the government. Single payer healthcare *should* also drive down prices significantly, because the government would set the rates for medical procedures, and have negotiating power to push for cheaper drugs.

Here's the rub: driving down prices is much harder when the government is negotiating with a powerful monopoly than when it is negotiating in a competitive market. Healthcare expert Phillip Longman has written several persuasive articles about consolidation in the drug market, and the healthcare industry more generally, and the risk that this consolidation poses to nationalizing plans. If a single payer plan was enacted without additionally addressing the monopoly problem, he argues, government could end up effectively subsidizing big pharma, and big hospitals, and keep paying enormously high prices. Those costs would shift back to the public—in the form of taxes.[12]

Single payer care is necessary for humane reasons, and for the extraordinary reduction in administrative costs. But why not demand both single payer and breaking up drug monopolies? Why risk skyrocketing prices that could cause single payer care to collapse on itself? The same logic holds for the other big consolidated regimes within healthcare: hospitals, medical device companies, insurance companies, and drugstores.

Hospitals—for-profit and nonprofit—have been on a consolidation spree, combining at electric speed. In the last few years, UnitedHealthcare bought up a major healthcare payments firm and over 300 doctors' clinics, all while being the largest insurer in the country. The hospital merger spree led to a single company, Ascension and Providence St. Joseph Health, owning 200 hospitals in 27 states. Twenty years ago, half of all community hospitals were part of a big multi-provider system; now two-thirds are.[13] As hospitals consolidate, their profits go up. Hospital mergers lead to prices that are 10% to 40% higher. And as one expert recently told the *New York Times*, "evidence from three decades of hospital mergers does not support the claim that consolidation improves quality."[14] Instead, consolidation hurts patients. Hospitals that dominate their local market charge much higher prices than hospitals in a competitive market, because they negotiate for higher prices with insurers, who feel they have no choice but to include a dominant hospital. Unsurprisingly, the hospitals with the highest prices earn the largest profits—whether or not they are for-profit or not-for-profit. The difference? A nonprofit hospital gets state and federal tax breaks for being a charity.

To illustrate the monopoly problem, Longman compares the imagined government-run insurance negotiations with one of these hospitals to existing Department of Defense negotiations with one of the big defense contractors. The DOD is an indisputably public program with no private rivals, and has struggled to keep down costs in contracting, now that there are fewer than five major defense contractors, down from over 65 a few decades ago, before a merger spree.

In theory, the DOD has enormous bargaining power; defense contractors care deeply about those federal dollars and should be doing everything they can to win those contracts, including pushing down prices. In practice, that power vanishes with the monopolization in the contracting industry, as contractors can essentially dictate how much they want to be paid. That power will be even more diminished if the government is negotiating with geographically bound hospitals. Longman writes, "If the Department of Health and Human Services tried to contract with the Cleveland Clinic or the University of Pittsburgh Medical Center to provide medical services under a single payer plan, it would have no more market power than our 'single payer' Pentagon procurement system does when it comes to bargaining with sole-source defense contractors."[15] The University of Pittsburgh Medical Center can give a take-it-or-leave-it price, and the government, bound to take it, will pay whatever Pittsburgh wants to charge, far more than whatever it costs to provide the service.

The same consolidation—and price-gouging—is playing out with medical devices. The "medtech" market is governed by a club of five companies, which make up 94% of the market.[16] Drugstores have also consolidated, from a diverse collection of neighborhood pharmacists to three megastores that all have relationships with the drug companies. Nearly 80% of Americans, 180 million people, rely on CVS Health, Express Scripts, or OptumRx to get their prescriptions.[17]

The concentration/cartelization of all these health-related sectors means that monopoly problems don't go away even if you support total nationalization of health, getting rid of for-profit and nonprofit hospitals and replacing them with government-run hospitals. For example, the United States could directly provide healthcare, as it does at the Veterans Affairs hospitals. Instead of paying the bills to Mount Sinai Hospital—as it would on the single payer plan—it could run Mount Sinai Hospital. There are good reasons to consider such an approach, or at least an expansion of the VA. But unless the government also manufactures the drugs, produces the devices, and grows the vegetables for the food eaten at the facilities, large, private-sector providers could hike up costs; they, too, need to be broken apart. Even within the VA, there is always some aspect of running the hospital that will involve private industry and can be controlled by monopolies, whether it is the drugs, the medical devices, or the sheets patients use.

In short, no matter what nationalizing reform we pursue in healthcare, anti-monopoly actions are necessary. Antitrust within and across industries will both enable competition *and* make it easier to pass national programs to provide better healthcare for everyone.[18] All of these can go hand in hand with single payer care. In other words, we need a massive national overhaul of private insurance, but also a reshaping of the drug market to make it more competitive, open, and decentralized.

Breaking up these private kingdoms is not a policy designed to replace Medicare for All, but a policy that would make single payer healthcare far less expensive.

ENERGY

When you use the word "monopoly," Standard Oil and the board game spring to mind. The name conjures the image of an octopus, one sticky, rapacious arm curled around a statehouse, another around the Capitol Building, three others crushing the steel, copper, and shipping companies, and a greedy tentacle raised to take over the White House. And then, other images may come to mind: Standard Oil as a snake about to eat other oil companies, and Standard Oil as a wealthy man in a tuxedo, astride an oil barrel, holding up the globe in one hand, a light in another, piles of cash in little loot bags at his feet. These cartoons of the Gilded Age echo across the last century.[19]

When Standard Oil was broken into parts in 1911, it became a symbol not of corporate tyranny but of hope, of the potential power of government to restrain monopoly power and reassert public power over private corporations.

Now, unlike in 1911, the world is burning: fossil fuel tycoons are making money as their industry causes floods and fires and conditions that spread diseases. Many of our cities are at risk as once-in-a-century floods have become routine, causing sewage to leak onto main streets. People are sick, dying, scared, choking *right now* because of climate events.

Ever since antitrust law was decimated in the early 1980s,

the fossil fuel industry has become re-concentrated. As in healthcare, much of that concentration has been created not by building fortresses around particular products, but by creating a web of vertically integrated companies. The companies are frequently described as engaged in business "from pit to pump"; a single company can own extraction teams, refining plants, storage facilities, and stations. The pit-to-pump club may be better described as pit-to-politician, as fuel companies have created powerful political arms to push back against anything that would shake profits.

The fossil fuel business is not a large club. In 2017, the Carbon Disclosure Project showed that over half of *all* global emissions in the last 20 years have come from 25 corporations.[20] Some of this concentration is justified in the name of efficiency; extraction, at its best, requires an enormous amount of investment and money and can't easily be split up into a truly decentralized system. Although that is partly true (and a non-climate-change reason why renewable energy markets are preferable), as with most efficiencies-of-scale arguments, the case is often overstated.

There are definitely significant economies of scale when it comes to the ability to shape politics. ExxonMobil, Chevron, Shell, BP, ConocoPhillips, Peabody Energy, Consol Energy, and Arch Coal are extremely active in lobbying, campaign contributions, and think-tank funding. Because those companies are so large and powerful, they have been able to fight against any attempts to hold them liable for the damage they have caused, the misinformation they have shared and the science they have fought to keep *un*shared, and the irreversible climate change they have caused. With roughly $2 billion spent directly on climate change lobbying between 2000 to 2016, big oil, utilities, and the transportation industry outspent climate change opponents ten to one.[21]

They have also, as the *Guardian* reported last year, taken over funding in certain fields of academia. The energy programs at Harvard, Stanford, and MIT are heavily funded by Shell, Chevron, and BP. David Koch, the oil billionaire, gave over $150 million to MIT. UC Berkeley's Energy Biosciences Institute has given BP power over which research projects are funded, in exchange for $500 million. Stanford's Global Climate and Energy Project is supported by ExxonMobil. As two Stanford students wrote in protest, "Fossil fuel interests—oil, gas, and coal companies, fossil-fueled utilities, and fossil fuel investors—have colonized nearly every nook and cranny of energy and climate policy research in American universities, and much of energy science too. And they have done so quietly, without the general public's knowledge."[22]

The fossil fuel companies' vertical expansion ensures that other companies have a vested interest in maintaining their grip on power. Coal, gas, and oil are prioritized by the grid. If private utilities have a choice between natural gas and wind, they will choose natural gas, because of our broken anti-monopoly laws, which allow the utilities to have financial relationships with and to profit from fossil fuel infrastructure building.

Utilities currently play a central role in blocking renewable energy, because they make most of their money by charging a "reasonable rate of return" on building the infrastructure that supports fossil fuels.[23] The profit center is not actually in selling electricity, but in building pipelines and power plants, and charging consumers for it. The build-out of 1.63 million miles of fossil fuel pipelines crossing America—six times as many miles of natural gas pipeline as miles of national highway—is fueled in part by the incentives of the utilities. When renewable, decentralized energy is prioritized—where individuals, small institutions, and small communities can contribute to the energy flowing through the grid—the for-profit utilities no longer make the same profits. As environmental expert Dave Roberts explains, "For utilities dependent on building power plants and power lines to make a return on investment, the new decentralized, low-infrastructure electricity system is anathema."[24]

Duke Energy, for instance, is the largest utility in the country, serving over seven million customers, with an energy portfolio that includes only 2% renewables. It has monopoly control over the energy sector and has actively fought competition from renewables. It has also fought net metering—systems that connect solar panels and local power generators to a grid, allowing customers to transfer excess power to the public grid, and in so doing offsetting the cost of the power they take from the utility.

Net metering would reduce Duke Energy's profits, and since the growth of community solar is tied to net metering, renewable energy actively threatens the business model, whereby utilities present weak public regulators with costs and demand that the public pay for building infrastructure. Duke Energy has fought for higher monthly charges, and can do so because it plays such a central role in the political economy of the states in which it operates that it dictates, instead of responds, to regulators. This kind of conflict of interest is a classic monopoly problem: while we allow for public utilities to operate as monopolies, we should generally not allow those utilities to engage in any other activity than providing the good that they have been granted monopoly power to provide.

I don't take seriously the question of whether we must switch to renewables: we must. Our planet is at stake. Solar, wind, and geothermal energy, and power from animal waste, are better for human health and the health of our climate. Wind, solar, and geothermal energy are all available everywhere, with different strengths in different places. Most states could meet their *existing* electrical needs with their own solar, wind, water, and geothermal sources of energy. With the exception of major dams and major offshore wind turbines, most renewable energy is modular. Every apartment building can have solar and geothermal sources of energy; every house can be weatherized; almost every town can have wind or water energy.

And so, since the question is not whether but how to switch to renewable energy, we run into a version of the healthcare question: nationalize or decentralize? One might ask, Why are we even talking about antitrust when what we need is to remove all subsidies for fossil fuels and replace them with an aggressive, top-down subsidization of renewable energy projects? Why talk decentralization when we need a big government project?

Assume we create a massive national program to transform our energy sector. Imagine a national Department of Green Energy (DGE), like the Department of Defense, but whose job it is to ensure the energy security of the country. It could do it in one of two ways: closely working with a few big companies to produce renewable energy, or using national power to subsidize millions of local producers, rigorously enforcing antitrust.

In the first model, we ignore anti-monopoly, and ask the DGE to contract out. Inevitably, the DGE would end up working with companies like Solar City (Elon Musk's effort to rent out solar panels from a massive, centralized, subsidized company) or ExxonMobil's renewable energy division. We would anticipate that the DGE would quickly come to work with just a handful of contractors. For instance, Royal Dutch Shell—one of the biggest oil and gas companies in the world—recently announced it is rebranding its consumer-facing company as "Shell Energy," emphasizing that it will provide energy from many different sources, including renewable, starting with a consumer base of 700,000 homes that will use renewable power. Shell Energy would quickly line up to be a preferred contractor with the DGE.

As has happened with the Department of Defense, the contractors would likely come to have far too much power over national policy, and their incentives might not align with those of the public.[25] As Matt Stoller and Lukas Kunce wrote in a chilling story about the monopoly weaknesses of the military-industrial complex, a 2018 Department of Defense report found that for critical military items—high-voltage cables, fittings for ships, inputs for missiles, tent materials—there are frequently only one or two domestic producers. These producers, in turn, frequently depend on foreign products. The report found that "China is the single or sole supplier for a number of specialty chemicals used in munitions and missiles."[26] Monopolization in the private sector of suppliers has led to a fragile system whereby the Department of Defense, the most national of national agencies, is dependent on Chinese contractors with close ties to the Chinese government.[27]

So let's look at option two: the DGE could work with anti-monopoly as a core value, along with—not opposed to—other core values.

The Green New Deal Resolution is a remarkable example of what such an anti-monopoly federal policy can look like. Decentralization is at its heart. Subsection (N) of the Green New Deal Resolution declares that it should be the policy of the United States to "ensure a commercial environment where every businessperson is free from unfair competition and domination by domestic or international monopolies."

The Green New Deal prioritizes "community-defined projects and strategies" and aims to "spur massive growth in clean manufacturing." It lays out a vision of "working collaboratively with farmers and ranchers," of supporting family farming, and of building sustainable, decentralized food systems. This is similar to the New Deal's Soil Conservation and Domestic Allotment Act, which paid farmers to plant beans and grasses and to restore the soil after the ravages of the Dust Bowl, and to the wildly successful Rural Electrification Act, which provided loans to farming cooperatives to generate electricity for their rural areas.

The Green New Deal will require, by its own terms, community grants, public banks, and other public financing systems to finance the decentralized green energy sector boom it imagines. To achieve Green New Deal goals, the Resolution requires investments to "deepen and diversify industry in local and regional economies, and build wealth and community ownership." It demands "democratic and participatory processes that are inclusive of and led by frontline and vulnerable communities and workers to plan, implement, and administer the Green New Deal mobilization at the local level." It demands union jobs.

It also requires some top-down programs of direct national investment, like investment in high-speed rail, hazardous waste cleanup, and research programs. Like the original New Deal, which created the Tennessee Valley Authority, which in turn directly hired people and built power stations in the desperately poor Tennessee Valley, the Green New Deal will directly hire people. What it won't do is allow Elon Musk or Shell to control the process. It represents the best of both nationalization and decentralization.

＊

Should we nationalize or decentralize? Big national solutions that ignore antitrust do so at their peril. In almost any industry, there is an option to nationalize, and in some instances that might make sense. But more often, a successful, sustainable model requires some national program in combination with a principle of decentralization.

12

Moral Markets

The other kind of freedom is the freedom to take
care of ourselves and of each other.

—Wendell Berry

It's an early February morning, and I am at a family-owned
greasy spoon diner in Central Harlem where the manager has
a loud, friendly, teasing relationship with most of the regulars.
He is a Mexican-American man in his midfifties who knows
his customers well and enjoys insulting them. The phone starts
ringing repeatedly, and he works as he picks up each call, the
phone cord dancing over and under orders of eggs and coffee.
Each time, he ends the call with, "Not today!" The delivery man
isn't working, and one of the regulars asks the manager if he'd
be willing to deliver the food himself. The manager laughs, says
"Never," and tells this story: A man once drove up just outside the diner and ordered, asking for delivery. The manager
could see him outside, but had no one to deliver, and decided
he didn't feel like walking outside. The customer waited 45
minutes.

"You wouldn't even walk outside?," the customer asks.

"Nope. It's not all about the money," the manager says.

"But isn't the customer always right?"

The manager doubles over with laughter. "Not here! Not
here! You've come to the wrong place!" The story finished, he
grins and takes another call.

That manager comes across as a free man. He works extremely hard, he cares about the money, he cares about the operation, but he also cares about his freedom to make choices—some idiosyncratic—that make his restaurant his. The same freedom that allows him to say, "I would prefer not to," as Bartleby famously did in Herman Melville's short story "Bartleby, the Scrivener," also allows him to treat his employees with respect and give them days off.[1] That same freedom is an engine for his own motivation and drive. He likes to be able to make his own decisions, to turn down customers, to make the menu. If someone comes in and bilks him on the check, he can choose to call the cops, or he can choose not to. The customer is *not* always right. At the heart of the owner's laughter is a fundamental insistence on his autonomy; a saying that includes the word *always* is itself a rejection of our total, messy, wonderful, discretion-filled humanity.

His neighbors to the east, the managers and franchisees at IHOP and Domino's and McDonald's, have none of that freedom. They are governed by strict handbooks setting out protocols and procedures, outlining how the restaurant must look and feel. They don't have the freedom to make judgments about how to deal with peculiar situations, but instead must follow rules from above. These restaurants work on a franchise model that closely resembles that of Tyson's chicken farmers: the restaurants are independently owned, so the owners take on the debt and risk, but lack the freedom to make many decisions. An Indeed.com post about being a general manager at a chain restaurant could apply to millions of jobs in America today: "Not a good place to work if you're not built in the culture, too many issues, you're just a baby sitter with no control of your job, too much micro managing."[2]

Wage laborers also have more or less freedom depending on

the structure of power. New York cable electricians who used to work a few miles south of the Harlem diner know that well. They remember working for Time Warner Cable before 2014, when TWC had competitors. It was a time when they felt their worth and felt sufficiently secure and dignified in their jobs to treat each other with humanity. The workplace was unionized by IBEW Local 3. The electricians felt respected and had enough money to take vacations, care for their homes, provide for their families. They knew that if they did their work, their salaries would increase, and they had good benefits. They recall fondly the pride they felt in their work and the joy they took in their fellowship with each other. Their union regularly disagreed with the company owners, and they certainly never got everything they wanted, but they knew that when they negotiated, their demands mattered. They knew they had some power.

Now, after the merger with Charter Communications, and over three years of striking, the company doesn't even try to bargain; the new entity, Spectrum counts on its workers gradually losing their will to strike as they become poorer, less powerful, and less and less visible.[3]

Every human being deserves at least a minimum of freedom in her personal and professional life. If the structure of an economy denies people the dignity of meaningful choice—both in matters moral and in those of personal expression—they may lash out, or they may curl inward, disappear, and disengage. If you have no power, anger can give you the feeling of being able to change something; and disengagement means you don't have to face the lack of your power. The ability to choose—or not choose—is necessary for a moral life, and it isn't just located at the polling booth or in community life: it is a state of being responsible and powerful that must exist to some degree in every part of life.

Our current society has a shrinking number of unionized workers collectively coming together to negotiate for good treatment. Instead, we have a growing number of temporary, non-union workers who are locked out of opportunities through non-compete clauses and corporate concentration. As a result, people are also locked out of structures that allow for solidarity and compassion. We have a collapse in the number of businesses like the one described at the beginning of this chapter, and a growing number of IHOP managers, middlemen, and workers subject to the arbitrary power of the one or two bosses who control them, monopolists who have all the money and all the power.

With this increasing chickenization comes the decreasing possibility of moral action and human connection. Many business owners and workers who look free are in fact overburdened by debt, reliant on a platform, losing their ability to speak up, and surveilled and trapped. Each subservient moment amplifies the next, until subservience is a constitutional habit.

But the inverse can also be true: each free moment amplifies the next, until freedom is a constitutional habit. A free worker, grappling with his local union on whether to strike or not, will necessarily generate dozens of conversations about power and class, which then spill over into politics. A free business owner in a community, wrestling with the hard moral choices of business life, also generates spaces of freedom for those around her—on a street with ten different breakfast establishments, customers and workers can both choose the restaurant that treats its workers better. When most businesses are independently owned, it creates millions of nodes of freedom, the restaurant owner making choices, the workers making choices, the clientele making choices—millions of moments when human agency comes into play.

We should aim for an economy in which the people who

make things, who buy things, who sell things, and who interact with each other do so from positions of dignity, with enough power to know that they matter. It should be possible for all actors—the buyer, the seller, the worker—to play their roles with integrity. The moral freedom of the medium-sized shop-keeper, producer, and business owner, of the farmworker and the electrician, is essential to the moral fabric of a democratic community. Public morality is a muscle that can atrophy—to ask people to be free once a year, on voting day, but governed in their economic life (while being told they are free) leads to cognitive disarray, as well as a tendency toward paranoia. It is also a muscle that can be strengthened.

Moral action, except as a form of window dressing, is close to impossible when most business is run by Wall Street; and the rare moments of business heroism shouldn't blind us to the sociopathy of the structure. Even giving investors the benefit of the doubt, financialization makes love and care and freedom and creativity and quirkiness difficult. Compassion is extremely difficult at a distance in the best of circumstances—it becomes nearly impossible when the human narrative is masked and when one chicken farmer's life is reduced to a few extra cents in an investment fund.

When people are allowed to amass great pools of capital, one of two things happens: The logic of investment overcomes the moral sensibilities of the people who hold the investments, and investment agents' instructions to maximize profit sever the moral relationship between people and their impact on the world. Or the logic of power overcomes the moral sensibilities of those who hold too much power, and they start govern-ing from a place of whimsy and self-importance, disconnected from human reality and unable to honestly perceive the world over which they trample. Both outcomes lead to destruction, instability, and cruelty.

In case there is any doubt, I strongly support living wage minimums and worker protections and stiff penalties for environmental and other harms. Human nature is vast and weird and wonderful and doesn't tend to the universal good: people will always be selfish, narrow, parochial, petty; freedom doesn't necessarily bring out the best in every person at every time. So it is critically important to demand basic rules of the road to ban cruelty, laws that create a floor of basic human treatment below which no company can go. But human nature doesn't tend to the universal bad, either. *Without* freedom in the workplace, people don't have space to be funny, wise, loving, and self-sacrificing, and to build community. You can't legislate against Scroogelike tendencies, but it is equally foolish to imagine we are all Scrooge. The key to human flourishing is the building of structures that support more loving and solidarity and less pettiness.

In order to allow for an economy in which people bring their full selves, we should actively encourage local control; a business owner who works where she lives will confront *as a human* the impacts of her decisions on the people she lives around—not just as a matter of shame, but as a matter of conscience. Instead of accommodating Wall Street owners who use spreadsheets to justify death and poisoning, we should encourage local business owners who take more responsibility for their actions.

We should build a market economy with lots of room for worker-owned and producer-owned cooperatives, where lots of small producers or farmers can come together to share costs and parts of production. The co-op model has been at the heart of the progressive vision for over 140 years. However, it is very difficult to achieve in a monopolized and financialized economy, because the monopolists squeeze them out, or Wall Street buys them out, and they become servants to the debt they owe.

We should aim for a market with tens of thousands of these co-ops, and medium-sized companies with unionized workforces, local banking and local entrepreneurship; an economy that starts ground-up, instead of one that is dictated top-down by a few billionaires and their political-economic institutions. I don't think most business owners go into business to maximize profit; I think they want to make a profit, create something, feel a sense of ownership and the satisfaction of responsibility, and enjoy the fruits of their labor. However, our current economic system, which rewards monopolization and financialization, doesn't leave room for the inventor or producer or farmer who wants to make money but not necessarily maximize it; and that's a tragedy. It rewards those who try to squeeze every cent out of workers and crowd out every opponent as if markets are a kind of terrible, heartless war. Our current fight about the kind of economy we want is necessarily a fight about human nature: people can be humane and compassionate, but need structures that support these tendencies.

THE DEEP PRICE OF CYNICISM

To have moral markets, one must first believe that moral markets are worth aiming for, that they are possible and desirable. Many on today's left and right reject this concept, but for most of human history, economists and philosophers have believed in moral markets. For instance, the Baron de Montesquieu, a political philosopher whose influence on the framers of America's Constitution was unmatched, believed that markets could bring out the best in people. It wasn't a Pollyannaish view—he also worried that some market-related cultures, including commodification, could be dangerous—but he saw political and economic freedom as absolutely intertwined. The economist Adam Smith, who is often cited in defense of a purely mechanistic understanding of markets, in fact believed that human contact and connection, through markets, were engines of empathy.

Even the influential right-wing economist Friedrich Hayek was committed to meaningful choice as a precursor to moral action. For Hayek, choice in the commercial sphere enables morality. He wrote, "It is only where the individual has choice, and its inherent responsibility, that he has occasion to affirm existing values, to contribute to their further growth, and to earn moral merit."[4] Hayek worried that systems with too much centralization transformed men into bureaucrats, taking them out of their capacity as decision makers and planners who try, fail, and thereby learn, and turning them into watchers of the system—working watchers, but essentially passive. One of the essential reasons for his support for the free market was the level of engagement it required.

We no longer have such a consensus on this issue. The modern conservatives who claim to admire these men have rejected their premises, and argue that the perfect market is a "morally free zone."[5] Markets are only designed to create stuff efficiently—efficiently enough that they raise one's standard of living and thus, in the words of the hugely influential libertarian Murray Rothbard, permit "man the leisure to cultivate the very qualities of civilization that distinguish him from the brutes."[6] This is dystopian stuff: it is like saying that we can have a moral life in one tiny corner, but not where we spend at least eight hours a day.

For today's neoliberal economists, market freedom does not mean moral action or thought in the commercial realm, it only frees the buyer and seller from state interference; the only morality in a market lies in cheaper consumer goods. Efficiency has become more than a value, it's become something approaching an unhealthy, elite obsession. The slightest risk that consumer goods prices *might* rise because of a merger is weighed against all the other values of an economy. Time and again, keeping consumer prices low has been treated as not just the most important metric, but the only metric.

The neoliberal economists don't reject the importance of people developing moral lives—in which we are kind, compassionate, and caring. But such lives exist entirely outside of the market. The money freed up by the market can be privately used to care for others, but inside the market, where a moral choice conflicts with increased profits, profits must always come first. Eric Posner, a law professor at the University of Chicago, exemplifies this belief. He compares *It's a Wonderful Life*, in which a local banker cares about more than his own bottom line, to *The Handmaid's Tale*, because both impose what he considers narrow, parochial, and dangerously moral approaches on market choices.[7]

The current structure of markets, propped up by neoliberal thought, depends on the belief that people are above all else consumers, and that their collection of idiosyncratic wants and needs and hopes and fears can be understood in consumer terms. The job of the economy, imagined as a kind of natural biological fact, is to produce cheap goods. As a result, freedom and dignity and humor and love and connection have become second-level values: they serve consumer needs. A person is a worker in order to be a consumer, and a person is a citizen in order to be a consumer. This simplistic economic model is attractive because of its radical reductiveness and the difficulty of arguing outside of it. If one says, for instance, that a person wants to spend time in their community, the economist will cheerfully nod and explain that "communing" is a form of consumer good that people can seek and purchase. But calling human connection a form of consumption does violence to language and experience.

This rejection of market morality is not an exclusively right-wing view. In fact, many on the modern left agree. The difference is that while the right celebrates the model's efficiency, to some on the left, the model makes market exchange itself morally irredeemable. In other words, all markets are inherently immoral, so if we *must* have markets to make shoes, chairs, and tablets, it doesn't matter how they are structured—strong ground rules are the best we can hope for.

In Harvard Law professor Michael Sandel's 2012 book, *What Money Can't Buy*, he concludes that markets on the whole play a negative force in modern society and moral and civic life. Sandel argues that what he calls "market values and market reasoning" have recently intruded far more aggressively into arenas of life that were once seen as sacrosanct. Sandel claims that when something enters into the marketplace it becomes a thing that we value for its exchange, and not for itself. For Sandel, "markets" become a shorthand for "price," and pricing is bad for us. He argues that the act of putting a price on things changes how we value them, and how we value each other.

He uses the example of the woman who sold advertising rights on her forehead, in the form of a tattoo, to an online gaming site. Selling her skin changed her relationship to her body. Sandel also argues that in child-rearing, procreation, civic life, and military endeavors, market reasoning erodes the value of the thing we seek. These are areas of life in which "markets don't belong," he says, and they corrupt the things themselves—"markets leave their mark."[8] These are fairly uncontroversial claims. But Sandel's real target is markets themselves, which he says lead to commodification across the board. We experience commodified things differently than we do uncommodified things, and the very existence of markets threatens democratic life. Markets threaten to destroy the institutions of democratic life by repurposing them for private gain. Another

theorist, Richard Dagger, put it this way: while "markets are fine in their place," they are not fine "when they spill into, and corrupt, other parts of life."[9]

Sandel and Dagger are wrong. They are confusing "market" with commodification, financialization, and monopolization. Society should clearly make rules to prohibit certain activities, including the sale of skin space. But we don't have to accept a mandate of maximizing profits, or to accept that our role in any market is primarily that of consumer. There is a gulf a mile wide between profit seeking and profit maximization. The former has been part of markets for all of human history, and so long as we allow any corner of life to have markets, it will continue to be; the latter is a modern perversion. Conflating profit seeking and profit maximization is like conflating a marriage in which sex is valued with a marriage that maximizes sex at the cost of all else; the former is healthy, the latter is dystopic. A market is a social human activity, and we should discourage any market forms that strip it of its social and human aspect. Markets do not have to involve distant Wall Street owners pushing for every scrap, penny, and ounce of extraction.

In Sandel's world, we are left with two choices: simply accept the idea that one of the most essential ways that we interact in the world is going to be soul crushing and devoid of all love, connection, and humanity, or flee the market and nationalize the production of everything, from shoes to toothpaste, and trust that a national government can deliver those products.

Sandel is not wrong that *regardless* of whether markets can be improved or not, there is still value in spaces existing separate from consumption. Public and private nonmarket spaces tap into separate parts of ourselves and offer different ways of interaction, allowing for celebrations of the plural parts of being human. When it comes to truly public places—public education, public streets, public infrastructure, public mails,

public libraries—there is a strong reason that they should be shielded from all business as fully as possible. We want jurors and voters and school board members to put the public interest above all else in their public roles; but they can have private roles in which they seek to put themselves and family first, have a secure, well-paid job with good benefits, and feel dignity in their workspaces. But establishing the need for nonmarket spaces, as Sandel does persuasively, should not mean that we abandon the project of making markets as open and compassionate as possible.

Sandel's approach is dangerous because it closes down an arena of moral action and redirects activism away from breaking up big corporations. It makes us ignore market-structure problems. If we treat markets as a kind of necessary infectious disease that one must cordon off, instead of institutions that can be wonderful or corrupt depending on how they are structured, we stop trying to fix them. And while a few people think the state should make shoes and grow carrots, most people—including myself—imagine most of economic life happening through private exchange.

The bottom line is that there is no escaping the moral nature of all markets. Every market must be structured by somebody, and the structure will necessarily tend to result in a particular outcome, which can be judged by the people to be more or less moral based on their understanding of the term. The question is not *whether* morality, but *which* morality.

THE MORAL ECONOMY AND
THE IDEA OF AMERICA

Most of this book is about what happens when markets are so concentrated and dysfunctional that monopolies overtake politics and courts and schools, crush people's spirits, inflame racism, create more poverty and inequality, destroy journalism,

and elevate a few men (and even fewer women) to powerful, unaccountable positions governing us. Obviously, it is urgent that we stop this trend, using antitrust, among other tools.

But we should aim our sights higher than just creating not-terrible markets; we should seek to enable markets that are actually part of our freedom, spaces for creativity, compassion, and warmth. Anti-monopolism is not just a way station on a quest to get rid of markets altogether, but an essential component of a free society.

Achieving a moral market is a big task, and though a moral economy may never be wholly achieved, it is always worth fighting to approach it. We shouldn't give up on equality, or on the cultivation and protection of a vibrant, morally engaged citizenry. Part of the liberty that the founders of this country sought in the American Revolution was the liberty to engage directly with each other in the commercial sphere, without being directed from above by a giant multinational corporation like the British East India Company. Madison and Jefferson believed that the structure of a political economy, and the activities and independence that it allowed or did not, had a huge effect on the character, thinking, and actions of citizens.[10]

As journalist Barry Lynn recently testified in front of the Senate Judiciary Committee, the founders of the country were committed both to "rough economic equality" among citizens and to freedom in economic affairs. Lynn argued that Madison saw the right to be free from arbitrary commercial power to be an essential right, and essential to just government. He quoted Madison: "[t]hat is not a just government . . . where arbitrary restrictions, exemptions, and monopolies deny to part of its citizens that free use of their faculties, and free choice of their occupations, which not only constitute their property in the general sense of the word; but are the means of acquiring property strictly so called."[11]

Anti-monopoly laws were seen as providing democratic and civic freedom in a way that enabled vigorous, engaged, moral citizens for most of the nineteenth and twentieth centuries.[12] Most observers assumed that anti-monopoly laws were designed to ensure that a market made up of small- and medium-sized companies could thrive, and that a decentralized market was inherently preferable to a highly concentrated one.[13] The goals of this preferred structure were economic, political, social, and moral.

We should treat the market sphere as an absolutely foundational sphere of freedom, and be very concerned about markets that are governed by monopolies. One way to think about it, as a friend of mine does, is that we need a "fuck off" economy—an economy where everyone always knows they can say "fuck off" to their boss, and still survive. Just knowing that it is possible to leave operates like a magic power, and changes people's relationship to the world, knowing they hold a power they can always choose to use. Work will always be an essential part of most people's lives, and my hope is that we can come to envision the workplace—whether of the business owner or the worker—as a place of relative freedom and potential moral action.

Freedom is no easy matter in a mass industrialized society. One of the most consequential political philosophers of the early twentieth century, Louis Brandeis, struggled with how to reconcile modern industrial economies with self-government.[14] To that end, he promoted engagement, dissent, disagreement, and contestation, and the support of institutions that enabled all of these practices, which he understood to be essential to freedom and citizenship and the cultivation of character.[15] Brandeis focused on the structure and nature of power, the relationship between rules and civic flourishing, and the relationship between human flourishing and civic flourishing.[16]

Brandeis understood that freedom—of speech, and within the market—is the essential sphere of development.[17] The exercise of being directly engaged in a market society as a seller is important for the character traits that enable freedom. A vigorous, moral, creative life depends upon the existence of a decentralized business world.[18]

According to Brandeis, people can be courageous or weak, fickle or reliable; they can have "fallible" judgment, feel confident or insecure, be fearful or optimistic; they are "wee things"—but above all, they have the capacity to learn and change.[19] Human development, he believed, could and should lead to moral courage, and to learning.[20] Responsibility, moral courage, and learning would in turn lead to overall societal well-being.[21]

And this virtuous chain of events begins with institutional structure.[22] Brandeis wrote, "[t]he great developer is responsibility. Participation in, and eventual control of, industry is likewise an essential of obtaining justice in distributing the fruits of the industry."[23] The difficult task of democracy requires moral fiber, and that fiber is forged through experience: "development is attained mainly in the process of common living."[24] For Brandeis, this common living required shared power over shared enterprises; monopoly was incompatible with shared power, because it located all power in a few hands.

Institutions and people are always in an ongoing dance: the institutions shape human character, human character shapes the institutions. Monopolies tend to destroy the best in human character; decentralized power allows it to flourish. Big corporations, Brandeis argued, threatened to throttle creativity and vitality: "only through participation by the many in the responsibilities and determinations of business can Americans secure the moral and intellectual development which is essential to the maintenance of liberty."[25]

There are different ways to approach the idea of America. In the middle of the Jim Crow era, Langston Hughes wrote his thesis about what America might be. "Let America be America again," he wrote, wryly mocking the MAGA-ists of his own era, and then sharply argued that America has never lived up to its aspiration, but could. America, for Hughes, was "the great strong land of love," where "never kings connive nor tyrants scheme / that any man be crushed by one above."[26]

As Hughes understood, the biggest, most powerful dream of America, the one we can't forget, the one that underpins the right to eat, breathe clean air, have dignity, is the dream that people, not kings or lords or dukes, should govern themselves. The basic dream of America is the fight against illegitimate power. Money is not a legitimate source of political power. Race is not a legitimate source of political power. The only source of legitimate power over others—the power to imprison, the power to tax, the power to make decisions—flows from we the people. After 240 years of good and bad history, this is still an extraordinary idea, one worth trying to make a reality.

We face a major fork in the road right now on the way to *that* American dream. We can continue down a path of corporate concentration, gradually ceding authority over our lives to a few hundred individuals, or we can rise up to break those companies apart, and then, with power appropriately distributed, begin the ongoing, endless, but beautiful, human, moral work of self-governance by free people.

Epilogue: 2040

It is a beautiful fall afternoon in October 2040, and Jhunu is just returning from her father's funeral, reflecting on how different her life has been from his. When she was in high school, she had assumed she would face the fate of her parents: low wages, long hours, uncertainty, suspicion, anxiety, and fear, with pockets of paranoia. Her memories of being a teenager are of sitting around the kitchen table, listening to her parents talking worriedly about Uber, where her father worked. They fretted about how they would afford the mortgage payments that month, how they would pay to fix the vehicle, and whether it would be a good or bad month; she remembers stranger conversations, too, verging on the paranoid, about whether Uber's "oversight team" had overheard her father's political conversation with a passenger where he'd expressed real anger. She remembers how loudly her mother laughed when she came home with a drawing of a man named Uber towering over her father and asked what his last name was. Her mother had died in 2020 of diabetes, after she had used the money from skipped insulin treatments to pay for Jhunu's community college. The family had buried her at a cemetery owned by the conglomerate SCI.

For the last ten years Jhunu has worked at a medium-sized shoe company, with good vacations and benefits. The state provides healthcare, which it started doing in 2030 after hospitals and big pharmaceutical companies were broken up: once the power of insurance companies, hospitals, and pharmaceutical companies was taken away, the organized opposition to universal healthcare was too weak to fight public opinion.

It is her second job in shoe design; she left another after a disagreement with a manager and was happy she had options. It took her just a year to leave after forcefully expressing her disagreement, and she had none of the anxiety that her father suffered under Uber's political spying. Her new company is unionized. Since 2025, more and more companies have become unionized, reversing a 100-year trend. The shift happened after Walmart and Amazon were both broken up. When the spinoff Amazon Marketplace became a neutral public utility, and the different markets for consumer goods were split up so no company owned more than 5% of the market, unionization became much easier. Labor found itself able to negotiate and no longer needed to beg.

Sometimes her shop steward annoys her, but he was there for her when she had a conflict over taking time off when her son was sick, and another time when she was being harassed at work. She wishes her father had had someone who had his back when he finally quit Uber because he couldn't make the payments on the car. He began working at a storage facility. Uber had been bad, but the storage facility was worse: they had a camera that tracked his every move. When he was hurt at work he thought about bringing a lawsuit but couldn't find a lawyer who thought he could win in arbitration, and he was worried about retaliation. Now, all federal statutory disputes happen in open court, because in 2024, the Senate got rid of all arbitration for employment and consumer claims.

Her own son is now eight years old and at an excellent public school. Funding for public schools has increased as small-
and medium-sized companies created good middle-class jobs
and Wall Street firms stopped pushing for education privatiza-
tion. Unlike at her school, he gets to see how he did on a test
after he takes it. In his history class, they write about what they
call the "Gates Era," where one man dictated education policy
and eroded the quality of education for decades.

Jhunu shares pictures of her family on Facebook and reads
the news there. She used to be scared of what Facebook knew
about her, but after 2025, when Facebook was split off from
the ad company and designated as an essential communications
infrastructure, it was no longer allowed to surveill her or fund
itself through digital ads, so she now lets her son use it, too.
Just last week he wrote his first post to a friend from school and
was so proud. She remembers losing her little brother to years
of Facebook addiction, where he stopped engaging socially because he was so committed to screen time. She is happy to pay
$1 a month for a service that doesn't have an incentive to keep
her son addicted.

Looking back, historians place the seeds of the golden age
of American democracy in September 2008, when the banks
crashed and the government bailed them out for trillions of
dollars, and nobody went to jail. The bailout of the banks shaped
the politics that came after it; anyone coming of age in 2008
started assuming the profound failure of representative government and the broken nature of our economy. Then, for almost a
decade, a new movement built up throughout the country, taking on established power. First, there was Occupy Wall Street in
2010–2011, and then the movement gradually spread to elective
office. In 2018, a handful of Social Democrats were elected to
Congress, and from 2016 to 2030, more and more mayors ran
on a promise of a total commitment to public life.

In the wake of the 2008 crash, four different economic visions were pitted against one another: data-driven technocracy attached to nostalgia for pre-2010 politics, anti-monopoly Democratic Socialism, top-down socialism, and anti-government libertarianism (the destruction of the state). A sharp generational divide showed up in the approaches toward these issues, in which most older Americans either tried to re-create the Obama years or leaned toward libertarianism, while younger Americans, who had never known any prosperity and started with a default suspicion of big business, demanded essential change, using government, not rejecting it.

In the last month of the 2020 Democratic primary, a scandal erupted. A whistleblower inside one of the three big tech platforms revealed that they had been directing search results toward positive stories about the front-runner, while top executives were also funding the front-runner. A few weeks later, an investigation by the *American Prospect* showed that the political team at Amazon had visited the Alexa offices to learn what people were asking for regarding political products. Amazon and the other tech platform defended their activities as entirely legal and well within their rights under the First Amendment. The impact was decisive. The top candidates who had defended the existence of big tech platforms suddenly saw their support eroding. A Democratic nominee who had been lagging leapt ahead, won a surprise victory, and beat Donald Trump.

In 2021, the new president of the United States announced a radical overhaul of the country's antitrust policy. In their first month in office, they turned the merger guidelines upside down, announcing that mergers would be challenged for any firm that controlled more than 10% of the national market, or 25% of a local market, purchasing any firm that controlled more than 5% of any related market. Wall Street–backed campaigners, shocked at the seriousness of the change, set out to slander the president and worked with members of Congress to try to block the action through legislation. They failed, and their overstepping—thereby clarifying how much Wall Street profits had come from unfair business practices—led to a groundswell of support for new laws that made it per se illegal to engage in predatory pricing and exclusionary practices. Mergers dropped from 50,000 in 2017 to 15,000 in 2027.

Because of the backlog of 30 years of bloated companies, attorneys general, eager to make a name for themselves, joined together in over 40 major lawsuits, splitting the work across state lines. A major investigation into Google led by the New York state attorney general revealed internal documents proving intent to monopolize, and the company was forced to peel off YouTube in 2023, followed by a major federal divestiture in 2026, when Google was broken into 57 component parts.

The real change happened in 2025, when Congress, led by a new crop of anti-monopolists elected in 2022 and 2024, passed key pieces of legislation against fierce opposition. They created a category of company called "essential infrastructure" and made clear rules: no behavior ads, no surveillance, and no cross-ownership of companies. Amazon, the marketplace, was split into four different marketplaces, and each of them was spun off from all Amazon brands that it had sold on its site: Stone and Beam, Homethreads, and Happy Belly became their own companies.

Essential communications legislation led to what is being called the second golden age of news. Newspapers, after the brutal beating of 2010–2022, revived income streams and used the billions to hire 200,000 new reporters in three years. The newly invigorated Congress passed a law honoring the late, great Senator Phil Hart, and put the 1968 merger guidelines into law, forcing big corporations to spin off after growing to a certain size.

Pioneering lawmakers were supported by fierce organizing. In 2020, a new group of activists calling themselves "The 30 Days" became the go-to watchdogs for all mergers. Prior to 2020, the overwhelming majority of deals went forward after the first review and a mere quick look over 30 days. But in 2020, the moment a major merger was announced, activists and politicians showed up for a 30-day sit-in, asking questions, demanding answers. Newspapers covered the 30-day period with the intensity of a political race.

Led by a 2020 set of congressional candidates who ran on breaking up big banks, Congress passed new laws related to banking in particular, reviving some old principles. They not only reinstated Glass-Steagall, which separated investment and depository banking, but built on it, limiting the overall size of any financial institution and radically limiting the power of private equity. Congress adopted the Glass-Steagall separation-of-functions approach across industries, prohibiting systems that lead to conflicts of interest. Dominant platforms (think: trains, distribution systems) could not use their powers over distribution to gain power over other parts of the marketplace. Congress passed sweeping pro-labor laws, making it easier to organize and to use union power in one industry to support unions in related industries. It passed laws that enabled worker-owned co-ops. It banned forced arbitration. It passed a robust system allowing for publicly financed elections.

In the years that followed, the set of cases culminating in *Citizens United* was overturned, and old laws prohibiting unlimited spending in campaigns were revived. Corporate law was totally restructured; big corporations needed workers on the board, and Congress preempted state laws that required corporations to maximize profit at all costs.

Jhunu lives in Toledo, Ohio, and her brother lives in a town of 3,000 in upstate New York. She remembers how they used to think it was crazy to live outside New York City, but after the antitrust era, rural America and smaller cities and towns began flourishing. The pharmacies returned to downtowns, and small- and medium-sized companies with local ownership spread everywhere.

After the antitrust explosion, black-owned businesses flourished, and owners used their newfound independence to push for reparations. They faced significant opposition but were able to fight back because they were not dependent. After a law to publicly finance elections was passed in the House and Senate, lobbyists could no longer use the promise of campaign contributions to reliably get access to lawmakers. The oil companies and gas companies started sending lobbyists to stand outside bathroom doors, which gave them a new name, "the oily men."

Three times a day Jhunu reads the news—one local, one national, and one international source. She laughs as she recalls how little she knew about her own community when she was a girl and is grateful to find out about local sports scores, the public school board, and her neighbor who has proposed a new method for water distribution in her borough.

Jhunu cries for her father that he had to struggle so much but also feels grateful that he lived to see another future. Before he died, he told her, "finally, this is the America I wanted to give you and your siblings when you were born."

She understands that power can always creep back, and politics has to be part of life, even when it seems overwhelming. Once every other month she goes to her school board meeting; once or twice a year to the city council for hearings;

and three times a year to Columbus, to petition her elected officials. She regularly strategizes with her coworkers about union demands. Every Thursday, the local subcommittee of the Democratic Party meets to research proposals and argue vigorously with other members about healthcare policy, gaming in schools, taxation, how to distribute water, and other matters important to the community. When she finds a proposal she cares about, she knows who to work with to push it through. She isn't scared to speak up.

Jhunu carries a deep love of her family, her community, and her country, and is full of optimism about her future and that of her son. She knows that when the people fought to take the power back, they won—and she is going to make sure they protect that victory for the future.

Acknowledgments

After organizing together to break up the big banks in the wake of the 2008 crash, Tiffiniy Chen, Donny Shaw, and I decided to write a book, "Break 'em Up": that was 2010. It didn't happen, but the seed of the idea was born. In 2013, when I started working with Barry Lynn and Lina Khan, we spent hours at whiteboards and in conversation, trying to make a map of power in America.

This book represents my effort to put down in one place the ideas developed in those conversations with Lina, Barry, and our sprawling anti-monopoly family—Matt Stoller, Sarah Miller, Phil Longman, Tiff, Donny, Marcellus Andrews, Sandeep Vaheesan, Joe Maxwell, Sally Hubbard, Tim Wu, Franklin Foer, Richard John, David Dayen, Stacy Mitchell, Chris Mitchell, and many more. Christopher Leonard's top-notch journalism in *The Meat Racket* led to the central metaphor of this book—chickenization. I am particularly grateful for the help of Barry, Lina, Matt, Sarah, Joe, and Phil for reading so many chapters and giving invaluable feedback.

I am indebted to the insights I gleaned from conversations with Katherine Stone, Charlotte Garden, Marshall Steinbaum, Julia Angwin, Lorraine Lewandrowski, Lalch Ispahani, Jose Oliva, Don Guttenplan, Alexander Colvin, Dan Berger, Sabeel Rahman, Frederic M. Scherer, Rob Sheehan, Noah Hutton, Mike Callicrate, Nathan Jensen, Teddy Downey, Jonathan Kanter, Kate Crawford, Tom Perriello, Don Guttenplan, Joseph Stiglitz, Zach Carter, Anya Shiffrin, Jed Britton-Purdy, Chris Hughes, Roger McNamee, Jameel Jaffer, Jack Balkin, Ezra Klein, Chris Hayes, Ethan Zuckerman, Ganesh Sitaramen, John Nichols, Alexis Grinell, Rebecca Katz, Leonie Haimson,

Cynthia Nixon, Mike Lux, and Larry Lessig and online conversations with Hal Singer, Jason Kint, Asher Schechter, Dan Riffle, Austin Frerick, Dina Srinivasan, Einer Elhauge, Emily Bell, Ioana Marinescu, Sanjukta Paul, and Veena Dubal. The Stigler Center conferences organized by Luigi Zingales and Guy Rolnick were so enlightening.

I am so grateful to Senator Bernie Sanders for his generous Foreword, for his consistent leadership in taking on corporate power, and for his incredible compassion for the human impact of disempowerment.

Senator Elizabeth Warren's leadership on big tech transformed the debate. Congressman David Cicilline's leadership on antitrust in Congress has been a true inspiration. Ro Khanna—I stole some ideas from your Twitter feed, and get constant joy from your leadership. Thanks to Pramilla Jayapal and Alexandria Ocasio-Cortez, for your friendship and antitrust leadership. My great New York Amazon allies—Michael Kink, Deborah Axt, Ron Kim, Jonathan Westin, Paul Sonn, Tony Perstein—in different ways, your ideas are in the book.

Special thanks to Lauren Jacobs, Bianca Wylie, Dania Rajendra, Ryan Gerety, Mariah Montgomery, Michelle Miller, and Hannah Jane Sassaman from the The Ford Foundation retreat in May 2019.

Thanks to Katie Zanecchia, my first agent! Now I really know how agents are helpful! And Gail Ross, for taking over and helping guide me as Katie pushed off to new adventures.

I am so grateful to the always free-thinking Adam Bellow at All Points Books for accepting the book before it had real shape, and Kevin Reilly, who was so patient and brilliant in his suggestions and interventions in getting it in shape. Alan Bradshaw and his top-notch team of editors took something muddy and made it shine. Kevin and Adam dragged me over the finish line when I would still be happily rewriting today.

Fordham Law School has been an incredible home for me during the last decade. Special thanks to Olivier Sylvain, Joel Reidenberg, Mark Patterson, Russ Pearce, Barry Hawk— the colleagues whose thinking on markets has most directly influenced my own.

Two people had a special role in the crafting of this book: Lorin Stein and Jennifer Dworkin, thank you for the brilliant editing. Scott Faber, my writing partner, like a workout partner—those Howers of Power!!!

My research assistants were pure gold. Tara O'Malley above all—you answered impossible questions at impossible times of day and night. Thank you also to Jared Milfred, Simon Popkin, Benjamin Klein, Nate Chumley, Michael Levario, Frank Piacenti, and Shanice Harris. Your research, creativity, and doggedness are in every page of this book. I really appreciate all the students in Market Structure and Democracy, who played with these ideas with me over the last five years.

Nick, thank you for your patience with weekends lost to research, your support and belief in this project, and to your help with chapter titles. Sage, thanks for letting me bounce ideas (rants) off of you. And to the little snuggler, who has a spectacular sense of humor, who listened to my mumbling about big tech in the womb and in the park.

Thanks to Mom & Dad, for expecting good writing. So much easier if you didn't! And to Lise, because I misspelled your name in my last book.

The men and women who were willing to talk to me about the human costs of monopolization—whose voices show up in these pages, often anonymously—thank you.

Finally, thanks to Cassava House, on 1st Avenue and 116th Street, where most of the book was written.

Further Reading

Elizabeth Anderson, *Private Government: How Employers Rule Our Lives (and Why We Don't Talk About It)*

Jonathan Baker, *The Antitrust Paradigm: Restoring a Competitive Economy*

David Dayen, *Monopolized: Life in the Age of Corporate Power*

Ariel Ezrachi and Maurice E. Stucke, *Competition Overdose*

Franklin Foer, *World Without Mind: The Existential Threat of Big Tech*

Rana Foroohar, *Don't Be Evil*

Thomas Frank, *Listen, Liberal: Or, What Ever Happened to the Party of the People?*

Alexander Hertel-Fernandez, *Politics at Work: How Companies Turn Their Workers into Lobbyists.*

Sally Hubbard, *Monopolists Suck*

Richard R. John, *Network Nation*

Simon Johnson and James Kwak, *13 Bankers: The Wall Street Takeover and the Next Financial Meltdown*

John Kwoka, *Mergers, Merger Control, and Remedies*

Christopher Leonard, *Kochland: The Secret History of Koch Industries and Corporate Power in America*

Christopher Leonard, *The Meat Racket: The Secret Takeover of America's Food Business*

Barry C. Lynn, *Cornered*

Barry C. Lynn, *Liberty from All Masters*

Roger McNamee, *Zucked*

Frank Pasquale, *The Black Box Society*

Sanjukta Paul, *Solidarity in the Shadow of Antitrust*

Victor Pickard, *America's Battle for Media Democracy*

Victor Pickard, *Democracy Without Journalism?*

K. Sabeel Rahman, *Democracy Against Domination*

Robert Reich, *Saving Capitalism*

Jeffrey Rosen, *Louis D. Brandeis: American Prophet*

Chris Sagers, *United States v. Apple: Competition in America*

Ganesh Sitaraman, *The Great Democracy*

Paul Starr, *The Creation of the Media: Political Origins of Modern Communications*

Joseph Stiglitz, *People, Power and Profits*

Matt Stoller, *Goliath*

Jonathan Taplin, *Move Fast and Break Things: How Facebook, Google, and Amazon Cornered Culture and Undermined Democracy*

Jonathan Tepper and Denise Hearn, *Myth of Capitalism*

Siva Vaidhyanathan, *Antisocial Media: How Facebook Disconnects Us and Undermines Democracy*

Siva Vaidhyanathan, *The Googlization of Everything (And Why We Should Worry)*

Amy Webb, *The Big Nine: How the Tech Titans & Their Thinking Machines Could Warp Humanity*

Tim Wu, *The Curse of Bigness*

Shoshana Zuboff, *The Age of Surveillance Capitalism: The Fight for a Human Future at the New Frontier of Power*

Notes

FOREWORD BY BERNIE SANDERS

1 "Meat Processing Industry," *Open Markets Institute,* https://concen
   trationcrisis.openmarketsinstitute.org/industry/meat-processing/.
2 "Domestic Airlines Industry," *Open Markets Institute,* https://concen
   trationcrisis.openmarketsinstitute.org/industry/domestic-airlines/.
3 "Eyeglasses and Contact Lens Stores," *Open Markets Institute,* https://concen
   trationcrisis.openmarketsinstitute.org/industry/eye-glasses-contact-lens
   -stores/.
4 Jun-Sheng Li, "How Amazon Took 50% of the E-Commerce Market and
   What It Means for the Rest of Us," *TechCrunch,* https://techcrunch.com
   /2019/02/27/how-amazon-took-50-of-the-e-commerce-market-and
   -what-it-means-for-the-rest-of-us/.
5 Reed Abelson, "When Hospitals Save Money, Patients Often Pay More,"
   New York Times, https://www.nytimes.com/2018/11/14/health/hospital
   -mergers-health-care-spending.html.
6 "The Economic Cost of Food Monopolies," *Food & Water Watch,* https://
   www.foodandwaterwatch.org/sites/default/files/Food%20Monopo
   lies%20Report%20Nov%202012.pdf; Martin Longman, "Joe Biden
   Needs to Catch Up to His Rivals on Antitrust," *Washington Monthly,*
   https://washingtonmonthly.com/2019/03/08/joe-biden-needs-to-catch
   -up-to-his-rivals-on-monopoly/.
7 National Farmers Union, Twitter Post, April 18, 2019, 5:01 p.m., https://
   twitter.com/nfudc/status/1118982840065101844?s=21.

INTRODUCTION

1 "Which Corporations Control the World?" International Business Guide,
   https://www.internationalbusinessguide.org/corporations/; "Who Are the
   Companies That Manufacture Electronic Voting Machines?" ProCon.org,
   https://votingmachines.procon.org/view.answers.php?questionID=000263.
2 Benjamin Gomes-Casseres, "What the Big Mergers of 2017 Tell Us About
   2018," *Harvard Business Review,* January 2, 2018, https://hbr.org/2017/12
   /what-the-big-mergers-of-2017-tell-us-about-2018.
3 Terry Gross, "How 5 Tech Giants Have Become More Like Governments
   Than Companies," October 26, 2017, in *Fresh Air,* podcast, MP3 Audio,
   35:00, https://www.npr.org/2017/10/26/560136311/how-5-tech-giants
   -have-become-more-like-governments-than-companies; Farhad Manjoo,
   "The Upside of Being Ruled by the Five Tech Giants," *New York Times,*

November 1, 2017, https://www.nytimes.com/2017/11/01/technology /five-tech-giants-upside.html.

4   A lot of what I will talk about in this book falls within what economists call monopsony power, which is a subset of monopoly power. Technically, this is when a corporation gains so much power that producers have no choice but to use it.

5   Louis D. Brandeis, "An Address Delivered to the Industrial Department of the National Civic Federation," April 25, 1905, https://louisville.edu/law /library/special-collections/the-louis-d.-brandeis-collection/the-desirable -industrial-peace-by-louis-d.-brandeis. For some in-depth discussions of the problems of power, see Robert Reich, *Saving Capitalism* (New York: Vintage Books-Penguin Random House LLC, 2015), p. 117; Joseph Stiglitz, *People, Power and Profits* (New York: W. W. Norton, 2019); Matt Stoller, *Goliath* (New York: Simon & Schuster, 2019).

6   Lauren Hertzler, "Don't Like Comcast-Time Warner Cable Merger? Clock Is Ticking to Tell FCC," *Philadelphia Business Journal*, July 14, 2014, https://www.bizjournals.com/philadelphia/news/2014/07/14/dont-like -the-thought-of-a-mega-comcast-clock-is.html.

7   Terrence T. McDonald, "Citing Chain Store Ban, Jersey City Aims to Block New CVS," NJ.com, May 5, 2017, https://www.nj.com/hudson /2017/05/citing_chain_store_ban_jersey_city_aims_to_block_n.html.

8   Karl Bode, "More Than 750 American Communities Have Built Their Own Internet Networks," Motherboard, *Vice*, January 23, 2018, https://motherboard.vice.com/en_us/article/a3np4a/new-municipal -broadband-map.

9   Organization for Competitive Markets, "1 Million Consumers Call on DOJ to Block Bayer-Monsanto Merger," Common Dreams, November 14, 2017, https://www.commondreams.org/newswire/2017/11/14 /1-million-consumers-call-doj-block-bayer-monsanto-merger.

10 "Farmers Overwhelmingly Oppose Bayer Monsanto Merger," Farmaid .org, March 8, 2018, https://www.farmaid.org/issues/corporate-power /farmers-overwhelmingly-oppose-bayer-monsanto-merger/.

11 Steve Lohr, "Chris Hughes Worked to Create Facebook. Now, He Is Working to Break It Up," *New York Times*, July 25, 2019, https://www.nytimes .com/2019/07/25/technology/chris-hughes-facebook-breakup.html.

12 EuroNews, "Bayer Monsanto Merger Plan Protests," YouTube video, 1:00, March 3, 2018, https://www.youtube.com/watch?v=W4oTq1bN70c.

13 Zlata Rodionova, "Thousands Protest Against Seed Giant Monsanto Ahead of Bayer Merger," *The Independent*, May 23, 2016, https://www .independent.co.uk/news/business/news/thousands-protest-against-evil -seed-giant-monsanto-ahead-of-bayer-merger-a7043196.html; "'Marriage of Death': Protesters Oppose Bayer Monsanto Merger," *DW*, https://www.dw.com/en/marriage-of-death-protesters-oppose-bayer -monsanto-merger/a-38631990.

14 "Banking Operations Come to Halt as Unions Protest Against Proposed Bank Merger," NewsClick.in, December 26, 2018, https://www

.newsclick.in/banking-operations-come-halt-unions-protest-against
-proposed-bank-merger.

15 "Traders Protest Walmart Merger," *The Hindu* (Mumbai), July 3, 2018,
https://www.thehindu.com/news/cities/mumbai/traders-protest
-walmart-merger/article24315164.ece.

1. THE CHICKENIZATION OF
THE AMERICAN MIDDLE CLASS

1 "'He Was My Everything': A Farmer's Wife Reflects on Her Husband's
Suicide," NPR.org, May 18, 2018, https://www.npr.org/2018/05/18
/611687746/he-was-my-everything-a-farmer-s-wife-reflects-on-her
-husband-s-suicide.

2 Jonathan Knutson, "'Still Adjusting, Still Farming' After Husband's Suicide, Minnesota Woman Carries On the Family Farm," *Bismarck Tribune*,
August 11, 2018, https://bismarcktribune.com/news/state-and-regional
/still-adjusting-still-farming-after-husband-s-suicide-minnesota-woman
/article_2521aa25-d07f-579c-ac6b-9fc1dfd2d77f.html.

3 Bryce Wilson Stucki and Nathan Rosenberg, "How a Simple CDC
Error Inflated the Farmer Suicide Crisis Story—and Led to a Rash of
Inaccurate Reporting," Newfoodeconomy.org, June 21, 2018, https://
newfoodeconomy.org/farmer-suicide-crisis-cdc-study/.

4 American Farm Bureau Federation, "Farm Groups Launch 'Farm
Town Strong' Campaign to Address Rural Opioid Epidemic" [Press re-
lease], January 3, 2017, https://farmtownstrong.org/2018/01/03/farm
-groups-launch-farm-town-strong-campaign-to-address-rural-opioid
-epidemic/.

5 Sam Hudzik, "Routine Mailing to Dairy Farmers Included a Rare Note:
Suicide Hotline Info," New England Public Radio, February 7, 2018,
http://nepr.net/post/routine-mailing-dairy-farmers-included-rare-note
-suicide-hotline-info#stream/0.

6 Morgen Davis (@morgendavis88), "All my life, literally all I wanted to be
was a farmer," Twitter, February 25, 2018, 6:08 p.m., https://twitter.com
/morgendavis88/status/967944509039546369.

7 Christopher Leonard, "Is the Chicken Industry Rigged?" Bloomberg,
February 15, 2017, https://www.bloomberg.com/news/features/2017
-02-15/is-the-chicken-industry-rigged.

8 Leah Douglas, "The Price Fixing Scandal Rocking Big Chicken," *Mother
Jones*, February 10, 2018, https://www.motherjones.com/food/2018/02
/chicken-poultry-price-broilers-tyson-perdue-lawsuits/.

9 Joshua Reichert, "Big Chicken: Pollution and Industrial Poultry Production in America," Pew Charitable Trusts, July 26, 2011, https://www
.pewtrusts.org/en/research-and-analysis/reports/2011/07/26/big-chicken
-pollution-and-industrial-poultry-production-in-america.

10 Hannibal Ware, "Evaluation of SBA's 7(a) Loans to Poultry Farmers: The U.S. Small Business Administration," U.S. Small Business Administration, Report No. 18–13, March 6, 2018, p. 7, https://www.sba.gov/sites/default/files/oig/SBA-OIG-Report-18-13.pdf.

11 Phone interview with Joe Maxwell, March 2019 (notes on file with author).

12 The dairy kings have brought their own innovation, with contracts that shift liability onto the farmer, away from the processor. Farmers agree to stay liable for problems with their milk even when it's on the grocery store shelves—and this is true even in the fake "co-ops." Leah Douglas, "How Rural America Got Milked," *Washington Monthly* (January 2018), https://washingtonmonthly.com/magazine/january-february-march-2018/how-rural-america-got-milked/.

13 Sonja Begemann, "2018 Corn Input Cost Per Bushel Lowest in 10 Years, 2019 to Jump," *Farm Journal's AgPro*, April 24, 2019, https://www.agprofessional.com/article/2018-corn-input-cost-bushel-lowest-10-years-2019-jump.

14 Donnelle Eller, "John Deere Enduring Despite Downturns in the Farm Industry," *Telegraph Herald* (Dubuque, IA), April 21, 2019, https://www.telegraphherald.com/news/agriculture/article_e40c55cb-c07e-5adf-b770-a1aea6e5c96e.html.

15 Begemann, "2018 Corn Input Cost Per Bushel Lowest in 10 Years, 2019 to Jump."

16 On gig economy as tragedy, see Sarah Kessler, *Gigged* (New York: St. Martin's Press, 2018). On suicides, see Reihan Salam, "Taxi Driver Suicides Are a Warning," *Atlantic,* June 5, 2018, https://www.theatlantic.com/ideas/archive/2018/06/taxi-driver-suicides-are-a-warning/561926/.

17 Bhairavi Desai, in-person interview, February 7, 2019 (notes on file with author).

18 Lawrence Van Gelder, "Medallion Limits Stem from the 30's," *New York Times*, May 11, 1996, https://www.nytimes.com/1996/05/11/nyregion/medallion-limits-stem-from-the-30-s.html.

19 Charles Vidich, *The New York Cab Driver and His Fare* (Rochester, VT: Schenkman, 1976), 73.

20 Biju Mathew, *Taxi!: Cabs and Capitalism in New York City* (Ithaca, NY: ILR Press, 2008), 50–52.

21 *Rudack v. Valentine*, 163 Misc. 326, 328, 295 N.Y.S. 976 (Sup. Ct.), aff'd, 274 N.Y. 615, 10 N.E.2d 577 (1937).

22 Travis Kalanick, "Uber Policy White Paper 1.0," Uber, April 12, 2013, https://www.benedelman.org/uber/uber-policy-whitepaper.pdf.

23 In-person interview with Bhairavi Desai, February 8, 2019 (notes on file with author). In-person interview with Biju Mathew, February 8, 2019 (notes on file with author).

24 Desai interview, February 8.

25 Ridester Staff, "How Much Does an Uber Driver Make in 2019? [The Inside Scoop]," *Ridester*, September 4, 2019, https://www.ridester.com/how-much-do-uber-drivers-make/.

26 Interview with Bhairavi Desai and Biju Mathew, February 8, 2019 (notes on file with author).

27 Noam Schreiber, "How Uber Uses Psychological Tricks to Push Its Drivers' Buttons," *New York Times*, April 2, 2017, https://www.nytimes.com/interactive/2017/04/02/technology/uber-drivers-psychological-tricks.html.

28 Brishen Rogers, "The Social Costs of Uber," *University of Chicago Law Review Online* 82, no. 1 (2015), article 6, https://chicagounbound.uchicago.edu/uclrev_online/vol82/iss1/6/. http://dx.doi.org/10.2139/ssrn.2608017; Temple University Legal Studies Research Paper No. 2015–28. Available at SSRN: https://ssrn.com/abstract=2608017 or http://dx.doi.org/10.2139/ssrn.2608017.

29 Interview with Biju Mathew, February 8, 2019.

30 Holly Everett, "19 Online Ordering Statistics Every Restaurateur Should Know in 2019," *Upserve Restaurant Insider,* February 12, 2019, https://upserve.com/restaurant-insider/online-ordering-statistics/. "Study: Delivery Sales to Outpace In-Restaurant Sales," *QSR Magazine*, https://www.qsrmagazine.com/news/study-delivery-sales-outpace-restaurant-sales.

31 David Yaffe-Bellany, "New York vs. Grubhub," *New York Times*, September 30, 2019, https://www.nytimes.com/2019/09/30/business/grubhub-seamless-restaurants-delivery-apps-fees.html.

32 Sunny Lee, "The Uncertain Future of Your Neighborhood Dry Cleaner," *The Outline*, October 1, 2019, https://theoutline.com/post/8026/korean-american-drycleaners-apps?zd=1&zi=fxetp6t2.

33 Kate Gibson, "Should McDonald's Be Responsible for How Its Franchises Treat Workers?" CBSNews, March 11, 2016, https://www.cbsnews.com/news/is-mcdonalds-on-the-hook-for-how-franchisees-treat-workers/.

34 Lina Khan, "Monsanto's Scary New Scheme: Why Does It *Really* Want All This Data?" *Salon*, December 30, 2013, https://www.salon.com/2013/12/29/monsantos_scary_new_scheme_why_does_it_really_want_all_this_data/.

35 See the great work of Brishen Rogers, who writes about the ways in which intrusive technologies are changing the future of work. Brishen Rogers, "Employment Rights in the Platform Economy: Getting Back to Basics," *Harvard Law & Policy Review* 10 (2016): 479–520. Available at SSRN: https://ssrn.com/abstract=2641305 or http://dx.doi.org/10.2139/ssrn.2641305.

36 Valerie Strauss, "Pearson Conducts Experiment on Thousands of College Students Without Their Knowledge," *Washington Post*, April 23, 2018, https://www.washingtonpost.com/news/answer-sheet/wp/2018/04/23/pearson-conducts-experiment-on-thousands-of-college-students-without-their-knowledge/.

37 Tom Super, "The Chicken Guarantees: Industry-Wide Standards for Broiler Chicken Welfare," *Chicken Check In*, October 20, 2017, https://www.chickencheck.in/blog/national-chicken-council-never-always-chicken-welfare-guarantees-people-can-expect/.

2. BIG TECH'S GOVERNMENTAL AMBITIONS

1 Chris Hughes, "It's Time to Break Up Facebook," *New York Times*, May 9, 2019, https://www.nytimes.com/2019/05/09/opinion/sunday/chris -hughes-facebook-zuckerberg.html.

2 Facebook, "Facebook Reports Fourth Quarter and Full Year 2016 Results," Press release (February 1, 2017), https://investor.fb.com/investor -news/press-release-details/2017/Facebook-Reports-Fourth-Quarter -and-Full-Year-2016-Results/default.aspx; Julian D'Onfro, "Here's How Much Time People Spend on Facebook Per Day," *Business Insider*, July 8, 2015, https://www.businessinsider.com/how-much-time-people-spend -on-facebook-per-day-2015-7?r=UK.

3 Tristan Harris, "Brain Hacking," interview by Anderson Cooper, *60 Minutes*, CBS, April 9, 2017, https://www.cbsnews.com/news/brain-hacking -tech-insiders-60-minutes/.

4 Josh Constine, "Facebook Pays Teens to Install VPN That Spies on Them," TechCrunch, January 29, 2019, https://techcrunch.com/2019/01/29 /facebook-project-atlas/.

5 "From Alibaba to Zynga: 40 of the Best VC Bets of All Time and What We Can Learn from Them," CB Insights, Research brief, January 4, 2019, https://www.cbinsights.com/research/best-venture-capital-investments /. See also Alison L. Deutsch, "WhatsApp: The Best Facebook Purchase Ever?" updated June 25, 2019, https://www.investopedia.com/articles /investing/032515/whatsapp-best-facebook-purchase-ever.asp; Sarah Frier, "Facebook $22 Billion WhatsApp Deal Buys $10 Million in Sales," Bloomberg, updated October 29, 2014, https://www.bloomberg.com /news/articles/2014-10-28/facebook-s-22-billion-whatsapp-deal-buys -10-million-in-sales.

6 Phone interview with Julia Angwin, January 17, 2019 (notes on file with author). Since the hearing, Zuckerberg has repeatedly refused to testify in front of the British and Canadian Parliaments and the International Grand Committee of legislators from thirteen countries investigating fake news. According to Zuckerberg, he has already said enough. Graham Kates, "Facebook's Mark Zuckerberg Declines Latest Invite to Appear Before International Lawmakers," CBS News, September 9, 2019, https:// www.cbsnews.com/news/facebooks-mark-zuckerberg-declines-latest -invite-to-questioning-by-international-lawmakers/; Alex Hern and Dan Sabbagh, "Zuckerberg's Refusal to Testify Before UK MPs 'Absolutely Astonishing,'" *Guardian*, March 27, 2018, https://www.theguardian .com/technology/2018/mar/27/facebook-mark-zuckerberg-declines-to -appear-before-uk-fake-news-inquiry-mps.

7 Ezra Klein, "Mark Zuckerberg on Facebook's Hardest Year, and What Comes Next," *Vox*, April 2, 2018, https://www.vox.com/2018/4/2 /17185052/mark-zuckerberg-facebook-interview-fake-news-bots -cambridge.

8 Henry Farrell, Margaret Levi, and Tim O'Reilly, "Mark Zuckerberg Runs a Nation-State, and He's the King," *Vox*, April 10, 2018, https://www.vox.com/the-big-idea/2018/4/9/17214752/zuckerberg-facebook-power-regulation-data-privacy-control-political-theory-data-breach-king.

9 Josh Constine, "Facebook Announces Libra Cryptocurrency: All You Need to Know," Tech Crunch, June 18, 2019, https://techcrunch.com/2019/06/18/facebook-libra/.

10 Kate Cox, "Facebook Plans Launch of Its Own 'Supreme Court' for Handling Takedown Appeals," *Ars Technica*, September 18, 2019, https://arstechnica.com/tech-policy/2019/09/facebook-plans-launch-of-its-own-supreme-court-for-handling-takedown-appeals/.

11 Rasheed Shabazz, "UC Berkeley Professor Dacher Keltner Explains 'How Power Makes People Selfish,'" Othering & Belonging Institute, UC Berkeley, January 20, 2015, https://belonging.berkeley.edu/uc-berkeley-professor-dacher-keltner-explains-how-power-makes-people-selfish.

12 Jake Dunagan, "Power Should Never Be Lonely," *Future Now: The IFTF Blog*, February 8, 2010, http://www.iftf.org/future-now/article-detail/power-should-never-be-lonely/.

13 Erik Sherman, "Amazon Says, Let the Employees Sweat—and the DVDs, Too," CBS News, September 29, 2011, https://www.cbsnews.com/news/amazon-says-let-the-employees-sweat-and-the-dvds-too/; Hamilton Nolan, "True Stories of Life as an Amazon Worker," *Gawker*, August 2, 2013, https://gawker.com/true-stories-of-life-as-an-amazon-worker-1002568208.

14 Michael Sainato, "Revealed: Amazon Employees Are Left to Suffer After Workplace Injuries," *Guardian*, April 2, 2019, https://www.theguardian.com/technology/2019/apr/02/revealed-amazon-employees-suffer-after-workplace-injuries.

15 Emily Guendelsberger, "I Worked at an Amazon Fulfillment Center; They Treat Workers Like Robots," *Time*, July 18, 2019, https://time.com/5629233/amazon-warehouse-employee-treatment-robots/.

16 Melissa Lemieux, "USA: Amazon Workers Protest After Employee Allegedly Fired for Exceeding Bereavement Leave by One Hour, to Care for Dying Relative," *Newsweek*, October 2, 2019, https://www.business-humanrights.org/en/usa-amazon-workers-protest-after-employee-allegedly-fired-for-exceeding-bereavement-leave-by-one-hour-to-care-for-dying-relative.

17 Adam Lashinsky, "Amazon's Jeff Bezos: The Ultimate Disrupter," *Fortune*, November 16, 2012, https://fortune.com/2012/11/16/amazons-jeff-bezos-the-ultimate-disrupter/.

18 Karen Hao, "Amazon Is the Invisible Backbone of ICE's Immigration Crackdown," *MIT Technology Review*, October 22, 2018, https://www.technologyreview.com/s/612335/amazon-is-the-invisible-backbone-behind-ices-immigration-crackdown/?mod=article_inline.

19 Stacy Mitchell, "Amazon Doesn't Just Want to Dominate the Market—It Wants to Become the Market," *The Nation*, February 15, 2018, https://

www.thenation.com/article/amazon-doesnt-just-want-to-dominate-the
-market-it-wants-to-become-the-market/.

20 Josh Dzieza, "Prime and Punishment: Dirty Dealing in the $175 Billion
Amazon Marketplace," *The Verge*, December 19, 2018, https://www
.theverge.com/2018/12/19/18140799/amazon-marketplace-scams-seller
-court-appeal-reinstatement.

21 Jay Greene, "Amazon Sellers Say Online Retail Giant Is Trying to Help
Itself, Not Consumers," *Washington Post*, October 1, 2019, https://www
.washingtonpost.com/technology/2019/10/01/amazon-sellers-say-online
-retail-giant-is-trying-help-itself-not-consumers/?arc404=true.

22 Ibid.

23 Stacy Mitchell and Shaoul Sussman, "How Amazon Rigs Its Shopping
Algorithm," Pro-Market, November 6, 2019, https://promarket.org/how
-amazon-rigs-its-shopping-algorithm/.

24 Lashinsky, "Amazon's Jeff Bezos: The Ultimate Disrupter."

25 Zephyr Teachout and Lina Khan, "Market Structure and Political Law: A
Taxonomy of Power," *Duke Journal of Constitutional Law & Public Policy* 9,
no. 1 (August 2014): 54, http://dx.doi.org/10.2139/ssrn.2490525.

26 Jonathan Shieber, "Blue Origin's Passengers Will Pay Hundreds of Thousands of Dollars for a Ticket on New Shepard," *Disrupt SF 2019*, October
2, 2019, https://techcrunch.com/2019/10/02/blue-origins-passengers-will
-pay-hundreds-of-thousands-of-dollars-for-a-ticket-on-new-shepard/;
Steven Levy, "Jeff Bezos Wants Us All to Leave Earth—for Good," *Wired*,
October 15, 2018, https://www.wired.com/story/jeff-bezos-blue-origin/.
"Everything You Need to Know About Blue Origin's New Glenn Rocket,"
Axios, May 27, 2019, https://www.axios.com/everything-you-need-to
-know-about-blue-origins-new-glenn-rocket-65ee886a-c181-492e-8628
-cd9d4cc229da.html.

27 Phone interview with Stacy Mitchell, January 23, 2019. Notes on file
with the author. Stacy Mitchell, "Amazon Doesn't Just Want to Dominate
the Market—It Wants to Become the Market," *The Nation*, February 15,
2018, https://www.thenation.com/article/archive/amazon-doesnt-just
-want-to-dominate-the-market-it-wants-to-become-the-market/.

28 Adrianne Jeffries, "How Google Eats a Business Whole," *The Outline*,
April 17, 2017, https://theoutline.com/post/1399/how-google-ate
-celebritynetworth-com?zd=1&zi=vlefm6sy.

29 Cat Zakrzewski, "Big Tech Went Big on Lobbying Spending—and Privacy Advocates Are Concerned," *Washington Post*, January 23, 2019,
https://www.washingtonpost.com/news/powerpost/paloma/the
-technology-202/2019/01/23/the-technology-202-big-tech-went-big-on
-lobbying-spending-in-washington-and-privacy-advocates-are-concerned
/5c475fae1b326b29c3778c69/?utm_term=.020610fa699f. See also Rana
Farahoor, *Don't Be Evil* (New York: Currency-Random House, 2019), 216.

30 Brody Mullins and Jack Nicas, "Paying Professors: Inside Google's Academic Influence Campaign," *Wall Street Journal*, July 14, 2017, https://
www.wsj.com/articles/paying-professors-inside-googles-academic

-influence-campaign-1499785286; Berkman Klein Center, "Past Support," https://cyber.harvard.edu/node/99967.

31 Franklin Foer, *World Without Mind: The Existential Threat of Big Tech* (New York: Penguin Books, 2017); Siva Vaidhyanathan, *Antisocial Media: How Facebook Disconnects Us and Undermines Democracy* (New York: Oxford University Press, 2018).

32 "Competitors say Google has leveraged that control of the internet's ad ecosystem to push companies to use its advertising technology and buy its ads" and "Regulators are considering whether Google unfairly leverages Android's dominance. Handset makers are effectively locked into Android because it is the only available smartphone software that hosts the apps that users demand, like Instagram and Uber." Jack Nicas, Karen Weise, and Mike Isaac, "How Each Big Tech Company May Be Targeted by Regulators," *New York Times,* September 8, 2019, https://www.nytimes.com /2019/09/08/technology/antitrust-amazon-apple-facebook-google.html. Matt Stoller, "Facebook, Google, and Amazon Aren't Consumer Choices. They Are Monopolies That Endanger American Democracy," *Tablet Magazine*, October 16, 2017, https://www.tabletmag.com/jewish-news-and -politics/246822/facebook-google-amazon-monopolies. See also Shoshana Zuboff, *The Age of Surveillance Capitalism: The Fight for Human Future at the New Frontier of Power* (New York: Hachette Book Group, 2019).

33 Adam Satariano, "The World's First Ambassador to the Tech Industry," *New York Times*, September 3, 2019.

34 P. J. Huffstutter and Tom Polansek, "Lost Hooves, Dead Cattle Before Merck Halted Zilmax Sales," Reuters, December 30, 2013, https:// www.reuters.com/article/us-zilmax-merck-cattle-special-report/special -report-lost-hooves-dead-cattle-before-merck-halted-zilmax-sales -idUSBRE9BT0NV20131230. Charles Fishman, *The Wal-Mart Effect: How the World's Most Powerful Company Really Works* (New York: Penguin Press, 2006), 2.

35 Tim Wu, *The Curse of Bigness: Antitrust in the New Gilded Age* (New York: Columbia Global Reports, 2018), 18: "Over the twentieth century, nations that failed to control private power and attend to the economic needs of their citizens faced the rise of strongmen who promised their citizens a more immediate deliverance from economic woes. The rise of a paramount leader of government who partners with monopolized industry has an indelible association with fascism and authoritarianism." See also pp. 80–83.

36 Zakrzewski, "Big Tech Went Big on Lobbying Spending—and Privacy Advocates Are Concerned."

37 Astead W. Herndon, "Elizabeth Warren Proposes Breaking Up Tech Giants Like Amazon and Facebook," *New York Times*, March 8, 2019, https://www.nytimes.com/2019/03/08/us/politics/elizabeth-warren -amazon.html.

38 U.S. House of Representatives, Committee Repository, "Questions for the Record from the Honorable David N. Cicilline, Chairman, Subcommittee

on Antitrust, Commercial and Administrative Law of the Committee on the Judiciary," HHRG-116-JU05-20190716-QFR005, https://docs.house.gov/meetings/JU/JU05/20190716/109793/HHRG-116-JU05-20190716-QFR005.pdf. The first set of answers came in late November 2019, just as this book was going to galleys. https://www.wired.com/story/amazon-gating-private-labels-antitrust/.

39 See, e.g., Siva Vaidhyanathan, *The Googlization of Everything (and Why We Should Worry)* (Berkeley: University of California Press, 2012).

40 See, e.g, Frank Pasquale, "Technology, Competition, and Values," *Minnesota Journal of Law, Science and Technology* 8, no. 2 (2007): 607, reprinted in K. Prasanna Rani, ed., *Law and Technology: An Interface* (Hyderabad: Icafi University Press, 2009); for another great recent book on tech and antitrust, see Jonathan Baker, *The Antitrust Paradigm: Restoring a Competitive Economy* (Cambridge: Harvard University Press, 2019).

41 Tony Romm, "50 U.S. States and Territories Announce Broad Antitrust Investigation of Google," *Washington Post*, September 9, 2019, https://www.washingtonpost.com/technology/2019/09/09/states-us-territories-announce-broad-antitrust-investigation-google/?arc404=true; Diane Bartz, "Facebook Probe by U.S. States Expands to 47 Attorneys General," Reuters, October 22, 2019, https://www.reuters.com/article/us-tech-antitrust-facebook/facebook-probe-by-u-s-states-expands-to-47-attorneys-general-idUSKBN1X1200.

42 Alison Durkee, "'So You Won't Take Down Lies?': AOC Blasts Mark Zuckerberg in Testy House Hearing," *Vanity Fair Hive*, October 24, 2019, https://www.vanityfair.com/news/2019/10/mark-zuckerberg-facebook-house-testimony-aoc.

43 Rachel Lerman and Marcy Gordon, "YouTube to Pay $170M Fine After Violating Kids Privacy Law," Associated Press, September 4, 2019, https://apnews.com/d84a8ba6b1434249bad5a3831b271eb1.

3. OH, JOURNALISM WAS MURDERED? TOO BAD!

1 Editorial, "Equal Justice for All Kids on Sexual Abuse," *New York Daily News*, March 30, 2016, https://www.nydailynews.com/opinion/equal-justice-kids-sexual-abuse-article-1.2581782.

2 Some observers will rightly note that the owner of the *Daily News* also played a role and that private equity has also played a significant role in killing the news (see, e.g., Alex Shephard, "Finance Is Killing the News," *The New Republic*, April 18, 2018, https://newrepublic.com/article/148022/finance-killing-news). While I agree with this analysis, unless the underlying model of advertising is addressed, all non-subscription, non-charitable, non-governmental news organizations are in trouble.

3 On the front page of the *Daily News*, May 25, 2016; you can see the image here: Rocco Parascandola, Graham Rayman, and Thomas Tracy, "Priest

Who Demanded Homosexuals Have a 'Celibate Life' Suspended After Being Accused of Molesting 15-Year-Old Boy in the Bronx," *New York Daily News*, September 6, 2016, https://www.nydailynews.com/new-york/bronx-priest-suspended-child-sexual-abuse-charges-article-1.2780156.

4 Joe Pompeo, "How Much Does the 'New York Post' Actually Lose?" *Politico*, August 30, 2013, https://www.politico.com/media/story/2013/08/how-much-does-the-new-york-post-actually-lose-001176.

5 "Google's Ad Revenue from 2001 to 2018 (in Billion U.S. Dollars)," Statista, https://www.statista.com/statistics/266249/advertising-revenue-of-google/.

6 Eric Jhonsa, "Why Is Groupon on Sale? Look No Further Than Facebook, Google and Amazon," *TheStreet*, July 9, 2018, https://www.thestreet.com/opinion/facebook-and-google-are-big-reasons-why-groupon-is-on-the-block-14645188.

7 Ashley Rodrigues, "Being Google Is Getting Very Expensive," *Quartz*, February 5, 2019, https://qz.com/1541705/being-google-is-getting-very-expensive/.

8 Andrew Orlowski, "Facebook and Google Gobble 99 Per Cent of New Digital Cash," *The Register* (UK), April 28, 2017, https://www.theregister.co.uk/2017/04/28/facebook_and_google_gulp_99_of_new_digital_ad_cash/.

9 Mathew Ingram, "The Platform Patrons: How Facebook and Google Became Two of the Biggest Funders of Journalism in the World," *Columbia Journalism Review*, May 16, 2018, https://www.cjr.org/special_report/google-facebook-journalism.php/.

10 Interview with Julia Angwin, January 17, 2019 (notes on file with author). See also Megan Graham, "Digital Ad Revenue in the US Surpassed $100 Billion for the First Time in 2018," CNBC, May 7, 2019, https://www.cnbc.com/2019/05/07/digital-ad-revenue-in-the-us-topped-100-billion-for-the-first-time.html.

11 Peter Kafka, "BuzzFeed's New Strategy: Fishing for Eyeballs in Other People's Streams," *Vox*, March 16, 2015, https://www.vox.com/2015/3/16/11560308/buzzfeeds-new-strategy-fishing-for-eyeballs-in-other-peoples-streams.

12 Mark Zuckerberg, "Mark Zuckerberg: Facebook Can Help the News Business," *New York Times*, October 25, 2019, https://www.nytimes.com/2019/10/25/opinion/sunday/mark-zuckerberg-facebook-news.html.

13 Josh Marshall, "A Serf on Google's Farm," Talking Points Memo, September 1, 2017, https://talkingpointsmemo.com/edblog/a-serf-on-googles-farm; Nicholas Thompson and Fred Vogelstein, "Inside the Two Years That Shook Facebook—and the World," *Wired*, February 12, 2018, https://www.wired.com/story/inside-facebook-mark-zuckerberg-2-years-of-hell/. *Wired*'s Nicholas Thompson called publishers "sharecroppers" on Facebook's farm.

14 Josh Marshall, "How Facebook Punked and Then Gut Punched the News Biz," *TPM*, June 29, 2018, https://talkingpointsmemo.com/edblog/how-facebook-punked-and-then-gut-punched-the-news-biz.

15 Shira Ovide, "Facebook's Profit Margin Is Shrinking, But Not for the Reason You Think," *Bloomberg Businessweek*, November 19, 2018, https://www.bloomberg.com/news/articles/2018-11-19/facebook-s-profit-margin-is-shrinking-but-not-for-the-reason-you-think.

16 Paul Moses, "In New York City, Local Coverage Declines—and Takes Accountability with It," *Daily Beast*, April 3, 2017, updated May 5, 2017, https://www.thedailybeast.com/in-new-york-city-local-coverage-declinesand-takes-accountability-with-it. See more generally Andrew McCormick, "There Is Nobody Who Will Cover This," *Columbia Journalism Review*, April 29, 2019, https://www.cjr.org/special_report/local-news-new-york-city.php.

4. REPLACING JUSTICE WITH POWER

1 "A Litigator's Take on Arbitration and the Demise of the Jury Trial," *The Recorder*, December 21, 2015, https://www.keker.com/news/news-items/john-kekers-take-on-arbitration-and-the-demise-of-the-jury-trial.

2 Robert Fojo, "12 Reasons Businesses Should Use Arbitration Agreements," Legal IO, May 11, 2015, https://www.legal.io/guide/5550f4df77777765ebb80100/12-Reasons-Businesses-Should-Use-Arbitration-Agreements.

3 This sample comes from Amazon, "Conditions of Use: 'Service Terms: Applicable Law'" section: https://www.amazon.com/gp/help/customer/display.html/ref=hp_551434_conditions?nodeId=508088.

4 Adam J. Levitin, *Consumer Finance Law: Markets and Regulation* (New York: Wolters Kluwer, 2018), 68; "Online Access Agreement," Wells Fargo & Company, accessed November 24, 2019, https://www.wellsfargo.com/referenced/secure-session/online-banking/online-access-agreement/.

5 David Dayen, "The Biggest Abuser of Forced Arbitration Is Amazon," July 10, 2019, https://prospect.org/article/biggest-abuser-forced-arbitration-amazon; Amazon, "Conditions of Use," last updated May 21, 2018, https://www.amazon.com/gp/help/customer/display.html/?nodeId=508088&tag=zxcv123-20.

6 See, e.g., Sandeep Vaheesan, "We Must End Rule by Contract," *Current Affairs*, August 19, 2019, https://www.currentaffairs.org/2019/08/we-must-end-rule-by-contract.

7 Katherine V. W. Stone and Alexander J. S. Colvin, "The Arbitration Epidemic: Mandatory Arbitration Deprives Workers and Consumers of Their Rights," Economic Policy Institute, Briefing Paper 414, December 7, 2015, https://www.epi.org/publication/the-arbitration-epidemic/.

8 *Alexander v. Denver-Gardner Co.*, 415 U.S. 36 (1974) (italics added).

9 Ibid. (italics mine).

10. Center for Public Resources, or the International Center for Conflict Prevention & Resolution, History, https://www.cpradr.org/about/history.

11 Eric Green, "Corporate Alternative Dispute Resolution," in Eric D. Green, ed., *Disputing in America: The Lawyer's Changing Role* (New York: Aspen Law and Business, 1988), https://kb.osu.edu/bitstream/handle /1811/76163/OSJDR_V1N2_203.pdf?sequence=1.

12 Phone interview with Katherine Stone, January 28, 2019 (notes on file with author); *Gilmer v. Interstate/Johnson Lane Corp.*, 500 U.S. 20 (1991), https://supreme.justia.com/cases/federal/us/500/20/.

13 Owen M. Fiss, "Against Settlement," *Yale Law Journal* 93(6) (1984): 1073–1090.

14 *Gilmer v. Interstate/Johnson Lane Corp.*

15 Tracey Kyckelhahn and Thomas H. Cohen, "Civil Rights Complaints in U.S. District Courts, 1990–2006," Bureau of Justice Statistics Special Report, August 2008, NCJ 222989, https://www.bjs.gov/content/pub/pdf /crcusdc06.pdf.

16 Kauff, McGuire & Margolis LLP, "Clause Requiring Arbitration of Title VII Claim Upheld by Ninth Circuit," April 1, 1992, https://www.kmm .com/articles-89.html.

17 Alexander Colvin, "An Empirical Study of Employment Arbitration: Case Outcomes and Processes," *Journal of Empirical Legal Studies* 8(1) (2011): 1–23, https://digitalcommons.ilr.cornell.edu/articles/577/.

18 Deepak Gupta and Lina Khan, "Arbitration as Wealth Transfer," *Yale Law & Policy Review* 35(2) (2017): 499–520, https://ylpr.yale.edu/arbitration -wealth-transfer.

19 Alexander J. S. Colvin, "The Growing Use of Mandatory Arbitration," Economic Policy Institute, April 6, 2018, https://www.epi.org /publication/the-growing-use-of-mandatory-arbitration-access-to-the -courts-is-now-barred-for-more-than-60-million-american-workers/.

20 Ibid.

21 Tim Ryan, "Democrats Fight to Curb Forced Arbitration Clauses," Courthouse News Service, March 7, 2017, https://www.courthousenews .com/democrats-fight-curb-forced-arbitration-clauses/.

22 Jacob Gershman, "As More Companies Demand Arbitration Agreements, Sexual Harassment Claims Fizzle," *Wall Street Journal*, January 25, 2018, https://www.wsj.com/articles/as-more-employees-sign-arbitration -agreements-sexual-harassment-claims-fizzle-1516876201.

23 Howard Berkes, "Federal Workplace Law Fails to Protect Employees Left Out of Workers' Comp," NPR, January 21, 2016, https://www .npr.org/2016/01/21/460257932/federal-workplace-law-fails-to-protect -employees-left-out-of-workers-compensation.

24 Kate Hamaji, "Justice for Sale: How Corporations Use Forced Arbitration to Exploit Working Families," Center for Popular Democracy, May 2017, https://populardemocracy.org/sites/default/files/Forced-Arbitration _web%20%283%29_0.pdf.

25 Colvin, "An Empirical Study of Employment Arbitration."

26 Phone interview with Katherine Stone, January 28, 2018. Notes on file with author.

27 Judith Resnik, "Diffusing Disputes: The Public in the Private of Arbitration, the Private in Courts, and the Erasure of Rights," *Yale Law Journal* 124, 2015; *Carnegie v. Household International Inc.*, 376 F.3d 656 (7th Cir. 2004), Nos. 04-8008, 04-8009, https://caselaw.findlaw.com/us-7th-circuit/1296172.html.

28 *Am. Express Co. v. Italian Colors Rest.*, 570 U.S __ (2013) (Kagan, dissenting), https://supreme.justia.com/cases/federal/us/570/12-133/.

29 Dayen, "The Biggest Abuser of Forced Arbitration Is Amazon"; Spencer Soper, "Amazon Is Accused of Forcing Up Prices in Antitrust Complaint," Bloomberg, November 8, 2019, https://www.bloomberg.com/news/articles/2019-11-08/amazon-merchant-lays-out-antitrust-case-in-letter-to-congress. Also interview in my office with Shaoul Sussman in September 2019, comments confirmed via email on file with author, November 2019.

30 Phone interview with Charlotte Garden, February 4, 2019 (notes on file with author).

31 "A Litigator's Take on Arbitration and the Demise of the Jury Trial," *The Recorder*, December 2015, https://www.keker.com/news/news-items/john-kekers-take-on-arbitration-and-the-demise-of-the-jury-trial.

32 Miriam Gilles, "Class Warfare: The Disappearance of Low-Income Litigants from the Civil Docket," *Emory Law Journal* 65, no. 6 (2016): 1531, 1568.

33 Phone interview with Tanuja Gupta, January 29, 2019 (notes on file with author).

34 Claire Bushey, "Kirkland & Ellis Dumps Mandatory Arbitration Agreements for Some," *Crain's Chicago Business*, November 26, 2018, https://www.chicagobusiness.com/law/kirkland-ellis-dumps-mandatory-arbitration-agreements-some.

35 Phone interview with Tanuja Gupta.

36 Alexia Fernández Campbell, "A Google Walkout Organizer Just Quit," *Vox*, June 7, 2019, https://www.vox.com/policy-and-politics/2019/6/7/18656562/google-walkout-organizer-stapleton-quits.

37 Phone interview with Tanuja Gupta.

5. THE BODY SNATCHERS

1 Willis John Abbot, *Carter Henry Harrison: A Memoir* (New York: Dodd, Mead & Company, 1895), 133.

2 "New York District 19 Race: 2016 Cycle Outside Spending," OpenSecrets.org, accessed November 24, 2019, https://www.opensecrets.org/races/outside-spending?cycle=2016&id=NY19&spec=N; "New York Wins, Contributors, 2016 Cycle," OpenSecrets.org, accessed November 24, 2019, https://www.opensecrets.org/pacs/pacgave2.php?cycle=2016&cmte=C00603365; "National Horizon, Contributors, 2016 Cycle," OpenSecrets.org, accessed November 24, 2019, https://www.opensecrets.org/pacs/pacgave2.php?cycle=2016&cmte=C00519363; Caroline Kormann, "Zephyr Teachout's Loss and the Fight Against Dark

Money," *New Yorker*, November 10, 2016, https://www.newyorker
.com/news/news-desk/zephyr-teachouts-loss-and-the-fight-against
-dark-money; Paul Blumenthal, "These Super PAC Donors Were Able
to Hide Their Identities Before the Election," *Huffington Post*, December
9, 2016, https://www.huffpost.com/entry/2016-super-pac-donors_n
_584a309de4b0e05aded34958.

3 Peter Schroeder, "Zephyr Teachout Challenges Paul Singer to a Debate,"
The Hill, August 18, 2016, https://thehill.com/blogs/ballot-box/house
-races/291820-dem-candidate-challenges-opponents-donors-to-debate.

4 This double-vision—or, really, cognitive whiplash—has become an everyday hazard for any serious journalist. If you're a newspaper editor, you may
run an article on Monday exposing the sugar trade association for what it
is—not an actual association of small businesses, but a syndicate controlled
by two big sugar companies. Then on Tuesday or Wednesday you'll report
that a trade deal has been condemned by this same "trade association." On
a Friday you'll run a story showing that the corporate donations in a political race reflect no particular ideology—just a concern for the bottom line;
then that Sunday you'll refer to corporate ads as "Republican-aligned" or
"Democrat-aligned," as if these ads conveyed political convictions.

5 Hannah Arendt, *The Human Condition*, 2nd ed. (Chicago: University of
Chicago Press, 1998), 52–53.

6 See Nancy Rosenblum, *On the Side of Angels* (Princeton, NJ: Princeton
University Press, 2008). Rosenblum explores the essential value that political parties play, despite being so universally hated. Without political
parties, the locus of deliberation in contemporary theory is ambiguous;
"the often invoked 'public sphere' is everywhere and nowhere."

7 Diana Evans, "Johnson versus Koskoff," in James A. Thurber, ed., *The
Battle for Congress: Consultants, Candidates, and Voters* (Washington, DC:
Brookings Institute Press, 2001), 76.

8 Center for Responsive Politics, "Outside Spending," OpenSecrets.org,
https://www.opensecrets.org/outsidespending.

9 "Indiana Senate 2018 Race, Candidates," OpenSecrets.org, accessed November 24, 2019, https://www.opensecrets.org/races/candidates?cycle
=2018&id=INS1&spec=N; "Indiana Senate Race, Outside Spending, 2018
Cycle," OpenSecrets.org, accessed November 24, 2019, https://www
.opensecrets.org/races/outside-spending?cycle=2018&id=INS1&spec=N;
"Missouri Senate 2018 Race, Candidates," OpenSecrets.org, accessed November 24, 2019, https://www.opensecrets.org/races/candidates?cycle
=2018&id=MOS2&spec=N; "Missouri Senate Race, Outside Spending,
2018 Cycle," OpenSecrets.org, accessed November 24, 2019, https://www
.opensecrets.org/races/outside-spending?cycle=2018&id=MOS2&spec=N.

10 "West Virginia Senate 2018 Race," OpenSecrets.org, accessed November
24, 2019, https://www.opensecrets.org/races/summary?id=WVS1&cycle
=2018; "West Virginia Senate Race," OpenSecrets.org, accessed November
24, 2019, https://www.opensecrets.org/races/outside-spending?cycle
=2018&id=WVS1&spec=N.

11 Americans for Prosperity, "AFP Commits Seven Figures to Judge Kava-
    naugh's Confirmation, Urges a Swift Action in Senate," July 9, 2018, https://
    americansforprosperity.org/afp-applauds-the-trump-administration-on
    -the-nomination-of-judge-kavanaugh-and-urges-a-swift-confirmation/.

12 Carl Hulse and Ashley Parker, "Koch Group, Spending Freely, Hones At-
    tack on Government," *New York Times*, March 20, 2014, https://www
    .nytimes.com/2014/03/21/us/politics/koch-group-seeks-lasting-voice
    -for-small-government.html; Jim Geraghty, "Koch World Faces Year
    Two of the Trump Era—and the 2018 Midterms," *National Review*, Janu-
    ary 29, 2019, https://www.nationalreview.com/2018/01/koch-brothers
    -network-faces-midterms-year-two-trump-administration/.

13 Alexis de Tocqueville, *Democracy in America: Historical-Critical Edition*, 3rd
    ed., Eduardo Nolla, ed., James T. Schleifer, trans. (Indianapolis: Liberty
    Fund, 2010), 950.

14 Phone interview with Rutgers business professor Michael Barnett, April
    2014, confirmed via email in November 2019, notes on file with author.

15 Phone interview with Lee Drutman, May 2014, notes on file with author,
    confirmed in email exchange in November 2019.

16 Comcast Corp., Summary, 2013, OpenSecrets.org, https://www.opensecrets
    .org/lobby/clientsum.php?id=D000000461&year=2013; National Assn. of
    Broadcasters, Summary, 2018, OpenSecrets.org, https://www.opensecrets
    .org/pacs/lookup2.php?strID=C00009985&cycle=2018.

17 Ben Fagan-Watson, "Big Business Using Trade Groups to Lobby Against
    EU Climate Policy," *Guardian*, April 15, 2015, https://www.theguardian
    .com/sustainable-business/2015/apr/15/big-business-trade-groups-lobby
    -against-eu-climate-change.

18 Matt Weinberg, "New Tech Trade Associations Will Have Big Role in Future
    Tech Policy," TechCrunch, May 2, 2017, https://techcrunch.com/2017/05
    /02/new-tech-trade-associations-will-have-big-role-in-future-tech-policy/.

19 Ibid.

20 Alexander Hertel-Fernandez, *Politics at Work: How Companies Turn Their
    Workers into Lobbyists* (New York: Oxford University Press, 2018), 90.

21 Chris Matyszczyk, "In a Startling New Study, Companies Admit to
    Spying on Employees Far More Than Employees Realize," *Inc.*, June 21,
    2018, https://www.inc.com/chris-matyszczyk/study-shows-how-much
    -companies-spy-on-employees.html.

22 Caroline O'Donovan, "Walmart's Newly Patented Technology for Eaves-
    dropping on Workers Presents Privacy Concerns," BuzzFeed News, July
    11, 2018, https://www.buzzfeednews.com/article/carolineodonovan
    /walmart-just-patented-audio-surveillance-technology-for#.ieNKjR6j6.

23 Abbot, *Carter Henry Harrison*, 133.

24 Hannah Knowles, "Amazon Spent $1.5 Million on Seattle City Council
    Races. The Socialist It Opposed Has Won," *Washington Post*, Novem-
    ber 10, 2019, https://www.washingtonpost.com/nation/2019/11/10
    /amazon-spent-million-seattle-city-council-races-socialist-it-opposed
    -has-won/.

6. RACE AND MONOPOLY POWER

1 "Wealth Gaps Rise to Record Highs Between Whites, Blacks, Hispanics," Pew Research Center, July 26, 2011, https://www.pewsocialtrends.org /2011/07/26/wealth-gaps-rise-to-record-highs-between-whites-blacks -hispanics/.

2 Mehrsa Baradaran, "A Bad Check for Black America," *Boston Review*, No- vember 9, 2017, http://bostonreview.net/class-inequality-race/mehrsa -baradaran-bad-check-black-america. Mehrsa not only looks at the obvi- ous examples of openly racist policies but the challenges of black capital access under a model of black capitalism: the institutions, including black banks, that are often imagined to be well positioned to provide better access are themselves trapped in a system that doesn't allow them to provide the much-needed credit, but forces them to transfer wealth to the increasingly concentrated and white-controlled financial sector. This is because while black banks might lend to black homeowners, the money borrowed was go- ing to white-owned real estate owners, who invested that money in white communities. See also Mehrsa Baradaran, *The Color of Money: Black Banks and the Racial Wealth Gap* (Cambridge, MA: Belknap Press, 2017), 95.

3 Gilbert Mason and James Patterson Smith, *Beaches, Blood and Ballots: A Black Doctor's Civil Rights Struggles* (Jackson: University Press of Mississippi, 2000).

4 Ibid.

5 Louis Fergeler and Matthew Lavallee, "How Black Businesses Helped Save the Civil Rights Movement," Institute for New Economic Thinking, Jan- uary 15, 2018, https://www.ineteconomics.org/perspectives/blog/how -black-businesses-helped-save-the-civil-rights-movement.

6 Kim Severson, "Another Role for Buses in Civil Rights History," *New York Times*, March 18, 2011, http://www.nytimes.com/2011/03/19/us /19birmingham.html.

7 Tiffany Stanley, "The Disappearance of a Distinctively Black Way to Mourn," *Atlantic*, January 26, 2016, https://www.theatlantic.com/business/archive /2016/01/black-funeral-homes-mourning/426807/?fbclid=IwAR3kvbtmq asds78IBdAFdpEoTGIGGssMMVwAA7ADwmqCPBmh4xgPR2WX2ow &utm_campaign=the-atlantic&utm_content=5c63c3fa00bd47000171b9e6 _ta&utm_medium=social&utm_source=facebook.

8 Brian Feldman, "The Number of Black-Owned Businesses Has Plum- meted Since the 1970s. Here's Why," *Washington Monthly*, March 15, 2017, https://washingtonmonthly.com/magazine/marchaprilmay-2017 /the-decline-of-black-business/.

9 Hilary Potkewitz, "Grave Situation for City's Funeral Homes as Death Rate Drops and Customs Change," *Crain's New York Business*, July 24, 2016, https://www.crainsnewyork.com/article/20160724/SMALLBIZ /160729946/once-seen-as-recession-proof-the-funeral-industry-is-in-a -death-spiral-some-owners-are-staving-off-the-end-by-cat.

10 Andrew Soergel, "Most of America's Businesses Run by White Men," *U.S. News & World Report*, September 1, 2016, https://www.usnews.com

/news/articles/2016-09-01/most-of-americas-businesses-run-by-white
-men-says-census-bureau.

11 Jeffrey McKinney, "Black Asset Management Firms Manage Only 1.1%
of the Total $71.4 Trillion in Assets," *Black Enterprise*, January 31, 2018,
https://www.blackenterprise.com/black-asset-management-firms
-manage-1-1-total-71-4-trillion-assets/.

12 Danielle Wiener-Bronner, "Soon, There Will Be Just 3 Black Fortune 500
CEOs," CNN Business, October 20, 2017, http://money.cnn.com/2017
/10/19/news/companies/black-ceos-fortune-500/index.html.

13 The modern efforts to gerrymander state legislatures in favor of Republicans were spearheaded by the Republican State Leadership Committee
(RSLC), a dark-money group that takes unlimited corporate contributions.
Walmart was consistently among the top donors to the RSLC during the
early years of its redistricting push. See Janet Burns, "Dear AT&T, Boeing, Pfizer, Comcast, Walmart, Etc: Stop Funding Abortion Attackers,"
Forbes, August 21, 2019, https://www.forbes.com/sites/janetwburns/2019
/08/21/dear-att-boeing-pfizer-google-comcast-stop-funding-abortion
-attackers/#41de78ef5f35.

14 Joshua Sophy, "Franchise Business Ownership Among Women and Minorities Hits Record Levels," Small Business Trends, June 2, 2018, https://
smallbiztrends.com/2018/03/women-and-minorities-franchise-owners
-statistics.html.

15 Nicholas Confessore, "Minority Groups and Bottlers Team Up in Battles over Soda," *New York Times*, March 12, 2013, http://www.nytimes
.com/2013/03/13/nyregion/behind-soda-industrys-win-a-phalanx-of
-sponsored-minority-groups.html; Lee Fang, "Comcast-Funded Civil
Rights Groups Claim Low-Income People Prefer Ads over Privacy," *The
Intercept*, March 29 2017, https://theintercept.com/2017/03/29/isp-civil
-rights/.

16 Steven Melendez, "Why Civil Rights Groups Are Siding with Telecom
Giants in the Net Neutrality Fight," *Fast Company*, February 14, 2017,
https://www.fastcompany.com/4030687/why-civil-rights-groups-are
-siding-with-telecom-giants-in-the-net-neutrality-fight.

17 William Wan, "Inside the Republican Creation of the North Carolina
Voting Bill Dubbed the 'Monster' Law," *Washington Post*, September 2,
2016, https://www.washingtonpost.com/politics/courts_law/inside
-the-republican-creation-of-the-north-carolina-voting-bill-dubbed-the
-monster-law/2016/09/01/79162398-6adf-11e6-8225-fbb8a6fc65bc
_story.html.

18 WLOS News 13, "Daily Show Sparks Local Controversy," You-
Tube video, November 19, 2013, https://www.youtube.com/watch?v
=5HSWmCqBshk.

19 *North Carolina State Conference of the NAACP v. McCrory*, 831 F.3d 204,
214, 229 (4th Cir. 2016).

20 Ari Berman, *Give Us the Ballot: The Modern Struggle for Voting Rights in
America* (New York: Picador, 2015).

21 Yvonne Wingett Sanchez and Rob O'Dell, "What Is ALEC? 'The Most
    Effective Organization' for Conservatives, Says Newt Gingrich," *USA To-
    day*, April 3, 2019, https://www.usatoday.com/story/news/investigations
    /2019/04/03/alec-american-legislative-exchange-council-model-bills
    -republican-conservative-devos-gingrich/3162357002/.

22 Wendy R. Weiser and Lawrence Norden, "Voting Law Changes in 2012,"
    Brennan Center for Justice, 2011, https://www.brennancenter.org/sites
    /default/files/2019-08/Report_Voting_Law_Changes_2012.pdf.

23 John Grooms, "Thom Tillis Is N.C.'s No. 1 Weasel," *Creative Loafing Char-
    lotte*, August 16, 2011, https://clclt.com/charlotte/thom-tillis-is-ncs-no1
    -weasel/Content?oid=2446580.

24 Alan Greenblatt, "ALEC Enjoys a New Wave of Influence and Criticism,"
    Governing the States and Localities, December 2011, https://www.governing
    .com/topics/politics/ALEC-enjoys-new-wave-influence-criticism.html.

25 Wan, "Inside the Republican Creation of the North Carolina Voting Bill
    Dubbed the 'Monster' Law."

26 Email correspondence with Marcellus Andrews, September 14, 2019
    (notes on file with author).

27 Ibid.

28 Gerald Berk, "Monopoly and Its Discontents," *American Prospect*, Oc-
    tober 9, 2019, https://prospect.org/culture/books/monopoly-and-its
    -discontents-stoller-goliath/.

29 Safiya Noble, *Algorithms of Oppression* (New York: New York University
    Press, 2018). See also Olivier Sylvain, "A Watchful Eye on Facebook's Ad-
    vertising Practices," *New York Times*, March 28, 2019, https://www.nytimes
    .com/2019/03/28/opinion/facebook-ad-discrimination-race.html.

30 Jonathan Cohn, "Google's Algorithms Discriminate Against Women and
    People of Color," *Bright Magazine*, May 16, 2019, https://brightthemag
    .com/googles-algorithms-discriminate-against-women-and-people-of
    -color-578abb8a47c1.

31 Salvador Rodriguez, "Facebook Apologizes After Employees Complain
    About Racist Company Culture," CNBC, November 8, 2019, https://
    www.cnbc.com/2019/11/08/facebook-racism-complaints-by-anonymous
    -employees-company-apologizes.html.

32 Farhad Manjoo, "Here's the Conversation We Really Need to Have About
    Bias at Google," *New York Times*, August 30, 2018, https://www.nytimes
    .com/2018/08/30/technology/bias-google-trump.html.

33 Emily Dreyfuss, "Facebook Changes Its Ad Tech to Stop Discrimina-
    tion," *Wired*, March 19, 2019, https://www.wired.com/story/facebook
    -advertising-discrimination-settlement/.

34 John Detrixhe and Jeremy B. Merrill, "The Fight Against Financial Ad-
    vertisers Using Facebook for Digital Redlining," *Quartz*, https://qz.com
    /1733345/the-fight-against-discriminatory-financial-ads-on-facebook/.

35 Queenie Wong, "Facebook Again Accused of Discriminatory Ad Target-
    ing," CNET, November 1, 2019, https://www.cnet.com/news/facebook
    -accused-of-discriminatory-ad-targeting-yet-again/.

36 Pema Levy, "Facebook Is Cracking Down on Ad Discrimination. But the Bias May Be Embedded in Its Own Algorithms," *Mother Jones*, July 12, 2019, https://www.motherjones.com/politics/2019/07/facebook-is -cracking-down-on-ad-discrimination-but-the-bias-may-be-embedded -in-its-own-algorithms/.

37 Frank Pasquale, "Paradoxes of Digital Antitrust," *Harvard Journal of Law and Technology*, https://jolt.law.harvard.edu/assets/misc/Pasquale.pdf.

38 Timothy Karr, "People of Color Need the Open Internet: Racial-Justice Coalition Urges the FCC to Preserve Net Neutrality Under Title II," FP News Release, July 20, 2017, https://www.freepress.net/news/press -releases/people-color-need-open-internet-racial-justice-coalition-urges -fcc-preserve-net.

39 Color of Change, "Tell the FCC to Protect Net Neutrality" [Petition], accessed November 7, 2019, https://act.colorofchange.org/sign/tell-fcc -protect-net-neutrality.

40 Steven G. Calabresi and Larissa Price, "Monopolies and the Constitution: A History of Crony Capitalism," Faculty Working Papers, Paper 214 (2012), http://scholarlycommons.law.northwestern.edu/facultyworkingpapers/214.

7. THE WAGE MYSTERY

1 Diana Hembree, "CEO Pay Skyrockets to 361 Times That of the Average Worker," *Forbes*, May 22, 2018, https://www.forbes.com/sites /dianahembree/2018/05/22/ceo-pay-skyrockets-to-361-times-that-of -the-average-worker/#1e93a259776d.

2 Yuki Noguchi, "Solving the 'Wage Puzzle': Why Aren't Paychecks Growing?" NPR, August 2, 2018, https://www.npr.org/2018/08/02 /634754091/solving-the-wage-puzzle-why-aren-t-paychecks-growing.

3 Robert J. Samuelson, "Wages Aren't Rising. These Theories Could Explain Why," *Washington Post*, July 11, 2018, https://www.washingtonpost.com /opinions/wages-arent-rising-these-theories-could-explain-why/2018/07 /11/eeb938f4-8529-11e8-8f6c-46cb43e3f306_story.html.

4 Ibid.

5 "Rising Prices, Flat Wages: The Economy's Booming, So Why Are Working People Still Broke?" IBEW Media Center, July 24, 2018, http://www .ibew.org/media-center/Articles/18Daily/1807/180724_RisingPrices.

6 Paul Krugman, "Is the Great Recession Still Holding Down Wages? (Wonkish)," *New York Times*, May 4, 2018, https://www.nytimes.com /2018/05/04/opinion/is-the-great-recession-still-holding-down-wages -wonkish.html.

7 Yasser Abdih, "Chart of the Week: An Answer to the U.S. Wage Puzzle," IMF Blog, International Monetary Fund, July 10, 2018, https://blogs .imf.org/2018/07/10/chart-of-the-week-an-answer-to-the-u-s-wage -puzzle/.

8 Ibid.

9 Simcha Barkai, "Declining Labor and Capital Shares," Stigler Center for the Study of the Economy and the State, University of Chicago Booth School of Business, New Working Paper Series No. 2, November 2016, https://research .chicagobooth.edu/~/media/5872FBEB104245909B8F0AE8A84486C9 .pdf. Arne Alsin, "The Ugly Truth Behind Stock Buybacks," *Forbes*, February 28, 2017, https://www.forbes.com/sites/aalsin/2017/02/28/shareholders -should-be-required-to-vote-on-stock-buybacks/#7c5ec43e6b1e.

10 José Azar, Emiliano Huet-Vaughn, Ioana Marinescu, Bledi Taska, and Till Von Wachter, "Minimum Wage Employment Effects and Labor Market Concentration," National Bureau of Economic Research, NBER Working Paper 26101 (July 2019), https://doi.org/10.3386/w26101.

11 Since part of the argument of this book is that we need to reclaim economic policy from economists who have failed us and who use jargon to make people feel inadequate in their ability to assess policy, I resist using their terms.

12 "In the status quo sans minimum wage, workers in such a labor market are paid below marginal productivity." Azar et al., "Minimum Wage Employment Effects and Labor Market Concentration."

13 Barkai, "Declining Labor and Capital Shares."

14 José A. Azar, Ioana Marinescu, Marshall I. Steinbaum, and Bledi Taska, "Concentration in US Labor Markets: Evidence from Online Vacancy Data," National Bureau of Economic Research, Working Paper 24395, March 2018, revised February 2019, https://www.nber.org/papers/w24395.pdf.

15 Paul Krugman, "Monopsony, Rigidity, and the Wage Puzzle (Wonkish)," *New York Times*, May 20, 2018, https://www.nytimes.com/2018/05/20 /opinion/monopsony-rigidity-and-the-wage-puzzle-wonkish.html.

16 Teresa Ghilarducci, "Why Wages Won't Rise When Unemployment Falls," *Forbes*, July 18, 2018, https://www.forbes.com/sites/teresaghilarducci /2018/07/18/why-wages-wont-rise-when-unemployment-falls /#2e93f0ff5d9d.

17 Many of these stores are themselves franchises.

18 Rachel Abrams, "Why Aren't Paychecks Growing? A Burger-Joint Clause Offers a Clue," *New York Times*, September 27, 2017, https://www .nytimes.com/2017/09/27/business/pay-growth-fast-food-hiring.html.

19 Nandita Bose, "Half of Walmart's Workforce Are Part-Time Workers: Labor Group," Reuters, May 25, 2018, https://www.reuters.com/article /us-walmart-workers/half-of-walmarts-workforce-are-part-time-workers -labor-group-idUSKCN1IQ295.

20. See Binyamin Applebaum, *The Economists' Hour: False Prophets, Free Markets, and the Fracture of Society* (London: Pan Macmillan, 2019).

21 Tony Abraham, "Healthcare Jobs Grow at Rapid Clip, but Wages Lag amid Consolidation Boom," HealthcareDive.com, April 16, 2019, https:// www.healthcaredive.com/news/healthcare-jobs-grow-at-rapid-clip-but -wages-lag-amid-consolidation-boom/552765/.

22 Kathleen Elkins, "Here's How Much Money the Average Millennial Has in Savings," CNBC.com, September 19, 2017, https://www.cnbc.com/2017 /09/14/how-much-money-the-average-millennial-has-in-savings.html.

23 On the other hand, CEO pay is increasingly arbitrary as well, and not only
   grotesque but disconnected from success or performance. CEOs whose
   companies failed or were bailed out by taxpayers made up a quarter of the
   top 500 best-paid CEOs. Richard Fuld was one of the highest-paid CEOs
   for eight years—and then Lehman Brothers collapsed. He wasn't an anom-
   aly. CEO salaries keep rising, regardless of value—nearly 40% of the top-
   paid CEOs led companies that were involved in serious fraud, went bust,
   or were bailed out. See Zoë Carpenter, "Paying CEOs Top Dollar for Poor
   Performance," *The Nation*, August 28, 2013, https://www.thenation.com
   /article/paying-ceos-top-dollar-poor-performance/; "9 Wall Street Execs
   Who Cashed In on the Crisis," *Mother Jones* (January/February 2010),
   https://www.motherjones.com/politics/2010/01/wall-street-bailout
   -executive-compensation/; Peter Eavis, "It's Never Been Easier to Be a
   C.E.O., and the Pay Keeps Rising," *New York Times*, May 24, 2019, https://
   www.nytimes.com/2019/05/24/business/highest-paid-ceos-2018.html.

24 Joseph Carino, "Uber Driver Tracking and Telematics," Geotab Blog,
   January 15, 2018, https://www.geotab.com/blog/uber-driver-tracking/.
   Caroline O'Donovan, "This Creepy Time-Tracking Software Is Like Having Your Boss Watch You Every Second," Buzzfeed News, August 7, 2018,
   https://www.buzzfeednews.com/article/carolineodonovan/upwork
   -freelancers-work-diary-keystrokes-screenshot.

25 Colin Drury, "Amazon Workers 'Forced to Urinate in Plastic Bottles Because They Cannot Go to Toilet on Shift,'" Independent Digital News and
   Media, *The Independent*, July 19, 2019, https://www.independent.co.uk
   /news/uk/home-news/amazon-protests-workers-urinate-plastic-bottles
   -no-toilet-breaks-milton-keynes-jeff-bezos-a9012351.html; Jodi Kantor
   and David Streitfeld, "Inside Amazon: Wrestling Big Ideas in a Bruising
   Workplace," *New York Times*, August 15, 2015, https://www.nytimes.com
   /2015/08/16/technology/inside-amazon-wrestling-big-ideas-in-a-bruising
   -workplace.html?_r=1&assetType=nyt_now. Amazon disputes these claims.

26 Alejandra Cancino and Jessica Wohl, "McDonald's Workers Allege Injuries, Unsafe Conditions," *Chicago Tribune*, March 16, 2015, https://www
   .chicagotribune.com/business/ct-mcdonalds-osha-complaints-0317-biz
   -20150316-story.html.

27 Cora Lewis, "America's Largest Meat Producer Averages One Ampu-
   tation Per Month," BuzzFeed News, February 18, 2016, https://www
   .buzzfeednews.com/article/coralewis/americas-largest-meat-producer
   -one-amputation-per-month#.pxxm3zY5Z.

28 "No Relief: The Denial of Bathroom Breaks in the Poultry Industry,"
   Oxfam America, 2016, https://www.oxfamamerica.org/static/media/files
   /No_Relief.pdf.

29 "Feeling Powerless Increases the Weight of the World . . . Literally," University of Cambridge, February 4, 2014, https://www.cam.ac.uk/research
   /news/feeling-powerless-increases-the-weight-of-the-world-literally. In an
   experiment, volunteers ranked a series of questions about their own perception of power in the world, like "I can get people to listen to what I say."

They were then asked to guess the weight of a series of boxes. The people who did not feel they could get others to listen to them guessed that the boxes were heavier. In another experiment, volunteers who had just reflected on a moment they felt powerful thought that the boxes were lighter, compared to those who had just reflected on a moment they felt powerless.

30 Jacob Passy, "Google Has More Temp and Contract Workers Than Actual Employees—But They Have Far Fewer Rights," MarketWatch, May 30, 2019, https://www.marketwatch.com/story/google-has-more-temp -and-contract-workers-than-actual-employees-but-they-have-far-fewer -rights-2019-05-30; Daisuke Wakabayashi, "Google's Shadow Workforce: Temps Who Outnumber Full-Time Employees," *New York Times*, May 28, 2019, https://www.nytimes.com/2019/05/28/technology/google-temp -workers.html.

31 Lisa Disselkamp, David Parent, and Werner Nieuwondt, "Workforce on Demand," Deloitte Insights, February 27, 2015, https://www2.deloitte .com/us/en/insights/focus/human-capital-trends/2015/on-demand -workforce-human-capital-trends-2015.html.

32 Aaron R. Hanlon, "America's Real-Life Dystopia: Wal-Mart Is Straight out of George Orwell and Aldous Huxley," *Salon*, December 2, 2015, https://www.salon.com/2015/12/02/is_wal_mart_more_like_orwells _1984_huxleys_brave_new_world_or_kim_jong_uns_north_korea/.

33 Bryan Menegus, "Amazon's Aggressive Anti-Union Tactics Revealed in Leaked 45-Minute Video," Gizmodo, September 26, 2018, https:// gizmodo.com/amazons-aggressive-anti-union-tactics-revealed-in-leake -1829305201.

34 Stephen B. Moldof, "Cross-Border Mergers and Acquisitions: A Union Perspective," Panel on Cross-Border Mergers and Acquisitions, American Bar Association, Labor & Employment Law Section Annual Meeting, Toronto, Canada, August 5, 2011, https://www.americanbar.org/content /dam/aba/administrative/labor_law/meetings/2011/annualmeeting/005 .authcheckdam.pdf.

35 Harold Pierce, "Healthcare Workers to Protest Dignity Mega Merger Tuesday at Mercy Hospital Southwest," Bakersfield.com, https://www .bakersfield.com/news/healthcare-workers-to-protest-dignity-mega-merger -tuesday-at-mercy/article_ac278c08-15d4-11e8-a466-73584dff738c.html.

36 Ibid.

37 Samantha Liss, "CommonSpirit Health Posts $600M Operating Loss in 2019," HealthcareDive.com, October 7, 2019, https://www .healthcaredive.com/news/commonspirit-health-posts-600m-operating -loss-in-2019/564460/.

38 S. E. Smith, "He Needed a Gender Affirming Procedure. The Hospital Said No," *Vox*, November 1, 2019, https://www.vox.com/the-highlight/2019 /10/25/20929539/catholic-hospitals-religious-refusal-rural-health-care -evan-minton.

39 "Largest Pay TV Providers in the U.S. 2019," Statista, https://www .statista.com/statistics/251793/pay-tv-providers-with-the-largest-number

-of-subscribers-in-the-us/; Maggie McGrath, "Comcast Strikes Deal with Charter to Divest Nearly 4 Million Subscribers," *Forbes*, April 28, 2014, https://www.forbes.com/sites/maggiemcgrath/2014/04/28/comcast -strikes-deal-with-charter-to-divest-nearly-4-million-subscribers /#273011cd7a45.

40 Chaim Gartenberg, "Charter-Spectrum Reaches $174.2 Million Settlement in New York AG's Speed Fraud Lawsuit," *The Verge*, December 18, 2018, https: www.theverge.com/2018/12/18/18146210/charter-spectrum-174 -million-settlement-new-york-state-attorney-general-internet-speeds; Liz Robbins, "A Victory for Spectrum Customers: Charter to Pay $75 Refunds and Offer Free HBO," *New York Times*, December 18, 2018, https://www .nytimes.com/2018/12/18/nyregion/charter-cable-settlement-lawsuit .html; Lauren Feiner, "Charter Communications Customers to Get Millions in Payments in Internet Speed Fraud Case," CNBC, December 18, 2018, https://www.cnbc.com/2018/12/18/charter-communications-settles-fraud -case-with-ny-attorney-general.html.

41 Jon Brodkin, "NY Says Charter Lied About New Broadband, Threatens to Revoke Its Franchise," *Ars Technica*, March 20, 2018, https://arstechnica .com/tech-policy/2018/03/ny-says-charter-lied-about-new-broadband -threatens-to-revoke-its-franchise/.

42 Notes on file with author. Asked not to be named.

43 Mark Brueggenjohann, "IBEW Supports AT&T Time Warner Merger," Press release, IBEW Media Center, November 29, 2017, http://www .ibew.org/media-center/Articles/17Daily/1711/171128_IBEWSupports.

44 "CWA Offers Full Support for AT&T–Time Warner Merger," Communications Workers of America, Press release, November 14, 2017, https:// www.cwa-union.org/news/releases/cwa-offers-full-support-for-att-time -warner-merger.

45 Josh Eidelson, "Union Says AT&T Reneged on Pact from Before Time Warner Deal," Bloomberg.com, July 18, 2019, https://www.bloomberg .com/news/articles/2019-07-18/union-says-at-t-reneged-on-deal-made -before-time-warner-merger.

46 United Steelworkers, "American, European and South American Labor Unions from Dow Chemical and DuPont Share Common Concerns at Dow North American Labor Council Meeting," September 30, 2016, https://m .usw.org/news/media-center/releases/2016/american-european-and-south -american-labor-unions-from-dow-chemical-and-dupont-share-common -concerns-at-dow-north-american-labor-council-meeting.

47 J. Adam Cobb and Ken-Hou Lin, "Growing Apart: The Changing Firm-Size Wage Premium and Its Inequality Consequences," *Organization Science* (May 2017), https://pdfs.semanticscholar.org/09eb/36fa81973b9d6d eacc82ea190f7faf131b69.pdf.

48 Nicholas Bloom, Fatih Guvenen, Benjamin S. Smith, Jae Song, and Till von Wachter, "The Disappearing Large-Firm Wage Premium," *AEA Papers and Proceedings* 108 (2018): 317–322, https://nbloom.people.stanford.edu /sites/g/files/sbiybj4746/f/pandp.20181066.pdf.

49 David Bacon, "Why These Farm Workers Went on Strike—and Why It Matters," *The Nation*, October 3, 2016, https://www.thenation.com /article/why-these-farm-workers-went-on-strike-and-why-it-matters/.

50 David Bacon, "The Cross-Border Farmworker Rebellion," *The American Prospect*, October 31, 2018, https://prospect.org/article/cross-border -farmworker-rebellion.

51 Ibid.

52 Phone interview with Jose Oliva, January 30, 2019, notes on file with author. See also Stephanie Strom, "Driscoll's Aims to Hook the Berry-Buying Shopper," *New York Times*, September 6, 2016, https://www .nytimes.com/2016/09/07/business/driscolls-aims-to-hook-the-berry -buying-shopper.html; "Driscoll's Workers Call for Global Boycott over Alleged Abuses at World's Biggest Berry Distributor," Democracy Now!, May 9, 2016, https://www.democracynow.org/2016/5/9/driscolls _workers_call_for_cross_border.

8. THE MONEY POWER

1 William Jennings Bryan, New York Reception, 1906.

2 Tami Luhby, "The Top 26 Billionaires Own $1.4 Trillion—as Much as 3.8 Billion Other People," CNN, January 21, 2019, cnn.com/2019/01/20 /business/oxfam-billionaires-davos/index.html.

3 Oxfam, "Just 8 Men Own Same Wealth as Half the World," Press release, January 16, 2017, https://www.oxfam.org/en/press-releases/just-8-men -own-same-wealth-half-world.

4 "The Richest People in the World," *Forbes*, March 5, 2019, https://www .forbes.com/billionaires/#6f92253e251c.

5 David Streitfeld, "Amazon's Antitrust Antagonist Has a Breakthrough Idea," *New York Times*, September 7, 2018, https://www.nytimes.com /2018/09/07/technology/monopoly-antitrust-lina-khan-amazon.html.

6 Felicity Barringer and Geraldine Fabrikant, "Coming of Age at Bloomberg L.P.," *New York Times*, November 4, 2019, https://www.nytimes.com /1999/03/21/business/coming-of-age-at-bloomberg-lp.html. See also Ben McLannahan, "Banks Back Rival to Bloomberg Messaging System," CNBC, July 21, 2015, https://www.cnbc.com/2015/07/21/banks-back -rival-to-bloomberg-messaging-system.html (discussing the dominance of Instant Bloomberg, the messaging service).

7 Charles Dickens, *Great Expectations* (New York: Shine Classics, 2014), 92.

8 David Dayen, "Special Investigation: The Dirty Secret Behind Warren Buffett's Billions," *The Nation*, February 15, 2018, https://www.thenation .com/article/special-investigation-the-dirty-secret-behind-warren -buffetts-billions/.

9 Jonathan Laing, "The Collector: Investor Who Piled Up $100 Million in the '60s Piles Up Firms Today," *Wall Street Journal*, March 31, 1977, http://online .wsj.com/public/resources/documents/1977Buffett0502.pdf.

10 Jonathan Tepper and Denise Hearn, *The Myth of Capitalism* (Hoboken, NJ: John Wiley & Sons, 2019), 2.

11 See excerpt in Jonathan Tepper and Denise Hearn, "Where Warren Buffett and Silicon Valley Billionaires Agree," Barrons.com, December 11, 2018, https://www.barrons.com/articles/myth-of-capitalism-book-excerpt -51544500404.

12 Mark DeCambre, "Goldman Sachs Thinks the Best Mergers Are Ones That Create Oligopolies," *Quartz*, February 14, 2014, https://qz.com /177395/goldman-sachs-thinks-the-best-kinds-of-mergers-create -oligopolies/.

13 Michael Porter, *Competitive Strategy: Techniques for Analyzing Industries and Competitors* (New York: Free Press, 1980).

14 James Currier, "70% of Value in Tech is Driven by Network Effects," Medium, November 28, 2017, https://medium.com/@nfx/70-of-value -in-tech-is-driven-by-network-effects-8c4788528e35.

15 Milind Lele, *Monopoly Rules: How to Find, Capture, and Control the Most Lucrative Markets in Any Business* (New York: Crown Business, 2005), 205. "Big Tech Hires Lawyers and Boosts Lobbying Groups to Repel Antitrust Onslaught," *The Gazette*, June 8, 2019, https://www.thegazette .com/subject/news/business/big-tech-hires-lawyers-and-boosts-lobbying -groups-to-repel-antitrust-onslaught-20190608.

16 Einer Elhauge, "The Greatest Anticompetitive Threat of Our Time: Fixing the Horizontal Shareholding Problem," ProMarket, January 7, 2019, https://promarket.org/greatest-anticompetitive-threat-horizontal -shareholding/.

17 Germán Gutiérrez and Thomas Philippon, "Investment-less Growth: An Empirical Investigation," Brookings Papers on Economic Activity (September 2017), https://www.brookings.edu/wp-content/uploads/2017/09 /2_gutierrezphilippon.pdf.

18 Miguel Anton, Florian Ederer, Mireia Gine, and Martin C. Schmalz, "Common Ownership, Competition, and Top Management Incentives" (June 1, 2018), Ross School of Business Paper No. 1328; European Corporate Governance Institute (ECGI)-Finance Working Paper No. 511/2017. Available at SSRN: https://ssrn.com/abstract=2802332 or http://dx.doi .org/10.2139/ssrn.2802332.

19 Einer Elhauge, "The Greatest Anticompetitive Threat of Our Time: Fixing the Horizontal Shareholding Problem," Pro-Market, January 7, 2019, https://promarket.org/greatest-anticompetitive-threat-horizontal -shareholding/. José Azar, Sahil Raina, and Martin C. Schmalz, "Ultimate Ownership and Bank Competition" (May 4, 2019). Available at SSRN: https://ssrn.com/abstract=2710252 or http://dx.doi.org/10.2139/ssrn .2710252.

20 Martin Schmalz, "Warren Buffett Is Betting the Airline Oligopoly Is Here to Stay," *Harvard Business Review*, November 17, 2016, https://hbr .org/2016/11/warren-buffett-is-betting-the-airline-oligopoly-is-here-to -stay; Eric A. Posner, Fiona Scott Morton, and E. Glen Weyl, "A Proposal

to Limit the Anti-Competitive Power of Institutional Investors," *Antitrust Law Journal* 81 (January 2017), https://scholarship.law.berkeley.edu/cgi /viewcontent.cgi?article=1100&context=law_econ.

21 Schmalz, "Warren Buffett Is Betting the Airline Oligopoly Is Here to Stay."

22 Ibid.

23 George Dallas, "Common Ownership: Do Institutional Investors Really Promote Anti-Competitive Behavior?" International Corporate Governance Network (ICGN), December 2, 2018.

24 Schmalz, "Warren Buffett Is Betting the Airline Oligopoly Is Here to Stay"; Posner, Morton, and Weyl, "A Proposal to Limit the Anti-Competitive Power of Institutional Investors."

25 Patrick Barta, "Do Predatory Lending Laws Hurt High-Risk Borrowers?" *Wall Street Journal*, October 14, 2002, https://www.wsj.com/articles /SB1034548477515572956. See also Kathleen Engel and Patricia McCoy, "A Tale of Three Markets: The Law and Economics of Predatory Lending," *Texas Law Review* 80, no. 6 (May 2002): 1258, http://lawdigitalcommons .bc.edu/cgi/viewcontent.cgi?article=1783&context=lsfp.

26 Lina M. Khan, "Amazon's Antitrust Paradox," *Yale Law Journal* 126, no. 3 (January 2017), https://www.yalelawjournal.org/note/amazons-antitrust -paradox.

27 Ibid.

28 Ward S. Bowman, "Restraint of Trade by the Supreme Court: The Utah Pie Case," *Yale Law Journal* 77 (1967).

29 Khan, "Amazon's Antitrust Paradox."

30 Ibid.; David Dayen, "Bring Back Antitrust," *The American Prospect*, November 9, 2015, https://prospect.org/justice/bring-back-antitrust/. "Judges began to require a higher threshold for merger challenges as well as a presumption against abuse of market power, as the Bork intellectual theories infected the entire apparatus."

31 Khan, "Amazon's Antitrust Paradox."

32 Michael J. Coren, "There's Precedent for Amazon Competing with So Many Companies. It Doesn't End Well," *Quartz*, October 28, 2017, https://qz.com/1107328/theres-precedent-for-amazon-competing-with -so-many-companies-it-doesnt-end-well/.

33 Emily Stewart, "Happy Prime Day! Experts Worry Amazon Is Building a Dangerous Monopoly," *Vox*, July 17, 2008, https://www.vox.com /2018/7/17/17583070/amazon-prime-day-monopoly-antitrust. See also Rana Foroohar, "Lina Khan: 'This Isn't Just About Antitrust. It's About Values,' " *Financial Times*, March 29, 2019, https://www.ft.com/content /7945c568-4fe7-11e9-9c76-bf4a0ce37d49.

34 Stacy Mitchell, "Amazon Doesn't Just Want to Dominate the Market—It Wants to Become the Market," *The Nation*, February 15, 2018, https:// www.thenation.com/article/amazon-doesnt-just-want-to-dominate-the -market-it-wants-to-become-the-market/.

35 "Technical Information on Anti-Dumping," World Trade Organization, https://www.wto.org/english/tratop_e/adp_e/adp_info_e.htm.

36 Corey Kilgannon, "Declare the Strand Bookstore a City Landmark? No Thanks, the Strand Says," *New York Times*, December 3, 2018, https://www.nytimes.com/2018/12/03/nyregion/strand-bookstore-landmark.html.

37 Carl Davis, "Tax Incentives: Costly for States, Drag on the Nation," Institute on Taxation and Economic Policy, August 12, 2013, https://itep.org/wp-content/uploads/taxincentiveeffectiveness.pdf.

38 Nathan M. Jensen and Edmund J. Malesky, *Incentives to Pander: How Politicians Use Corporate Welfare for Political Gain* (New York: Cambridge University Press, 2018).

39 Ibid.

40 Caroline Buts and Marc Jegers, "The Effect of Subsidies on the Evolution of Market Structure," http://www.stateaid.gr/images/article-attachments/The_effect_of_SA_on_competition_Cresse.pdf.

41 Aaron K. Chatterji, "The Main Street Fund: Investing in an Entrepreneurial Economy," Hamilton Project, policy proposal, June 2018, http://www.hamiltonproject.org/assets/files/Chatterji_20180611.pdf.

42 Ibid.

43 Jeff Stein, "As Bank Profits Soar, Wall Street's Political Spending Hits New High, *Washington Post*, April 30, 2019, https://www.washingtonpost.com/business/2019/04/30/bank-profits-soar-wall-streets-political-spending-hits-new-high/.

9. NO, YOU DON'T HAVE TO QUIT FACEBOOK

1. Adam Hochschild, *Bury the Chains* (New York: Houghton Mifflin Harcourt, 2006) 190.

2 Mike Kaye, "The Tools of the Abolitionists," British History, bbc.co.uk, http://www.bbc.co.uk/history/british/abolition/abolition_tools_gallery_07.shtml. See also Andrea Major, "'Not Made by Slaves': The Ambivalent Origins of Ethical Consumption," OpenDemocracy.net, April 30, 2015, https://www.opendemocracy.net/en/beyond-trafficking-and-slavery/not-made-by-slaves-ambivalent-origins-of-ethical-consumption/; Clare Carlile, "History of Successful Boycotts," EthicalConsumer.org, May 5, 2019, https://www.ethicalconsumer.org/ethicalcampaigns/boycotts/history-successful-boycotts; and William Fox, *An Address to the People of Great Britain on the Utility of Refraining from the Use of West India Sugar and Rum* (London: M. Gurney and W. Darton, 1791), https://archive.org/details/addresstopeopleo1791foxw/page/4.

3 In later years, American abolitionists joined in. William Cooper, the founder of Cooperstown, New York, sold maple syrup as a form of "free sugar," an alternative to slave-made sugar. The protest never gained traction in America. At most, tens of thousands, not hundreds of thousands, joined in, but it may have played a role in binding together some of the abolitionists.

4 Daniel Zamora and Niklas Olsen, "How Decades of Neoliberalism Led to the Era of Right-Wing Populism," *Jacobin*, https://jacobinmag.com/2019/09/in-the-ruins-of-neoliberalism-wendy-brown.

5 Nicole Aschoff, *The New Prophets of Capital* (New York:Verso Books, 2015).

6 Credit to Jeet Heer for pointing out this tweet. See Jeet Heer, "The Left Can't Rely on Boycotts Alone," *New Republic*, August 19, 2017, https://newrepublic.com/article/144418/left-cant-rely-boycotts-alone.

7 Zeynep Tufekci, "Social Movements and Governments in the Digital Age: Evaluating a Complex Landscape," *Journal of International Affairs* 68, no. 1 (Fall/Winter 2014): 15, http://blogs.cuit.columbia.edu/jia/files/2014/12/xvii-18_Tufekci_Article.pdf.

8 Michael Livingston, "Here's When Boycotts Have Worked—and When They Haven't," *Los Angeles Times*, March 1, 2018, https://www.latimes.com/nation/la-na-boycotts-history-20180228-htmlstory.html. Some of the more recent successful boycotts have targeted states, not companies—but with major companies and other states participating—such as the boycotts of Arizona and North Carolina after the passage of controversial laws. I take that as a different category.

9 Ruth Graham, "The Uncanceling of Chick-fil-A," *Slate*, March 7, 2019, https://slate.com/human-interest/2019/03/chick-fil-a-boycott-liberals-forgot-chicken-too-good.html.

10 James Rainey, "Farm Workers Union Ends 16-Year Boycott of Grapes," *Los Angeles Times*, November 22, 2000, https://www.latimes.com/archives/la-xpm-2000-nov-22-mn-55663-story.html.

11 Jack Nicas, "They Tried to Boycott Facebook, Apple and Google. They Failed," *New York Times*, April 1, 2018, https://www.nytimes.com/2018/04/01/business/boycott-facebook-apple-google-failed.html.

12 Ibid.

13 Leonard Castañeda, "Berkeley: Is Amazon Too Big to Boycott?" *Mercury News*, February 20, 2019, https://www.mercurynews.com/2019/02/20/berkeley-is-amazon-too-big-to-boycott/.

14 Poll appears in Megan Brenan, "Most Americans Try to Eat Locally Grown Foods," Gallup, August 7, 2018, https://news.gallup.com/poll/240515/americans-try-eat-locally-grown-foods.aspx.

15 Phone interview with Stacy Mitchell, January 23, 2019. Notes on file with author.

16 Debra Tropp, "Why Local Food Matters: The Rising Importance of Locally-Grown Food in the U.S. Food System," Agriculture and Rural Affairs Steering Committee, Subcommittee on Agriculture, National Association of Counties Legislative Conference, March 2, 2014, https://www.ams.usda.gov/sites/default/files/media/Why%20Local%20Food%20MattersThe%20Rising%20Importance%20of%20Locally%20Grown%20Food%20in%20the%20U.S.%20Food%20System.pdf.

17 Michael Hobbes, "The Myth of the Ethical Shopper," *Huffington Post*, https://highline.huffingtonpost.com/articles/en/the-myth-of-the-ethical-shopper/.

18 Ibid.
19 Zeynep Tufekci, "Online Social Change: Easy to Organize, Hard to Win," filmed October 2014 at TED Global, Rio de Janeiro, Brazil, Video, 15:52, https://www.ted.com/talks/zeynep_tufekci_how_the_internet_has _made_social_change_easy_to_organize_hard_to_win.
20 Tufekci, "Social Movements and Governments in the Digital Age: Evaluating a Complex Landscape."
21 "Martin Luther King Jr.'s 'Letter from Birmingham Jail,'" *The Atlantic*, February 2018, https://www.theatlantic.com/magazine/archive/2018/02 /letter-from-birmingham-jail/552461/.
22 Ibid.
23 Henry David Thoreau, "Resistance to Civil Government," Aesthetic Papers, 1849, http://xroads.virginia.edu/~hyper2/thoreau/civil.html.
24 David Streitfeld, "Activists Build a Grassroots Alliance Against Amazon," *New York Times*, November 26, 2019, https://www.nytimes.com/2019/11 /26/technology/amazon-grass-roots-activists.html.

10. WE HAVE THE TOOLS

1 *The Labour Annual, 1898* (London: Clarion; Manchester: Labour Press), 64.
2 See "Antitrust Men Speak," *New York Times*, February 13, 1900; "Antitrust Conference," *New York Times*, January 25, 1900; "Antitrust Conference Ends," *New York Times*, February 15, 1900.
3 Charles Sumner, *His Complete Works* (Boston: Lee and Shepard, 1900).
4 Chronicled in Lawrence Goodwyn, *The Populist Moment: A Short History of the Agrarian Revolt in America* (New York: Oxford University Press, 1978).
5 James Hudson, "Modern Feudalism," *North American Review* 144, no. 364 (March 1887): 277–290; D. M. Mickey, "Trusts," *American Law Review* 22, no. 538 (1888). I am indebted to John Millon for these quotes. See, generally, David Millon, "The Sherman Act and the Balance of Power," *Southern California Law Review* 61 (1988), 1219.
6 James May, "Antitrust in the Formative Era," *Ohio State Law Journal* 50, no. 257 (1989).
7 63rd Cong., 2d Sess., *Congressional Record* 51, pt. 16 (September 25, 1914–October 24, 1914): 15663–16978.
8 Barry Lynn, *Liberty from All Masters: The New American Autocracy vs the Will of the People* (New York: St. Martin's, forthcoming 2020).
9 Franklin Delano Roosevelt, Speech, March 9, 1933, https://www.fdic .gov/bank/historical/firstfifty/prologue.pdf.
10 *United States v. Aluminum Co. of America*, 148 F.2d 416, 427 (2d Cir. 1945).
11 Ibid.
12 *Northern Pacific R. Co. v. United States*, 356 U.S. 1, 4 (1958).

13   370 U.S. 294 (1962).

14   Ibid.

15   *United States v. Philadelphia National Bank*, 374 U.S. 321, 363 (1963).

16   Jonathan Baker, *The Antitrust Paradigm: Restoring a Competitive Economy* (Cambridge, MA: Harvard University Press, 2019), 139.

17   Harlan M. Blake and William K. Jones, "In Defense of Antitrust," *Columbia Law Review* 377 (1965): 383.

18   United States Federal Trade Commission, Office of Policy Planning and Evaluation, "Mergers Policy Session," edited version, 1978. A. O. Sulzberger Jr., "Kennedy Introduces Bill to Curb Mergers Among Biggest Companies," *New York Times*, March 9, 1979, https://www.nytimes.com /1979/03/09/archives/kennedy-introduces-bill-to-curb-mergers-among -biggest-companies.html.

19   "1982 Merger Guidelines," US Department of Justice, updated August 4, 2015, https://www.justice.gov/archives/atr/1982-merger-guidelines.

20   Howard M. Metzenbaum, "Is William Baxter Anti-Antitrust?" *New York Times*, October 18, 1981, https://www.nytimes.com/1981/10 /18/business/is-william-baxter-anti-antitrust.html. Howard Kurtz, "Amid Many Failures, Meese Makes a Mark," *Washington Post*, July 13, 1987, https://www.washingtonpost.com/archive/politics/1987/07/13 /amid-many-failures-meese-makes-a-mark/677c6f28-b496-4deb-8f62 -6f1387aba624/.

21   William E. Kovacic, "Reagan's Judicial Appointees and Antitrust in the 1990s," *Fordham Law Review* 60, no. 1 (1991), https://ir.lawnet.fordham .edu/cgi/viewcontent.cgi?referer=https://www.google.com/&httpsredir =1&article=2941&context=flr.

22   Sandeep Vaheesan, "Resurrecting 'A Comprehensive Charter of Economic Liberty': The Latent Power of the Federal Trade Commission," *University of Pennsylvania Journal of Business Law* 645 (2017).

23   Sandeep Vaheesan, "Resurrecting 'A Comprehensive Charter of Economic Liberty': The Latent Power of the Federal Trade Commission," *University of Pennsylvania Journal of Business Law* 645, 654-55 (2017).

11. NATIONALIZE OR DECENTRALIZE?
BIG PHARMA AND THE GREEN NEW DEAL

1   All the citations re Shane are in his social media accounts. See also https:// www.menshealth.com/health/a19545397/high-cost-diabetes-drugs -insulin-kills-man/.

2   Jan Hoffman, "Johnson & Johnson Ordered to Pay $572 Million in Landmark Opioid Trial," *New York Times*, August 26, 2019, https:// www.nytimes.com/2019/08/26/health/oklahoma-opioids-johnson-and -johnson.html.

3   David Ingram and Ros Krasny, "Johnson & Johnson to Pay $2.2 Billion to End U.S. Drug Probes," Reuters, November 4, 2013, https://www

.reuters.com/article/us-jnj-settlement/johnson-johnson-to-pay-2-2
-billion-to-end-u-s-drug-probes-idUSBRE9A30MM20131104.

4 "Eli Lilly Fined Nearly $1.5B in Drug Marketing Case," CNNMoney, January 15, 2009, https://money.cnn.com/2009/01/15/news/companies /eli_lilly/.

5 Ekaterina Galkina Cleary, Jennifer M. Beierlein, Navleen Surjit Khanuja, Laura M. McNamee, and Fred D. Ledley, "Contribution of NIH Funding to New Drug Approvals 2010–2016," *Proceedings of the National Academy of Sciences* 115, no. 10 (March 6, 2018): 2329–2334, https://pnas.org/content /115/10/2329.

6 Soutik Biswas, "Is the World Heading for an Insulin Shortage?" BBC News, November 30, 2018, https://www.bbc.com/news/world-asia-india -46354989.

7 Aaron S. Kesselheim, Jerry Avorn, and Ameet Sarpatwari, "The High Cost of Prescription Drugs in the United States: Origins and Prospects for Reform," *JAMA Network*, August 23/30, 2016, https://jamanetwork.com /journals/jama/article-abstract/2545691.

8 Jef Feeley and Robert Langreth, "Novo Nordisk, Lilly, Sanofi Must Face Insulin Drug Pricing Suit," Bloomberg, February 15, 2019, https://www .bloomberg.com/news/articles/2019-02-15/novo-nordisk-lilly-sanofi -must-face-insulin-drug-pricing-suit.

9 Open Markets Institute, Explainer, "High Drug Prices and Monopoly," https://openmarketsinstitute.org/explainer/high-drug-prices-and -monopoly/.

10 Alfred B. Engelberg, "How Government Policy Promotes High Drug Prices," Health Affairs blog, October 29, 2015, http://healthaffairs .org/blog/2015/10/29/how-government-policy-promotes-high-drug -prices/.

11 Andrew Lakoff, *Disaster and the Politics of Intervention* (New York: Columbia University Press, 2010), 117.

12 Phillip Longman, "How Big Medicine Can Ruin Medicare for All," *Washington Monthly* (November/December 2017), https://washingtonmonthly .com/magazine/novemberdecember-2017/how-big-medicine-can-ruin -medicare-for-all/.

13 Emily Gee, "Provider Consolidation Drives Up Health Care Costs," Center for American Progress, December 5, 2018, https://www .americanprogress.org/issues/healthcare/reports/2018/12/05/461780 /provider-consolidation-drives-health-care-costs/.

14 Austin Frakt, "Hospital Mergers Improve Health? Evidence Shows the Opposite," *New York Times*, February 11, 2019, https://www.nytimes .com/2019/02/11/upshot/hospital-mergers-hurt-health-care-quality .html.

15 Phillip Longman, "Why Universal Healthcare Needs Antitrust," *Democracy*, January 2, 2018, https://democracyjournal.org/arguments/why -universal-health-care-needs-antitrust/.

16 "Reprocessed Medical Devices Market Is Rising to a Valuation of US $3.35bn in 2024, Says TMR," Market Watch, June 7, 2018, https://www .marketwatch.com/press-release/reprocessed-medical-devices-market-is -rising-to-a-valuation-of-us335-bn-in-2024-says-tmr-2018-06-07.

17 David Dayen, "The Hidden Monopolies That Raise Drug Prices," *American Prospect*, March 28, 2017, https://prospect.org/health/hidden -monopolies-raise-drug-prices/.

18 Ibid.

19 Joseph Keppler, "Next!" *Puck Magazine*, September 1904, https://digital .library.cornell.edu/catalog/ss:19343487; Grant Hamilton, "A Monopoly That Requires Crushing," January 1888, Getty Images, https://www .gettyimages.com/detail/news-photo/political-cartoon-of-tidewater-pipe -line-fighting-with-news-photo/514882610; Schultzy, "Standard Oil: A Company So Effective Only the Government Could Compete with It," *Harvard Business Review*, December 2015, https://digital.hbs.edu/platform -rctom/submission/standard-oil-a-company-so-effective-only-the-u-s -government-could-compete-with-it/.

20 "Report Shows Just 100 Companies Are Source of over 70% of Emissions," Disclosure Insight Action, July 10, 2017, https://www.cdp.net /en/articles/media/new-report-shows-just-100-companies-are-source-of -over-70-of-emissions.

21 Joe Romm, "Fossil Fuel Industry Spent Nearly $2 Billion to Kill U.S. Climate Action, New Study Finds," Think Progress, July 19, 2018, https:// thinkprogress.org/fossil-fuel-industry-outspends-environment-groups -on-climate-new-study-231325b4a7e6/; Robert J. Brulle, "The Climate Lobby: A Sectoral Analysis of Lobbying Spending on Climate Change in the USA, 2000 to 2016," *Climatic Change* 149, no. 3–4 (August 2018): 289–303, https://doi.org/10.1007/s10584-018-2241-z.

22 Benjamin Franta and Geoffrey Supran, "The Fossil Fuel Industry's Invisible Colonization of Academia," *Guardian*, March 2017, https://www .theguardian.com/environment/climate-consensus-97-per-cent/2017 /mar/13/the-fossil-fuel-industrys-invisible-colonization-of-academia.

23 Rebecca Smith, "Utilities Profit Recipe: Spend More," *Wall Street Journal*, April 2015, https://www.wsj.com/articles/utilities-profit-recipe-spend -more-1429567463.

24 John Farrell, "The Challenge of Reconciling a Centralized v. Decentralized Electricity System," Institute for Local Self-Reliance, October 17, 2011, https://ilsr.org/challenge-reconciling-centralized-v-decentralized -electricity-system/.

25 Matthew Stoller and Lucas Kunce, "America's Monopoly Crisis Hits the Military," *American Conservative*, June 27, 2019, https://www .theamericanconservative.com/articles/americas-monopoly-crisis-hits-the -military/.

26 Ibid.

27 Ibid.

12. MORAL MARKETS

1 Herman Melville, "Bartleby, the Scrivener: A Story of Wall-Street" (Brooklyn, NY: Melville House Publishing, 2010), 15.
2 "IHOP Culture Reviews: General Manager," Indeed.com, https://www.indeed.com/cmp/Ihop/reviews?fcountry=ALL&fjobtitle=General+Manager&ftopic=culture.
3 Michael Sainato, "When a Company Tries to Decertify Its Union," In These Times blog, February 25, 2019, https://inthesetimes.com/working/entry/21757/charter-communications-strike-workers-replacement-decertify-spectrum-brand.
4 F. A. Hayek, "The Moral Element in Free Enterprise," Foundation for Economic Education, July 1, 1962, https://fee.org/articles/the-moral-element-in-free-enterprise/.
5 David Gauthier, *Morals by Agreement* (New York: Oxford University Press, 1986), 16.
6 Murray N. Rothbard, *Man, Economy, and State* (Princeton, NJ: David Van Nostrand, 1962).
7 Eric A. Posner and E. Glen Weyl, *Radical Markets: Uprooting Capitalism and Democracy for a Just Society* (Princeton, NJ: Princeton University Press, 2019).
8 Michael J. Sandel, *What Money Can't Buy: The Moral Limits of Markets* (London: Penguin, 2013); Michael J. Sandel, "What Isn't for Sale," *Atlantic,* April 2012, https://www.theatlantic.com/magazine/archive/2012/04/what-isnt-for-sale/308902/.
9 Richard Dagger, "Republican Punishment: Consequentialist or Retributivist?" in Cécile Laborde and John Maynor, *Republicanism and Political Theory,* 219–245 (Oxford: Blackwell, 2008).
10 Samuel Fleischacker, "Adam Smith's Reception Among the American Founders, 1776–1790," *William and Mary Quarterly* 59, no. 4 (2002): 897–924, doi:10.2307/3491575.
11 U.S. Congress, Senate, Committee on the Judiciary, *The Consumer Welfare Standard in Antitrust: Outdated or a Harbor in a Sea of Doubt? Hearing Before the Subcommittee on Antitrust, Competition and Consumer Rights of the Sen. Comm. on the Judiciary,* 116 Cong. 2017 (testimony of Barry Lynn, Executive Director of Open Markets Institute).
12 Prateek Raj, "'Antimonopoly Is as Old as the Republic,'" Pro-Market blog, University of Chicago Booth School of Business, May 22, 2017, https://promarket.org/antimonopoly-old-republic/.
13 Ibid.
14 K. Sabeel Rahman, *Democracy Against Domination* (Oxford: Oxford University Press, 2017), 173–180.
15 Daniel A. Farber, "Reinventing Brandeis: Legal Pragmatism for the Twenty-First Century," *University of Illinois Law Review* (1995), http://scholarship.law.berkeley.edu/cgi/viewcontent.cgi?article=1353&context=facpubs.

16 John Dewey, *Moral Principles in Education* (New York: Houghton Mifflin, 1909); Joel Goldstein, "Justice Brandeis and Civic Duty in a Pluralistic Society," *Touro Law Review* 33, no. 1 (2017), https://digitalcommons.tourolaw.edu/cgi/viewcontent.cgi?article=2800&context=lawreview.

17 Mary W. Atwell, "Louis Brandeis," The First Amendment Encyclopedia, Middle Tennessee State University, https://www.mtsu.edu/first-amendment/article/1316/louis-brandeis (accessed October 18, 2019); John Dewey, *Democracy and Education* (New York: Macmillan, 1916), https://www.google.com/books/edition/Democracy_and_Education/uWMWAAAAIAAJ?hl=en&gbpv=1&printsec=frontcover.

18 To be clear, in both *Liggett* and *Whitney* Brandeis does not express these as his own views, but as the views of "some" or "the framers"; his ventriloquism, however, is traditionally understood to barely mask his own views.

19 Melvin I. Urofsky, *Louis D. Brandeis: A Life* (New York: Pantheon Books, 2009), at xii (quoting a letter to Harold Laski).

20 Louis Brandeis, *Letters of Louis D. Brandeis: Volume V, 1921–1941: Elder Statesman* (Albany: State University of New York Press, 1978).

21 Ibid.

22 Jonathan Sallet, "Louis Brandeis: A Man for This Season," *Colorado Tech Law Journal* 15, no. 2 (2018): 396.

23 Jeffrey Rosen, *Louis D. Brandeis, American Prophet* (New Haven, CT: Yale University Press, 2016).

24 Brandeis, *Letters of Louis D. Brandeis.*

25 *Liggett Co. v. Lee*, 288 U.S. 517, 541, 580 (1933) (Brandeis dissenting).

26 Langston Hughes, *Let America Be America Again and Other Poems* (New York: Knopf Doubleday, 2004).

Index